THE REAL THIRTEENTH STEP

THE *REAL* THIRTEENTH STEP

Discovering Confidence,
Self-Reliance, and
Autonomy Beyond
the 12-Step Programs

Tina Tessina, Ph.D.

JEREMY P. TARCHER/PERIGEE

Jeremy P. Tarcher/Perigee Books
are published by
The Putnam Publishing Group
200 Madison Avenue
New York, NY 10016

Library of Congress Cataloging in Publication Data

Tessina, Tina B.
    The real thirteenth step : discovering confidence, self-reliance, and autonomy
beyond the 12-step programs/Tina Tessina.
        p.   cm.
    Includes bibliographical references
    ISBN 0-87477-713-5
    1. Compulsive behavior—Treatment.   2. Twelve-step programs—
Psychological aspects.   3. Alcoholism—Psychological aspects.   4. Autonomy
(Psychology)   5. Self-reliance.   I. Title.   II. Title: Thirteenth step.
RC533.T47   1991
362.29′18—dc20

Jeremy P. Tarcher, Inc.
5858 Wilshire Blvd., Suite 200
Los Angeles, CA 90036

Manufactured in the United States of America
10   9   8   7   6   5   4   3   2   1

This book is printed on acid-free paper.
∞

To my father
who made his share of mistakes,
but who challenged and encouraged
me to think for myself,
and who loved me first.
He has been gone for thirty years,
but his influence remains.

Contents

Acknowledgments

J ean Stine, my friend and my editor. Because writing requires far more rigorous organization than the creative thinking required to do therapy and conceptualize ideas, I needed lots of help. Jean's editorial brilliance and capacity for organizing ideas is what made this book readable and logical. She is truly "God in plain clothes" and her notes ("Tina, why? Explain.") made the crucial difference. She is a writer's necessity, an editor who cares about content.

No one but a writer's spouse knows what patience and tolerance a spouse must have to hang in there. Richard Sharrard has all that, and more. His unflagging love and support are a miracle in my life.

The cosmic support team, in alphabetical order: Isadora Alman, Maggie Bialack, Scott Blackson, Victoria Bryan, Ron Creager, Sylvia McWilliams, Bill and Joan Mueller, and Riley Smith who listened with interest, encouraged me with "I love you" phone calls, and even got me away from it all. You guys are my other miracles, and life would be a lot less fun without you.

There are so many others: Andree Morin, Vince the electrician, Bob Butler, computer whiz—the team who got me through the horrors of a dead computer at deadline time. Kathy DeMille and Bernice Eidy for secretarial support, and Michelle

Pellette, for service, cheerfulness, and energy beyond the call of duty.

Many thanks also to Denton Roberts, mentor and teacher, whose wisdom appears throughout this book. Richard FX O'Connor, colleague and correspondent extraordinaire, who read the manuscript and added bits of wisdom. The librarians at Long Beach Public Library, especially Laurie Wills, for their help and patience.

Last but never least, Jeremy Tarcher, who had enough faith to invest in me, who provided challenge and both emotional and practical support, and who has a most extraordinary book production and promotion team: Lisa Chadwick, Mike Dougherty, Lisa Ives, Robert Welsch, and several others whose names are unknown to me. I am fortunate to have such a caring, expert team behind me.

Preface

Support groups are the answer for 15 million Americans . . . 500,000 . . . will be attended . . . this week. . . . Support groups work.

NEWSWEEK

In my work as a consultant, I have observed clients becoming addicted to the twelve-step program and unable to transcend it.

Drug Counselor Bob Holder
NEW AGE MAGAZINE

S ince the founding of Alcoholics Anonymous in 1935, twelve-step-based recovery programs have proved very effective in helping victims of addictive, obsessive, and compulsive behavior put a stop to that behavior and the damage it has created in their lives. Up to now, these programs have provided almost the sole support, hope, encouragement, and successful examples of people who were able to arrest their addiction and enter recovery.

In a nation that has eight million "problem drinkers," more than two hundred *national* Alcoholics Anonymous–style groups, and over two thousand meetings each week of support groups catering to those caught up in "relationship addiction" *alone*—and where millions of others attend groups specifically formed for recovery from problems such as substance abuse, alcoholic families, eating disorders, and obsessive/compulsive behavior—there is no doubt that all these recovery programs based on the original Alcoholics Anonymous Twelve Steps have done a tremendous amount of good. In fact, to my knowledge, they are the most effective programs known: most reputable alcohol and substance abuse treatment centers use the Twelve Steps or some variant of them in their own programs; and many therapists will not work with substance abuse patients unless they attend a twelve-step-style recovery program. For the last twenty years, these programs have done exactly what they were designed to do: to help people free themselves from whatever substance or behavior holds them in addiction.

No wonder a Scripps Howard News Service story of June 18, 1989, maintains: "Throughout the country, there is a rush to . . . Alcoholics Anonymous, Cocaine Anonymous, and Narcotics Anonymous. Nationally, AA membership has easily doubled in the last decade. The country's Cocaine Anonymous groups have seen an even more dramatic rise, from 169 to 1,042 in four years." Ask any experienced recovery counselor, and you'll hear that twelve-step programs definitely work.

But recently another series of voices has begun to question certain aspects of the program. One of the foremost of these is psychologist Stanton Peele, author of *The Diseasing of America: Addiction Treatment Out of Control*, who criticizes the twelve-step process as "a religious conversion experience" and terms it "a kind of brainwashing."

"The . . . AA philosophy . . . that alcoholics . . . are unable to control their drinking from birth," writes Peele, means they "are obligated to think of themselves as having a lifetime condition. . . . Alcoholics are taught to believe that they are exactly one drink away from total relapse and the need to start again at day one." Others criticize the program's insistence that "recovery is forever" as undermining self-esteem, the way groups absorb members' time to the exclusion of all outside activity, and the way many members seem to just transfer their addiction to the program without attempting any further growth or progress.

U.S. News and World Report called this "America's addiction to addiction." One social worker employed by a veteran's hospital alcohol treatment program voiced this concern recently when he said: "We need a Twelve Steps Anonymous to handle peoples' addiction to the program."

In fact, as the number of support groups and the problems they focus on have mounted, so has the controversy. Concern over whether they are to be viewed as effective methods for arresting addictions or simply as a means for transferring the addictions to a more benign and less disastrous form is becoming more widespread.

This growing doubt has penetrated so deeply among the public at large that it has even become the subject of comic strips. A recent Feiffer cartoon featured a woman worrying because she goes to her support groups "seven nights and three afternoons a week" for her eating, drinking, smoking, and intimacy "disorders." She couldn't "live without them," the woman says, and then concludes, somewhat crestfallen, that she may have a "support group disorder."

Recently, I have noticed that therapy clients who had been in recovery groups and long ago stopped their addictive behavior were also beginning to voice these concerns and felt restless with the program. Among them are clients who have come to me feeling discouraged and disappointed with *themselves* because they couldn't achieve satisfying lives through the recovery programs alone, and clients who—after years spent going from one kind of group to another (AA to Al-Anon to CoDA to Overeaters Anonymous) as they quit one addiction only to discover they still had others—are kept by the groups from noticing that the underlying *cause* of all these compulsions had yet to be addressed.

Friends also have expressed frustration with being "in recovery" for years, and wanting to get *beyond* it. And colleagues have expressed concern about clients who seem to be stuck *because* they can't transcend their recovery programs. Members of my weekly drop-in therapy group attend to work on issues *not* addressed in their twelve-step programs. Even as I write this Preface, after overhearing a phone conversation about this book a young man who works for me (and incidentally is in recovery) said, "Were you just talking about a book about something beyond the Twelve Steps? Where can I get three copies?"

Although I recognize the limitations of twelve-step programs, I don't believe their effectiveness can or should be discounted. Nor should any of the ideas in this book, or even its analysis of the Twelve Steps' shortcomings, be taken as an attack on them. Instead, it is my hope to show recovery group members how they can build on the foundation of continued long-term recovery from addictive behavior that these groups have made possible to a full, autonomous life free of addiction and the fear of relapse, outside the group and without the program's support.

My clients are justly grateful for the help they've gotten within these groups. "The twelve-step program saved my life" is a statement I hear often. As a therapist, I am also grateful for the way these groups supply an ongoing, twenty-four-hour-a-day support structure and friendship that is both beyond the scope of, and an excellent adjunct to, private therapy.

But for many long-term recovery group members, it is no longer enough to remain "clean and sober," to learn the Steps, to be a part of the "family." Life beyond the group, beyond recovery, calls to them; human beings have an innate need to grow, to accomplish, to achieve.

Their recovery program has done its work; its objectives have been achieved. But there is no culminating celebration, no movement to a new level. Something feels wrong about this. When students study diligently and learn their lessons in school or college, they get to graduate and move on to a higher level. But for members of recovery groups there is no graduation or recognition that they might have completed their work—no *Thirteenth Step beyond recovery to a health and wholeness that transcends any further permanent dependency on the program* to keep them free from addiction.

But the whole philosophy and perspective of the twelve-step programs as they are currently constructed is against the view that permanent recovery of any kind is possible. They are convinced that nothing like a Thirteenth Step can *ever* exist, and they are convinced that addiction is a lifelong "illness" that can never be cured, that there is no such thing as graduation, and that all attempts to leave the group can only end in failure.

To them I would say that although addiction is indeed a very serious problem, and very difficult to heal, that just as people doubted the ability of anything to arrest addiction until Alcoholics Anonymous introduced the Twelve Steps and proved its effectiveness in the face of many doubts, there is increasing evidence that once addictive behavior has been stopped through the intervention of a recovery program, people can recover further beyond the likelihood of relapse.

Unfortunately, because they do not believe in "recovery beyond recovery," as they define it, most recovery programs actively discourage members from leaving the group. As a result, even members who feel they've gotten all they can from the program and eventually leave feel burdened by a sense of incompleteness, self-doubt, and guilt.

Helping clients, friends, and colleagues resolve these conflicts and find meaning beyond their self-help programs led to the writing of *The Real Thirteenth Step*, which addresses the following questions.

- How do you know you are ready to move beyond the program, and are not just in denial?
- What criteria must you meet to be ready for graduation from twelve-step programs?
- Does graduation mean you must leave the program forever? What is appropriate program participation once you achieve independence?
- How is self-reliant living different from arrogance and selfishness?
- What is healthy autonomy? Is it lonely?
- Why are some people on a treadmill of self-help group after group, and how do you stop the cycle?

The methods, exercises, and ideas in this book build on what you have already learned in your recovery program, and are based on proven psychological theory and techniques. Through following the teachings here, you can both honor the accomplishments you achieved in recovery and effectively move beyond them to normal, functional living. You can learn how to heal old dependency, old pain, and free yourself to enjoy the challenge of life. Because they are based on time-tested theories, some of the exercises and teachings in this book may seem familiar—but never before has such a coherent, complete outline of the basic tools been presented in a way that you can use *on your own* to effectively learn autonomy and create permanent, lasting recovery from the patterns of dependency that lie embedded in your subconscious mind.

Although this book is intended for people who are recovering from severe problems of addiction and codependency with the help of a recovery group, because of the social bias in most societies against independent thought and action almost every individual develops some degree of dependency and has his or her growth toward autonomy impaired. Therefore, the ideas and exercises in this book will also be useful for anyone striving to achieve a greater degree of personal freedom and autonomy in her or his daily life.

You may never have had problems with addiction or obsessive/compulsive behavior, but sometimes you might find it difficult to assert yourself in groups, to initiate conversations about painful topics, to ask salesclerks or repairpeople to correct errors, or to confront friends or relatives who need it. If so, by following the suggestions contained in this book you'll find yourself able to deal with most of life's difficulties with greater ease and self-confidence.

I invite you to turn the page, and begin to take the Thirteenth Step toward autonomy, self-confidence, and self-reliance.

AUTHOR'S NOTE

As a member of a twelve-step recovery program, you may have heard the term *thirteenth stepping* used disparagingly to mean having inappropriate sexual intimacy with new members. In this book, the phrase *Thirteenth Step* is used to mean completing recovery and achieving appropriate intimacy with yourself. Although I do believe that sexual intimacy between group members in recovery and brand-new members can be inappropriate,

I do not believe that *thirteenth stepping* is the correct phrase to describe it.

To me, *taking the Thirteenth Step means taking the next step beyond the Twelve Steps* and graduating from the group to healthy, fully autonomous living. That's why I have chosen to call this book *The Real Thirteenth Step*, and any time I use the phrases *Thirteenth Step* or *Real Thirteenth Step* it is this healthy intimacy with self, not inappropriate intimacy with others, that I mean.

Although Alcoholics Anonymous programs are among the best known of the self-help recovery groups, there are many others that are based on the Twelve Steps (such as Adult Children of Alcoholics (ACA), Overeaters Anonymous (OA), Gamblers Anonymous (GA), CoDependents Anonymous (CoDA), Debtors Anonymous (DA), and Al-Anon) or that, though they differ in the number of steps or in some details, take basically the same approach. Many incest survivor, codependency, or adult children of dysfunctional family and other self-help groups use a program based on the therapist's own feelings about the appropriate number of steps. But they are all very similar in their focus on a Higher Power, on fearlessly facing the self, and in making amends to those who have been injured. Since they all share the same focus on recovery through the support of the group, I have chosen to refer to them most often as *recovery groups* or *programs*. When you see these phrases, you will know I'm speaking about recovery groups in the most inclusive sense, and not exclusively AA-type twelve-step programs.

Addiction, obsession, compulsion, and codependency all share common elements, since addictive behavior is compulsive and we become obsessed about anything we are dependent on. Although therapists and programs consider these to be technically different behaviors, for the purposes of this book I have used the terms *addiction* and *addictive behavior* to include them all, and I have used the term *alcoholism* and related words (drunk, dry, sober, abstinent) to include all compulsions, obsessions, and addictions.

I

Recovery: Our Newest Addiction

CHAPTER 1

Autonomy: The Real Thirteenth Step

The trouble with twelve-step programs is that they just replace the addiction—then you're stuck with the program for life. I know people who've been going to three meetings a week for ten years.

WAYNE CURTIS
Psychologist

O ver many years of doing therapy, I have seen numerous clients who benefited enormously from a recovery program, but then came to me for private therapy either on the recommendation of a sponsor or a fellow member, because they recognized the need for something more than just arresting their addictions. Once their addictive behavior was overcome, they found out that group meetings were taking too much of their lives, and they felt something was missing. The stronger they felt in recovery, the more they felt that life should be more than endless attendance at meetings, and that there must be other meaningful things than the program. They were grateful for their recovery, but they wanted more. Here are some examples:

Richard O., 45, a self-employed professional: "The program created a miracle for me, my freedom from addiction. Moreover, I have never seen any other recovery program work the way AA's works. It works! But it took *me* to govern my mind and control my excesses. I am entering my tenth year of being sober. I stopped attending meetings after six months, primarily because they were repetitive. I don't want, desire, nor have a yen for booze and I keep a fully-stocked bar in my home for guests." He discovered the importance of autonomy on his own.

Bob D., 62, an aerospace engineer who began having heart problems: "I'm grateful to AA, I really feel the meetings saved my life. But, now that I've been sober for three years, I realize that there's more I need to do, and I can't seem to find it in AA."

Mary L., 33, a successful real estate agent, and divorced mother of two: "I found that my whole life, my friends, my activities were all limited to the program. For a while it felt great, being surrounded by recovering people, but then I wanted more variety. I wanted a life of my own! I'm grateful to the program, more grateful than I can say; but I never felt completely healthy until I left."

If you are a successful member of a recovery program and feel you've benefited enormously, but are beginning to sense that your progress toward life as an individual, able to function on your own in the outside world, is being hindered by the program itself—then the time may have come for you to graduate from your dependence on the group to help you manage your problems. It may be time now for you to learn how to rely on yourself and to develop the skills to cope successfully and fearlessly on your own.

If you are a member of a twelve-step or other recovery group, you may be trapped in the Twelve Steps, an unwitting victim of America's newest addiction—addiction to recovery. Here are some telltale signs of your need for independence:

- You have remained free from the destructive behavior for several years.
- You are realistically confident that your life is no longer unmanageable.
- You are happy to be in recovery and particularly to be clean/abstinent/sober, but are still at a loss about how to run the rest of your life.

- You are tired of being told you are an addict/alcoholic/codependent and will always be an addict/alcoholic/codependent.
- You are feeling restless and confined in the group.
- You are beginning to feel you may have just traded one crutch for another.
- You feel you are missing out on life because of the pressure to constantly attend group meetings.
- You realize that all your former friends were connected to your addiction, all your present friends are involved in the Program, and you have trouble forming friends with others outside these groups.
- You would like to let go of the program and try your "wings" as an independent, fully recovered human being, but are afraid you may slip back into your old, destructive behavior, because you have been told no one ever recovers.
- You sense you may be cured and ready for life outside the group, but are not sure you possess the skills for coping with the world successfully by yourself.

Twelve-step style recovery programs are unsurpassed in transforming destructive addiction, compulsion, or dependency into a much healthier dependency on the Program (see Chapter 2 if you are not familiar with the Twelve Steps). This is a significant accomplishment, but your recovery remains incomplete. It still leaves you dependent on the group.

Your current doubts about the group and feelings of restlessness may be the promptings of your inner awareness of this lack of completeness. If so, you may be ready to complete your recovery and take the Thirteenth Step: graduate to self-reliance, to self-confidence, to complete autonomy—to full and complete charge of your own life.

The word *autonomy*, which means to be self-governing or self-regulating, may seem cold and scientific, but it represents personal empowerment. Rather than being cold, autonomy is a source of emotional warmth, because only when you feel able to care for yourself can you successfully take the necessary risks to love and be loved. Through reading *The Real Thirteenth Step,* you will come to understand that achieving autonomy means to graduate beyond recovery and to build the essential foundation you need to create intimacy with yourself and others.

But recovery programs don't provide for graduation. So, this book will show you how to take the forgotten step in the twelve-step programs: the Thirteenth Step—recovery from recovery. In other words, recovery from your final dependency on the group to keep you from becoming dependent, addictive, or obsessive again. The Twelve Steps are like a tourniquet that stops a hemorrhage; they have saved your life, but the wound itself still needs to be treated. Unless the injury is healed, you will always be, as the programs put it, "recovering" but never "recovered."

Although vastly more functional than your original addiction and dependency, your replacement addiction to a sponsor, the Steps, and the meetings (which fill your time and take all your attention, much as your original addiction did) eventually limits your ability to live a full and emotionally complete life outside the group.

Perhaps you have abandoned old friends or left an addictive or compulsive mate or dysfunctional family, because they were harmful to your recovery. In the beginning, you found "instant friends" at AA or another group. This produced initial euphoria, but eventually you found that these new friends also have difficulties and problems—like yours, a result of the factors that created their addiction.

After a while, you may have longed for people who had other things in common (music, sports, art, intellectual pursuits, entertainment preferences, and so on) with you than addiction. But, because you believed you must attend the group regularly to remain in recovery, you could not take the time to go out and look. Also, if you came from a severely dysfunctional family, you may have felt at a loss about *how* to find new friends. Few recovery programs provide information, encouragement, or guidance for you to learn to make friends outside of the group.

After years of dependency and addictive behavior, becoming an autonomous, confident, and self-reliant adult for the first time in your life may sound like an impossible goal. It is possibly the one thing you always have been afraid you couldn't do successfully. You probably began drinking, eating, shopping, loving, working—or whatever your dependency problem was— too much in the first place to distract you from this fear that you were too weak or stupid to cope with, and make sound decisions about, managing your own life. And, ironically, you may feel that your destructive behavior patterns are the proof that you are right.

But the truth is that even after years of apparent failure, others who have had exactly the same problems and background have learned to end their addictions—and so can you! Instead of remaining dependent on something outside yourself (even a self-help program) to maintain your recovery, you can learn to depend only on yourself. You can become *self*-dependent, or, as it is more commonly put, *in*dependent. You can take the same step Carl, a thirty-three-year-old long-haul truckdriver, took— the Thirteenth Step, beyond mere recovery from addiction to full health and autonomy:

CARL

Carl began drinking at age fourteen. It was the "in thing to do." His buddies would steal alcohol from home, or talk an older guy into buying some beer. At first, it just seemed "grown up" and exciting, but soon it helped him forget his problems at home and school. His father was a truckdriver, and gone a lot. Carl missed having a father like the other kids', but he liked it better when Dad was gone. When Carl's dad was home, with nothing to do, he drank, became angry and violent, and Carl and his mother got the brunt. With his inner turmoil about the abuse, and no guidance from his troubled parents, Carl was unable to cope with school. Drinking became his only relief, and a big problem. Carl had hangovers, blackouts, arrests for drunk driving, and disastrous relationships.

Carl tells how he got to AA at age twenty-eight: "I went to the first meeting because I was ordered to by the judge after a DUI. I hated it, but they said 'keep coming back,' and I had to anyway." Being arrested for a DUI got his attention, and the court's referral to AA got him moving. "I went to meetings because I had been ordered to, but I never shared [spoke]. When I first said, 'My name is Carl, and I'm an alcoholic,' I began to face my problem. The Twelve Steps changed my life. For the first time, I had some hope."

Carl spent four years in AA, working the Steps, attending daily meetings, and even speaking at hospital alcohol programs to introduce AA. "AA was all I needed—until I fell in love. Suddenly, I had no idea what to do. It was a disaster. When that relationship broke up, I was afraid to meet other women. I had nothing in my life to talk about except AA. I discovered that meetings were not a good place to meet women. They were there because they needed to work the Steps—they were not ready for healthy relationships. I got restless. Meetings seemed repetitious, I had gotten what I needed, but I was afraid to leave, because I knew I was supposed to be in recovery forever. I didn't know what to do instead."

Carl had several relapses in his first six months in AA, and he didn't trust himself to stay sober without frequent attendance, but after a year of sobriety he wasn't learning anything new. Carl felt he needed more help than his sponsor had to offer.

Carl came into therapy, because although he was a handsome, well-built man, he needed to learn how to relate to women, and how to meet people outside AA. As I helped him confront himself, he discovered his awkwardness and shyness around people he didn't know was a result of internal emotional pain and a poor self-image.

As Carl practiced the exercises and processes I taught him, he learned to face his own feelings, and heal the trauma of his childhood. His confidence and energy were increasing. As he learned autonomous thinking and self-governing, he found his self-esteem grew, and he began to be able to trust himself to know what was good for him, and to do it. Carl reclaimed his life, from the painful legacy of a dysfunctional and abusive family, from the ravages of out-of-control drinking, and, finally, from dependency on AA.

Carl says, "I will always be grateful to AA. Nothing else would have gotten me sober. But I'm glad I found a way to graduate. Now, my involvement is voluntary—I can do it if I want to help someone, or to remind myself of what drinking was like, but I don't have to do it to stay sober or keep my serenity. Life is more fun, I'm enjoying myself more, I have more friends, and I'm successfully in love."

HEALING IS MORE THAN RECOVERY

You're one of the millions of men, women, and young people who have successfully stopped a destructive behavior—involving addictive substances, food binges, spending, gambling, abuse of others, or codependent relationships—through participation in one of the many twelve-step or twelve-step inspired recovery groups. You have learned, grown, and with the help of your recovery program become able to manage the biggest problem in your life: addiction. Through the powerful examples and support of others in the program, you have achieved a status called being *in recovery*—you've stopped an addictive habit, and its devastating effects are gone from your life.

The support system of the twelve-step program, and the "family" feeling that develops among members, rebuilt your self-esteem, which was so devastated by addictive behavior. This self-esteem begins to develop in much the same way it develops in a small child, based on rewards and approval for "good behavior" (maintaining abstinence or sobriety, and attending meetings). For many, it may have been the first time that their productive, healthy behavior has been rewarded.

Building self-esteem in those who have had it damaged can be a long-term process; in some cases, the damage began in early childhood, and takes considerable support and encouragement to repair. The stronger your self-esteem gets, the greater your investment in your recovery and the greater your chances of remaining free of your addiction.

The particular genius of the recovery program is to help people caught up in overwhelming addictions to get into, and stay in, recovery. There are several components that contribute to keeping members emotionally invested in recovery, even when it's difficult:

- the support of the group
- the accountability of knowing you'll be going to a meeting (especially once you have made friends you must face there)
- the constant availability of the sponsor
- the continuity provided by receiving *chips* (tokens given for each month of sobriety) and celebrating *birthdays* (the anniversaries of your sobriety.)

But most recovery programs, though they help stop the initial addiction, also unwittingly ignore or create an equally serious problem: As a member, you can never complete and move beyond recovery, because the underlying dependency (such as low self-esteem, lack of self-control, inability to establish intimacy, lack of motivation, inability of self-expression) that made you addictive is not addressed. The difference between "recovery" and full healing is confronting and correcting this internal dependency. There are more accurate ways to measure health than just looking at the duration of your sobriety. Your health can be measured, in part, by your attitudes about your independence, self-esteem, abilities, change, problems, emotions, and self-awareness.

Overcoming dependency, rather than remaining forever in recovery, means having the self-confidence to face your problems on your own, learning to think calmly and rationally about stressful situations, and knowing you can handle difficulty without having to hide in an addiction to people, sub-stances, or behaviors—in short, achieving autonomy.

A twelve-step group devotes all its efforts to stopping your addiction and simply accepts that you will continue to remain addicted forever, no matter how long you have abstained. That's why you are told to "keep coming back" and that "recovery is forever." The program does not correct the *mental* patterns that accompany the addiction. For example: you may have stopped drinking, but still have difficulties forming lasting relation-ships; you may have overcome bingeing, but still are unable to work out problems on the job; you may have stopped working compulsively, but don't know how to get along with your spouse and children. From a therapist's viewpoint, addiction is not the problem but the *symptom* of greater underlying prob-lems. What are these problems? What are the causes of ad-diction?

Many recovery counselors believe, with some justice, that addictive behaviors are actually ineffective attempts to heal or relieve intolerable pain. According to addiction expert Anne Wilson Schaef, when we have our addiction to hide in, "we do not have to deal with our anger, pain, depression, confusion, or even our joy or we feel them only vaguely. We stop relying on our knowledge and our sense and start relying on our confused perceptions to tell us what we know and sense. In time, this lack of internal awareness deadens our internal processes, which in turn allows us to remain addicted."

Although this explanation comes close, it does not com-pletely explain the causes of addiction. Many people have faced enormous pain and suffering from childhood on without re-sorting to addictive behaviors to help them hide from it. People who are disabled, disadvantaged, or come from broken homes or otherwise *dysfunctional* families can often successfully cope with pain on their own in a healthy, functional manner, every day of their lives.

The difference is that those who turned to addiction had al-ready been made to feel that they were not strong, capable, or smart enough to cope with life on their own and had to *depend* on someone or something stronger than they were to help them through life's pain and suffering. The cause of their addiction was not pain, but the fact that dysfunctional parents had made them perceive themselves as *unable to cope* with pain. Since these people *knew* in advance that they could not handle difficulty when it arose, they began to look for a place to hide, for a person, substance, or behavior they could *depend* on to help avoid the problem. Therapists call this condition *dependency*, and it, not the pain, is the cause of addiction, compulsion, obsession, and codependency.

In order to free yourself from the underlying factors that lead to addiction, and develop into an autonomous individual dependent only on yourself, you will need to overcome the mental attitudes that perpetuate dependency.

> *Hopelessness*—a feeling of "What's the use" or "I'm not capable anyway"; often accompanied by a feeling that you're undeserving
>
> *Helplessness*—related to hopelessness, a doubt that you can set intentions and keep them, or that you can take care of yourself when necessary
>
> *Dependence on others*—looking for motivation, support, and comfort from *outside* yourself
>
> *Fear of pain*—the inability to heal your old hurts; constant self-criticism; and unresolved emotions: fear, rage, and guilt
>
> *Self-abandonment*—lack of understanding of your responsibility to yourself, and no experience of the joys of self-awareness and self-love
>
> *Mindlessness*—avoiding thinking or being aware by looking for answers to problems from others; lack of willingness to think about options; lack of choice

Inherent in this belief pattern is a feeling of powerlessness. (I *cannot* help myself, I am not strong enough to cope with life, fear, pain, helplessness, relationships, and so on.) Dependency is a conviction that you cannot survive without the addiction, person, substance, or behavior that you rely on. When you try, feelings of rage, fear, and panic begin to emerge, overwhelming you, and sending you back to the "safety" of addiction, which you depend upon to numb or deaden them. These unresolved feelings, the result of your painful history, seem more terrifying than the ravages of alcohol, abusive mates, or even the risk of a fatal heart attack from compulsive smoking, overeating, or workaholism, because you do not believe yourself strong enough to resolve them without help.

Anne Wilson Schaef, author of *When Society Becomes an Addict*, writing in *New Age Journal*, proposes a definition of addiction that emphasizes this sense of powerlessness and dependency:

> An addiction is any process over which we are powerless. It takes control of us, causing us to do and think things that are inconsistent with our personal values and leading us to become progressively more compulsive and obsessive. . . . An addiction is anything we feel *tempted* to lie about. An addiction is anything we are not *willing* to give up (we may not *have* to give it up *and* we must be *willing* to do so to be free of addiction).

One of the underlying pains of addiction comes from the buried fear of helplessness and dependency. This dependency is a result of growing up in a dysfunctional family. As Dr. Timmon Cermak, founder of the National Association of Children of Alcoholics, writes in *A Time to Heal*, "In the midst of this unhealthy environment, COAs [children of alcoholics] must pass through the critical stages of developing trust, autonomy, mastery, identity and the ability to separate themselves from those around them." In a healthy family, your parents would help you progress through these stages from an infant's normal dependency through childhood exploration and adolescent separation to autonomous adulthood. However, when your family situation prevents you from completing this process, you remain stuck in the dependency stage, never feeling strong enough or confident enough to cope with life on your own, and looking to something outside yourself to help you through it. The result can be addiction to anything from work to religion.

If instead of learning dependency, you had grown up in a

healthy, functional family, you would have been gradually encouraged to become increasingly autonomous and more self-
reliant. You would have received support when your efforts
went wrong, and approval when they turned out successfully.
You would have learned you could trust and depend on your
own abilities to cope with the problems you encounter in life,
and that you did not need to depend on others to do so for you.
As a self-dependent or independent person, able to face life on
your own two feet, you would be far less likely to turn to addiction to help you through painful experiences.

Although addiction is merely a symptom of a dysfunctional
childhood, it becomes so destructive and so all-absorbing that
you have to stop the addiction and begin recovery before you
can begin to handle the true, underlying problem. As Schaef
says, "At some point we must choose to recover—to arrest the
progress of the addiction—or we will die." By getting into a
program, you have made that choice.

By numbing feelings, addiction also blocks learning and
growth for the period of time covered by an addiction. For this
reason, the AA *Big Book* defines alcoholism as "a state of being
in which the emotions have failed to grow to the stature of the
intellect." So that if you first became addicted to gambling, substances, or codependent relationships when you were fifteen
years old, and you stopped the behavior when you were thirty-
two, it is very likely that your emotional development, attitudes, and reactions will still be those of an adolescent. This
means that whatever physical age you might be when you finally end your cycle of destructive behavior, your social, emotional, and many mental skills will not have advanced much
beyond the level of development they had reached when your
addiction started.

For example, Carl, the alcoholic we met earlier who drank
heavily from age fourteen through age twenty-eight, had
achieved five years of sobriety at age thirty-three, but was left
with the social skills and the emotional development of an
abused fourteen-year-old. He did not know socially polite
"small talk" or etiquette, the correct approach to ask a woman
for a date, or how to develop a lasting relationship. After getting

sober, Carl had to catch up with his contemporaries by learning social skills, information, and knowledge that he had missed. He came to me wanting to know "how to talk to women" and completely mystified about how to make friends, ask for a date, or develop a relationship. He had missed all the skills adolescents and young adults are supposed to learn.

The following chart shows the differences between the attitudes of dependent recovery and of healthy adult autonomy:

RECOVERY	AUTONOMY
Self-control: Overcoming my addiction/compulsion is the most important thing—I still occasionally feel strong urges to revert to old behavior. I need a lot of support and encouragement.	*Self-control:* Addiction is no longer a big issue: a temptation may come up now and then, but I know how to control my impulses.
Gratification: I am focused on instant gratification. I feel deprived when I don't get what I want.	*Gratification:* I understand the value of long-term goals and delayed gratification, and I can motivate myself to keep my long-term goals.
The program: I work hard at the Steps of my program. I do it because it works, but I don't really understand why.	*The program:* I understand what keeps me emotionally healthy. I've modified the Steps and developed my own program to suit my individual nature.
Honesty: I struggle to tell the truth—to myself and others.	*Honesty:* Telling the truth to myself and others is easier for me because my life works better when I do.
Competence: I have a lot of unanswered questions: What is functional living? What is a healthy relationship? I don't think I have everything I need to make my life work.	*Competence:* I feel effective in everyday life. I have the skills I need to be successful, and when I need new skills to achieve my goals, I know I can learn them.

Change: Changes are scary—I want security, and I'm afraid of disappointment.

Change: Change is fun, a challenge, inevitable, an opportunity for growth. Disappointment is a part of learning and growth.

Problems: Problems seem huge and difficult; they might threaten my recovery.

Problems: Problems may be frustrating, but usually can be solved. I can trust myself to refrain from addiction even when things go wrong.

Feelings: I don't know what to do about my intense emotions. They frighten me.

Feelings: Emotions are natural, welcome, easy to handle. My feelings are important and I know what to do about them.

Self-awareness: I don't know who I am and I usually don't know what I feel and can't figure out what I want.

Self-awareness: I know myself well, including what I want and how I feel. I am my best friend, my partner in life.

To complete recovery, to move beyond addiction and dependency, you need to replace the dysfunctional skills of the past with new skills for

- effective communication
- taking risks
- problem solving
- coping with failure
- facing pain
- learning
- forgiveness
- independent behavior

Such skills will help you achieve autonomy.

Clearly, recovery can be only a halfway point. It is not possible or appropriate for recovery groups to attempt to fill all of a member's needs. The specific intent of a program is to steer you into recovery and halt addiction. It is not the program's job to move you beyond recovery. Restructuring the psychic system that created the dependent behavior in the first place is beyond its scope.

At first, having a definite program of steps to follow was an enormous aid to your progress. It gave you the first concrete plan for dealing with your addiction and you welcomed the structure, even though you may have struggled with it. You learned and grew a lot.

But you may have expected that ending your addiction would create a life-changing revelation, and so you may have experienced the disappointment that comes from discovering that though you've stopped your destructive behavior, you still have the same internal problems as before. Frequent meetings and endless talks with sponsors and members help, but when you are alone, your doubt and disappointment are still there.

You may feel the need for something more than what your recovery program is giving you, but you're afraid to tamper with an effective formula that you don't understand because you've been warned you can have a relapse at any time. "Keep coming back," which was encouraging before, has begun to sound oppressive. So you're now feeling better—but you are also feeling trapped.

RECOVERY: DOES IT HAVE TO BE FOREVER?

One reason all twelve-step programs insist you identify yourself as a lifelong addict is that, until you have addressed the underlying dependency, relapses are far more likely if you leave the continuing influence of the group. This is a truth learned from experience, and not as unreasonable or arbitrary as it might seem at first glance. Instead, it is a response to many actual relapses suffered when members, even of long standing, leave the support of the group.

Another reason they insist you identify yourself as a lifelong addict is that people caught up in addictive behavior have a truly astounding capacity to deny problems, to block them out. Such people often have learned to rationalize away even very destructive behavior such as losing jobs and loved ones because of drinking, repeatedly going back to a battering spouse, or gambling away the rent money. They tell themselves:

I can stop anytime.
He/she really needs me.
I'll win it all back next week.
It's all my husband's/wife's/boss's fault.
I just can't resist a good bargain.
No one else will get the work done right.
It's not so bad.
Everyone messes up.

Because of this lifelong tendency of addictive people to deny or minimalize the extent of their problems, as soon as the twelve-step program begins to help them gain control and they stop the damaging behavior, denial kicks in, and they minimalize the problem and believe they're cured. This attitude prompts many people to leave the program's support prematurely, *before* completing the work of the Twelve Steps and learning all they have to offer. Hence, the danger of continual relapses (frequently demonstrated by public figures such as David Crosby, Kitty Dukakis, and Washington Mayor Marion Barry) after proclaiming freedom from the old, destructive behavior.

Child star Drew Barrymore learned this fact the hard way, when she prematurely announced that she was "cured" of her alcoholism in media interviews, then had several public relapses. She told *People* magazine: "The truth is that you are never fully mended. There is no happy ending because there is no end to the struggle for a clean and sober life."

The addict's "quick fix" mentality is another factor in causing relapses for those who leave the program prematurely. If you have been addictive, compulsive, or obsessive you are probably familiar with this tendency to look for a quick or easy answer.

The twelve-step programs and most of the other recovery groups combat the relapses caused by denial and the quick-fix mentality by reminding you that quitting destructive behavior alone is not enough and telling you that you *will never get beyond recovery*. That's why the twelve-step programs urge you not to refer to yourself as "recovered," but "in recovery." In order to tell your story at meetings, you must first say, "I am a recovering alcoholic (addict, overeater, and so on) . . ." As an AA pamphlet states: "Alcoholism does not go away . . . recovery is forever."

But recovery only lasts forever when nothing is done to combat addiction's underlying causes, when the emotional problems and dependent attitudes that precipitated the addictive behavior still exist.

One sign of the failure to address underlying problems is a condition Alcoholics Anonymous calls a *dry drunk*. A dry drunk occurs when someone has stopped drinking but still exhibits "absence of favorable change in . . . attitudes and behavior . . . or the reversion to these attitudes and behavior by the alcoholic who has experienced a period of successful sobriety." A dry drunk is someone who is not recovering from the addictive behavior and the unhealthy attitudes that created it.

As Dr. R. J. Solberg, alcoholism expert, puts it in *The Dry Drunk Syndrome*, "The alcoholic, when drinking, has learned to rely on a deeply inadequate, radically immature approach to solving life's problems. And this is exactly what one sees in the dry drunk." Dr. Solberg describes the "obvious traits" of a "full-blown dry drunk":

Grandiosity—unrealistic expectations of your own abilities

Judgmentalism—being highly critical of others

Intolerance—not accepting others' individual mistakes or differences

Impulsivity—acting without thinking

Indecisiveness—inability to make up your mind

Dishonesty—lying, cheating, making false promises

Controlling—pressuring others into doing what you want

Self-centeredness—unable to consider others' feelings and needs

According to Anne Wilson Schaef, the "dry drunk syndrome" means you can be in recovery and still be addicted: "Individuals who are not chemically dependent and yet function in the addictive process are on a dry drunk." Recovery literature implicitly recognizes the connection between relapse and failure to address the causes of addictive behavior. Dr. Solberg writes that the condition is dangerous because "every relapse is preceded by a dry drunk which was allowed to go untreated."

One final reason that the twelve-step programs believe that recovery is forever is that those who created and maintained the programs did so as a result of their own involvement with compulsion and obsession. In short, their conviction that recovery is forever may be a symptom of the very lack of self-trust and self-confidence that led to their own difficulties in recovering from addiction. Having spent years unsuccessfully struggling, unable to manage their own addiction without the constant support of a group, they become convinced that no one can. In fact, their very expertise in the field may be a resolution of a dilemma: How do you continue to grow and challenge yourself and still remain in recovery? The answer is: Become more and more expert about addiction.

However, the constant pressure to "keep coming back" can also mean that a member who has recovered sufficiently to venture out independently from the group will be made to feel guilty for leaving. The results can be tragic. Members either abandon their fledgling impulses toward autonomy and further growth, returning to an even more complete dependency on the group, or the resulting guilt feelings undercut their developing self-esteem and they escape back into their old addictive behavior.

Because twelve-step programs often "feel like family," they can have a powerful influence. To the degree that they undercut your autonomy, and keep you dependent, they are like your original, dysfunctional family.

SUSAN

Susan, a thirty-two-year-old recovering codependent, faithfully worked her program for two years, and began to feel stronger. She sought the encouragement of friends outside the program, and began to realize her dream: to open her own flower shop. Things went very well at first, because Susan had a flair for floral design and was personable with customers.

Then the shop began to get very busy. Susan felt stressed. She was attending three meetings a week, and working constantly at her shop. After being exhausted and stressed for several months, she decided to drop her meetings. This gave her the extra time she needed for herself, but it had consequences: she felt guilty and afraid of relapse, and her friends from meetings began telling her she needed her meetings, and she was making a big mistake. Soon, they stopped calling her. Susan ignored her fear and stress for a while, but without emotional support, her enthusiasm for her business began to falter. She began overeating and bingeing, she became panicky and disorganized, and she eventually gave up her store lease and moved the faltering floral business into her home. She was in despair, and ready to give up, go back to being a secretary (which she hated), and attend all her old meetings. Susan says: "I was a mess— worse than before I joined CoDA. I even talked to a doctor and tried prescription drugs, but they just made me drowsy. The anxiety was still there. I began to feel suicidal."

Then, a concerned friend suggested she come to see me. Susan was overloaded with guilt and self-doubt, so we examined her decisions of the past year. Soon she was able to see that her problems had merely been the normal things that happen with a new business, and her relapse occurred because she let her guilt and fears override her thinking ability. We worked to resolve her fear of failure, which originally came from a family belief that she was the "pretty one" and "not too bright"; but was exaggerated by her twelve-step friends' insistence that she would fail if she left the group. She got in control of her eating again, made friends among other people in the floral business, and reevaluated what she wanted to do with floral design. This time, she designed her business to meet her needs and desires, kept it smaller, to be less overwhelming, took some courses in business, and ignored what friends thought she should do. Susan is now enjoying a small, exclusive, and thriving business, and she has time for a social life, recreation, friends, and romance. She says, "Without advice or help from anyone who knew floral business skills, I got frightened and confused, and stopped doing *what I already knew how to do to keep myself healthy.* I know now that it's my responsibility—not the program's, to keep me doing what I know is right, and to learn what I need to know."

Being trapped in the Twelve Steps is like being admitted into school to learn a skill, but never being allowed to graduate no matter how competent you become. In this (twelve-step) school, a student may turn around and become a teacher (a sponsor), but may not graduate honorably and finally.

This begins to undermine the self-esteem so painstakingly won through the program. Although people have successfully withdrawn from the program, they generally feel guilty and insecure about their ability to succeed on their own for years after leaving. This guilt and insecurity, coupled with a lack of information about independent living, is often a cause for relapse, which provides an excuse to return to the safety of the group. The less adventurous never leave at all. To encourage health and growth, twelve-step programs need a provision for graduation and moving on. They need a Thirteenth Step.

Of course, recovery is not a quick and easy process. Yet, although the skepticism caused by relapses is understandable, recovery does not really have to be forever. The whole history of psychology and human beings proves over and over again that it is possible for a dysfunctional or "radically immature" person to mature, to become functional, and to develop a permanent and enduring ability to remain free from dependency and addiction.

You may feel that you are ready for graduation and to take the Thirteenth Step to personal autonomy. Or, if you still believe that recovery is forever, you may be ready to take the Step and not be aware of it: you may have dismissed the restless signs as denial, or as further evidence of your own emotional problems. Either way, how do you tell if your feeling of restlessness and of having gotten all you can out of the group is not simply a wish to be healed (denial), or if it is a legitimate indication that you are ready to move on to healing and autonomy? The following quiz is designed to help you decide if you have completed the work of recovery and are ready for the Real Thirteenth Step. Answer the questions *yes* or *no*:

QUIZ: ARE YOU TRULY READY TO COMPLETE RECOVERY?

1. Have you identified and admitted your obsessive, compulsive, or addictive behavior?
2. Have you maintained abstinence or sobriety for six months to one year without relapse?
3. Have you completed each of the Twelve Steps at least once, or followed another recovery program through completion?
4. Have you been following your program faithfully for at least this time period?
5. Do you have a sponsor, buddy, therapist, or other knowledgeable person with whom you discuss your problems in recovery?
6. Do you devote some time each day to meditation, prayer, or solitary contemplation?
7. Have you become aware of the difference between your conscious personality and the Higher Power within?
8. Have you learned to recognize and handle successfully the triggers and mechanisms that set off your compulsive/addictive behavior?
9. Have you shared your story repeatedly with others, and listened to theirs?
10. Are you able to rely on others for support and ask for help when you need it?

11. Have you had a successful relationship with a sponsor, buddy, or other support person for a significant time?

12. If you are from a severely dysfunctional family, or a survivor of abuse or incest: have you had sufficient therapy, individually and/or in group, to heal the damaging legacy of your childhood?

13. Have you severed or limited all relationships with people who supported your addictions and compulsions, unless they are also fully in recovery?

14. Can you say "No" when tempted or pressured?

15. Do you know the difference between instant and deferred gratification, and can you choose intelligently between them?

16. Can you *act* on thoughtful decisions instead of impulsively *react* to events and circumstances?

17. Do you have a clear sense of who you are, and what your goals are?

Of course, these questions are somewhat arbitrary, since only you possess your own unique blend of accomplishments, situations, and personal growth, but if you have answered yes to most of these seventeen questions, you are probably ready to take the Thirteenth Step.

If you answered no to any of the above questions, but still want to aim toward autonomy, you may need to do further work within a recovery group until you have arrested the worst of your dependency and addiction. Then, when you can honestly answer yes to most of the above questions, consider whether it is appropriate for you to move on into graduation.

SURRENDERING THE DREAM OF DEPENDENCY

But what is completing recovery? It begins, of course, with entering recovery in the first place. "My Wednesday night meeting has so many new people . . . I need to hear more recovery," said Ava, thirty-five, describing her changing attitudes after a few years in CoDA. "It's good for me to go to that meeting and share *my* recovery, that's my Twelfth Step; but I'm also joining another meeting where I can hear less of 'I'm having this terrible problem, and it's awful' and more of 'I'm having a problem, and here's what I'm doing about it.'" Ava's description pinpoints the essence of recovery—moving from absorption with the problem to focus on the solution. In order to move *beyond* recovery toward a healthy and independent life, you must have laid that groundwork; but there are still hurdles to overcome. "As the price of liberty is vigilance—so the price of independence is self-determination, the price of dignity is self-assertion, and the price of respect is self-respect," wrote psychiatrist Dr. Thomas Szasz.

Self-determination and self-respect are the necessary keys most dependent people need to grasp the concept of taking full responsibility for and control over their own lives. Until they find these keys, dependent people are like Teddy, a well-educated and talented man who, when he began to be aware of his internal attitudes, said in frustration, "I'm thirty-six, and I still live my life as though *someone else* is in charge of it." Why does Teddy feel this way? Because he has turned his life over to others he believes can take care of him and advise and protect him from harm better than he could himself. Teddy has not yet learned that to feel wholly in charge of himself and his life he must give up what I call the Dream of Dependency—the dream that there is someone else who can make it better, who can take total care of you, who can be responsible for you more effectively than you can yourself.

We have this dream for two reasons: 1) when we were little our parents led us to believe that someone *would* take care of us and make it better; 2) dysfunctional parents failed to teach us the skills necessary to take care of and feel capable of being responsible for ourselves. Autonomy is what begins when we realize how false and destructive this dream is—when we understand that no one can take care of us better and that only we are responsible for our lives—and when we start to learn effective methods for doing these things ourselves. Autonomy is composed of many things:

Self-reliance—this is the dictionary definition of autonomy; making your own rules and living by them; also called self-governing

Self-determination—deciding your own future through planning and careful action

Higher purpose—self-motivation; a desire to create and accomplish regardless of outer rewards, for the *satisfaction* of accomplishment

Self-confidence—the security that comes from having a sense of purpose, and the confidence to accomplish your purpose

Self-esteem—appreciation of your talents and abilities; the recognition that you are a healthy, capable, and lovable person

Self-love—learning to care for yourself the way you care for your friends

By achieving autonomy, you gain three important possessions. First, you acquire the emotional strength necessary to free yourself from dependency. Dependent people, when faced with a problem, wait helplessly (or demand hysterically) for someone else to solve it. To be responsible is to be able to make effective decisions and choices for yourself, to weigh alternatives, and to evaluate ethical dilemmas and solve problems. When a problem arises, instead of blaming someone else or running away through denial or addictive behavior, the autonomous person faces it squarely, learns as much as possible about it, considers many options, weighs the possible outcome of each option, and perhaps seeks advice and counsel before reaching a decision. As an autonomous person, you can ask directly for help, but you remain in charge of how much and what kind of help you accept, and you make clear agreements about what is expected in return.

Second, you develop the role model that enables you to

choose appropriate friends and a suitable mate. The interaction you have with yourself is a role model for all your other relationships. For example, if you criticize yourself frequently, you're more likely to stay around others who are critical because it feels familiar. Likewise, learning about autonomy in yourself also helps you see it in others. When you have a caring, responsible relationship with yourself, you develop an interal relationship model to use as a basis for your friendships and intimate relationships with others. As you become more experienced at identifying healthy friendships, your circle of good friends grows—beginning with your relationship with yourself, expanding to a few new friends, and eventually growing into a supportive "family of choice," who reinforce your autonomy and independence.

Third, you acquire the understanding that you are responsible for yourself and must learn whatever you need to make your life successful, functional, and happy.

Taking care of and being responsible for yourself requires skills that are usually learned in early childhood. However, those of us born in dysfunctional families don't always get the healthy, positive examples we need, so we grow up without the necessary learning. Christina Crawford, of *Mommie Dearest* fame, eloquently describes her situation:

> Maybe I never knew who I was. Maybe I never had time to spend knowing who I was. My life as a child was spent concentrating on saving myself from a crazy person. But when, as an adult, you can't get your needs met because as a child no one was there to validate and love you and you never developed interpersonal life skills, that is how you live.

This is not unusual, or entirely the fault of our parents. If you were gradually taught and encouraged to be self-reliant from early childhood, you would learn the necessary skills and attitudes for autonomous living one step at a time. Unfortunately for many of us, our parents were not trained in autonomy either, and could not teach us. Dr. Charles Whitfield, author of *Healing the Child Within*, notes this fact:

Rarely does anyone find a mother, other parent figure or close friend who is even *capable* of providing or of helping us to meet all our needs. . . . Many mothers or other parent figures are mentally and emotionally impoverished. A likely reason is that *their* needs were not met as infants, children and/or adults.

The pressure of growing up dependent on adults who are themselves dependent distorts the child's development, writes Timmon Cermak, in *A Time to Heal*:

Children of alcoholics are forced to crystallize their identities under circumstances that are far from optimal. Their environment lacks a core feeling of safety. Communication is distorted by denial, leading to the deafening silence of secrets. Self-care is misinterpreted as selfishness. Roles become rigid so that the family can protect itself from change. A sense of continuity does not exist. Neither is there any significant privacy. In the midst of this unhealthy environment, CoAs must pass through the critical stages of developing trust, autonomy, mastery, identity and the ability to separate themselves from those around them.

Even the popular idea of parents' responsibility for children can be counterproductive. Because parents think in terms of *controlling* their offspring rather than teaching them to make choices on their own, most children are taught dependency, not autonomy. The result of this emphasis on dependency, writes editor Connie Zweig in *To Be a Woman*, is far-reaching:

Psychologically, deep within, many of us do not fully separate from one or both of our parents or from the stereotyped expectations of society . . . most people do not develop fully balanced egos or a sense of real individuality in our society; we remain dysfunctional in some essential ways. We continue to carry mother and father within us, not only following in their footsteps but often actually walking in their shoes. We re-create our parents' patterns, becoming second-generation alcoholics, abusive parents, or compulsive high achievers. Or we rebel against them, believing ourselves to have broken the patterns, but actually remaining unconsciously trapped within them.

Another reason autonomy can seem difficult is because most of our society actively discourages it. Media images of love and caring, a parental "I know what's best for you" attitude among helping professionals, religious and political leaders, and the generally accepted idea of parents' duty create an atmosphere in which autonomy appears to be selfish and alien. We are taught to value caring for others to the point of martyrdom, and to regard caring for ourselves as self-centered and egotistic. Alice Miller, the famed psychoanalyst who writes about harmful attitudes of parenting, says parents often operate on false beliefs:

A high degree of self-esteem is harmful in children. Such parents punish, denigrate, and belittle their children, producing "good little boys and girls" who learn to look outside for approval. This is the "spare the rod and spoil the child" attitude.

A low degree of self-esteem makes a child altruistic. Such parents often express their belief as: "It is better to give than to receive," with the added idea that you don't deserve to receive anyway.

A feeling of duty produces love. Such parents do not believe that their children will love them if allowed to choose autonomously. It is child-management by guilt: "If you love me, you'll . . . " or shame: "You're a bad little girl/boy if you don't . . . "

Such parental attitudes prevent children from learning self-esteem and the pleasure of self-love. As we shall see in the next chapter, children who don't learn self-esteem grow into dependent adults. Children who don't learn self-love and self-control (rather learning guilt and duty) become addictive adults. Those children who are taught self-esteem and autonomy and who therefore take care of themselves are viewed with disbelief ("She can't be that good"), suspicion ("Yes, but if we only knew . . ."), and envy ("Some people have all the luck") by other parents.

Recovery programs are challenging the social attitudes of addictive and dependent adults by defining caring for others without regard for self as *codependency* and *enabling*. Books such as *CoDependent No More* by Melody Beattie and *When Society Becomes an Addict* by Anne Wilson Schaef have popularized a concept long established in psychology theory: that it is unhealthy to be too dependent on another. However, although all these have indicated that dependency is unhealthy, they haven't yet learned to value *autonomy*.

Contrary to these beliefs, independence and autonomy actually enhance relationships with others, and allow giving and receiving to be truly unconditional. Only a person who is fully able to care for him- or herself can be free to love and give freely; deprived people give grudgingly. The chart on the next page will help you compare what autonomy is and isn't.

As children, our natural curiosity is powerful. In fact, young children are small "learning machines"—their whole being is focused on learning through their five senses. Research shows that children are "turned on" by situations in which they can learn. Their bodies produce hormones such as adrenaline and endorphins—natural substances that produce a "natural high"—the body's own, internal motivation and reward system for learning.

When faced with a new experience, as long as they feel safe and unthreatened, young children are highly motivated to explore and learn. Secure toddlers are irresistibly drawn to bright colors, new sounds, and new experiences—they find your jingling car keys fascinating. To a child who has supportive, loving, functional parents, the world is a fun, safe place to be, and learning is exciting and exhilarating. Children who feel secure are compelled by their joy in learning to venture forth, to begin to take small risks, and begin to act independently of their parents. In taking these risks, under parental supervision and support at first and increasingly independently as the child grows older, the necessary skills of autonomy are first learned.

Autonomy grows out of these healthy learning experiences. Through taking risks, we learn how to solve problems, and also how to deal effectively with disappointment and failure. When we have learned these skills, our experiences with life are successful, producing confidence that we can rely on ourselves to experiment, to solve new problems we encounter, and to comfort our disappointment and correct our mistakes. When we know how to do these things, we know we are capable of autonomy.

Frightened, insecure children, in contrast, are dependent on the adults around them. Their world is too insecure for them to

AUTONOMY IS	AUTONOMY IS NOT
Knowing yourself	Narcissism
Liking yourself	Being selfish
Being committed to take care of yourself—no matter what	Dependence or neediness
Being able to enjoy your own company	Loneliness, hiding out, rudeness, rejecting behavior
Making your own decisions and carrying them out	Procrastination, helplessness
Doing what's important and good for you even when others don't like it	Codependency, pleasing others at great cost to your well-being or self-esteem
Enjoying others, but not making them more important than yourself	Sacrificing and martyrdom, rescuing (helping those who haven't asked for it)
Making thoughtful decisions	Avoidance
Thinking clearly in a crisis	Hysterical panic
Being a competent adult who can play and be childlike, but always think like a grown-up loving wholeheartedly but still thinking clearly about yourself, your lover, and your relationship	Childishness, reacting, acting out, grimness, joylessness, limerance, self-destructive love, loving those who are unavailable

risk, and they look to others to solve their problems and care for their feelings. Being unaware of your motives, feelings, wants, and attitudes toward yourself leaves you out of control, unable to figure out how to satisfy yourself. It is indeed as though you don't own your life, as though someone else must be running it.

Here are several situations that are common for people who have dependency problems—first as they are usually handled by dependent people, and then as they are handled by those who have achieved autonomy.

You find yourself letting your exercise routine go, because your new lover doesn't exercise. *Dependency*: You notice this, but you do nothing about it. *Autonomy*: You notice it, and go on to discuss the situation with your lover, explain how important your routine is to you, and discuss possible solutions until you find a mutually satisfactory plan.

Your raise is due, and you deserve it, but it hasn't been mentioned. *Dependency*: You're afraid to ask about it. *Autonomy*: You request an appointment with your supervisor, and calmly remind her of the due date.

You call a plumber to fix a stopped-up drain, and he wants to tear out the whole wall and replace all the pipes. *Dependency*: Even though you think he's wrong, and you'd like another opinion, you let him do it. *Autonomy*: You ask him for a clear explanation of why he wants to do the extra work. When you find out that boring the drain out would be a temporary solution, you ask him to do that, and give yourself time to get another estimate on the larger job. When you have two or three estimates, you make your decision.

You feel anxious, and you go to the doctor to see if your thyroid is overactive. Your physical says everything's OK, but the doctor prescribes Valium to calm you down. *Dependency*: You don't think it's good for you, but you take it because he said so. *Autonomy*: You tell her that you're unwilling to take tranquilizers or relaxants, and ask for alternatives. She recommends therapy, yoga, or meditation. You ask your friends for recommendations and join a class in relaxation techniques.

Your friend, who has had a number of accidents, asks to borrow your car. *Dependency*: You worry about it, but you give him the car keys. *Autonomy*: You say, "I'm sorry. I'd like to help, but I can't loan you my car. Can I drive you somewhere?"

Your brother, who's always in debt and never pays you back, asks for money. *Dependency*: You resent it, but you give it to him. *Autonomy*: You explain that you don't have extra to give away, and carrying the debt he owes you is beginning to hurt your relationship. You care too much about him to let it go any further.

Your wife always wants to spend Thanksgiving at her mother's. *Dependency*: Even though you miss holidays at your family, and they complain that they miss you, you give in to keep the peace at home. *Autonomy*: You tell her that you miss holidays at your family, and they complain that they miss you, so you want to talk about other options. Together, you discuss the problem, talk to your respective families, and decide that this year you'll go to your parents on Thanksgiving, and your wife's family on the Sunday after.

Your husband is much harsher with your children than you think is right. *Dependency*: You say nothing because you are afraid of him. *Autonomy*: You call a child psychologist to get an independent opinion, and when the psychologist says the behavior is abusive, you request that your husband go with you to family counseling. If he refuses, you go to counseling yourself to find out how to protect yourself and your children.

Your former roommate has too much to drink at your party. *Dependency*: You don't think she should drive home, but when she insists, you let her. *Autonomy*: You don't think she should drive home, so you call a taxi and keep her car keys. The next day, you call and make arrangements for her to get her car.

You hear that your friend spread a rumor about you. *Dependency*: You're hurt and confused, but you don't ask her about it; you just let the friendship deteriorate. *Autonomy*: You're hurt and confused, so you ask her to have lunch with you. At lunch, you tell her what you heard, ask her if it's true, and get an explanation that clears things up.

A solid sense of autonomy makes graduating from your recovery program feel like a natural next step. You begin to choose your friends independently of the group, keeping those friends from the program that enhance your life and making other friends outside the program. You will want to do more and more activities that are not program-related. As your life becomes more fulfilling and active, you will need meetings less. You will begin to revise and change your original program to a discipline and pattern that expresses your own uniqueness, and incorporates what you've learned about yourself. For example, your Twelfth Step may evolve into sharing your experience of autonomy with others, both in and out of recovery programs, rather than continuing to attend meetings and sponsor people.

Many people ask: "Does taking the Real Thirteenth Step mean I can safely engage in my old addictive behaviors again without relapsing?" However, no client of mine, who has worked a program and been sober for a while, has ever asked this question. Their attitude is: "I feel so great without it, why should I hurt myself?" Or, as Richard O. said earlier, "I don't want, desire, nor have a yen for booze."

Mary L. seconds this idea: "The last thing I would want to do is go back to my old, dependent relationships—I'm finally free, and I don't need my old behavior any more."

Susan, when asked if she misses her old overeating behavior, says: "The food I eat now is right for me. It's healthy, delicious, and satisfying. I don't feel deprived at all—why would I want to mess this up?"

There are many addictive substances: cocaine, cigarettes, alcohol, fat, sugar, salt, caffeine, marijuana, some over-the-counter medicines, prescription drugs, and all street drugs. In small doses, some of the above are not a serious health problem; so, if you can limit your intake to small doses, it might be safe for you. But (unless your doctor prescribes something) you don't need them; so why ingest what's not good for you? Some people choose to have small amounts—they have only one cigarette a month, or one glass of wine a week, or only drink decaf coffee. Small amounts of fat, salt, and sugar can be part of a healthy, balanced diet.

Dr. Andrew Weil, professor of addiction studies at the University of Arizona, in a lecture on our confusion about drugs, gave an excellent overview of the autonomous person's attitude toward substances with a potential for abuse:

> Drugs, sex and food are the areas most concerned with pleasure and the areas of human experience that I see emotion most strongly affect. . . . Think of the psychological effects. . . . Does it make you calm and centered? Does it make you jangled? Does it make you sexually aroused? Do you feel like going out and beating someone up? Pay attention to those kinds of things . . . try to be aware of how they affect you and make some conscious choices about what happens to you. Make conscious choices about how and with what you nourish yourself.

Achieving autonomy means knowing your sensitivity and capacity, being realistic about it, and acting accordingly. Achieving autonomy means acquiring the self-confidence and self-reliance you need to cope with and overcome the temptation of a relapse (because you understand the inner dynamics that underlie your struggle, and how to handle them) without the need to go to a meeting or call a sponsor every time the issue comes up. Learning to do that is part of completing the Real Thirteenth Step.

Denton Roberts, a minister and psychotherapist, describes autonomy in his book *Able and Equal*:

> Autonomy is the knowledge that we are the *owners* of our lives. We are not owned by parents, bosses, government, church, neighbors, spouses, children or cars. . . . We are not, sometimes much to our dismay, victims of people and institutions. No longer being a victim means we determine our lives and what to do with them. Our ability to respond to life is both an asset and a challenge. Without the indul-

gent feeling of being victimized by the world or circumstances, we take possession of life.

After completing the exercises and processes in this book, you will have enough experience in what autonomy feels like to build upon what you know and, with practice, to take full and complete responsibility for your life. You will also begin to be aware of how well the people around you have developed their own autonomy, and how to choose appropriate partners for friendship and intimate relationships. You will have a sense of your value to yourself, your worth within the society, and your power as a healthy individual. As Denton Roberts writes, "When we possess a healthy sense of our autonomy we are no longer willing to define ourselves by what we are against; instead we define and direct ourselves by what we are for."

The kind of personal power that comes from taking care of yourself feels good, so once you experience it, it is quite easy to develop the motivation you need to maintain it. The lack of it becomes obvious. It is similar to the experience of serenity found while working your recovery program. Once you feel serenity, a sense of inner peace, you can tell when it's missing. Once you feel the joy and power of taking full responsibility for yourself, and the satisfaction of a life you have carefully chosen for yourself, your motivation to maintain the feeling will be high.

CHAPTER 2

Addicted to Recovery

I loved drinking. The most difficult part . . . is ad-
mitting: "I have a problem I can't control. . . ." In
this area you have to be willing to give up, willing
to be helped . . . you will get nowhere, until you
are ready to admit defeat . . . and thereby win a
victory you may never have thought was possible.
JACK LEMMON

Have you joined several twelve-step programs, each designed to help you overcome a different addiction, yet still
feel your life is somehow seriously out of your control?

The failure of recovery programs to provide a context for
achieving healthy, independent living leaves members with no
alternative but to remain with the group if they are to avoid relapsing to their old addictions. Having spent years developing
destructive habits, it is very easy for members to let their addiction to the group become equally destructive. If they were rigid,
dominating, and overcontrolling with family and loved ones
before, they now become equally so in the name of the Twelve
Steps, demanding that everyone under their influence join
groups or act in the way these groups do. If they were insecure
and frightened before, they remain that way now except when
they are surrounded by the warmth and support of the group—
attending meetings almost every free moment—or they move
from programs devoted to one kind of addiction (alcoholism)

to another (codependency) in a vain attempt to solve every problem they have through the Twelve Steps.

This pattern has led many therapists and addiction counselors to believe that something is needed to help "meeting junkies," twelve-step members who cannot get beyond constant attendance at meetings, or cope with life on their own. Therapist Bob Holder wrote to *New Age Magazine:* "In my work as a consultant, I have observed clients becoming addicted to the twelve-step programs and unable to transcend [them]." The experts feel that a Twelve Steps Anonymous is called for to handle peoples' addiction to the program.

Undoubtedly, you have heard something of the controversy reflected in the conflict among professionals about the Twelve Steps and the ultimate effect of recovery programs. For example, Dr. Stanton Peele, author of *The Diseasing of America,* believes that the program is emotionally destructive: "The chief innovation in AA philosophy is the idea that . . . alcoholism is inbred, . . . also irreversible. . . . Alcoholics are obligated to think of themselves as having a lifetime condition . . . they are exactly one drink away from total relapse and the need to start again at day one."

In contrast, Gerald Goodman, director of the UCLA Self-Help Center, takes the opposite view and sees the program as an important benefit: "If you look beneath those controversial Twelve Steps into actual AA method, you'll find a remarkable set of psychological mechanisms that have changed the way the world thinks about repairing the addict."

The specific intent of the Twelve Steps is to help you overcome your addiction and achieve sobriety, serenity, and recovery. Although you can overcome substance abuse, correct some dysfunctional thinking, and establish a foundation for self-esteem by completing the Twelve Steps, you cannot learn independent thinking, choice making, self-reliance, or healthy relating. Eliminating alcohol or other addictive substances or compulsive behaviors is essential because it makes it possible for you to think clearly enough to learn; but the information given in the program is nowhere near sufficient to retrain and reeducate the habits of a lifetime, or to replace destructive, dysfunctional family patterns with healthy habits. Restructuring the mental patterns and the often abusive history that create the need for obsessive/compulsive/addictive behavior is beyond the program's scope.

Ironically, the same Twelve Steps that help you recover from your addiction, allowing the growth that has prepared you for autonomy, can also act to undermine that autonomy even before it can begin to develop. By making you dependent on meetings and the Steps, the program keeps you involved long enough to overcome your denial and resistance to sobriety and serenity; but, once you are far enough along in your recovery, that same new dependency may hold you back from further growth.

In this chapter we take a close look at how the recovery programs, so effective at putting a stop to addiction, can also work to foster dependency on the group—creating an addiction to recovery—and what you need to do to overcome the limitations, and even destruction, this new addiction creates and to "kick the habit" of recovery.

THE POWER AND PERIL OF THE TWELVE STEPS

The steps quoted here are adapted from the original Twelve Steps, as formulated by Alcoholics Anonymous (although exact wording of the steps can vary slightly from group to group, they remain the same in essence). Except for the additions in brackets, they are quoted from *Alcoholics Anonymous*.

Step One
We admitted we were powerless over [your addiction: alcohol, gambling, drugs, food, and so forth]—that our lives had become unmanageable.

Why this step aids recovery. Step One was created to help confront the four forms of denial:

Grandiosity: I'm in control. I can stop drinking/smoking/ shooting up whenever I want to. I don't have a problem.

Blaming self: He doesn't mean to beat me up, I really deserved it. He'll change. He loves me.

Blaming others: I drink because she nags me. If she left me alone, I wouldn't have a problem.

Despair: Oh, what's the use, I'll never change. Nothing can be done.

Until you confront and accept the fact that your addictive behavior *is* your problem, no healing can occur, because your mechanisms of denial keep the truth out of your awareness and your addictive behavior too well defended.

As Jim Munsen writes in "From Denial to Surrender," addictive behavior "is a disease of denial. If you confront a practicing alcoholic with the possibility that he is an alcoholic, the response will be 'No, I'm not!' ninety-nine times out of a hundred." Denial can still be at work even when you get to the program: "I didn't come to AA to stop drinking, I just wanted to stop getting into trouble. I knew that every time I got into trouble alcohol was involved, but I never considered alcohol to be the cause of the trouble." This is typical alcoholic thinking.

Those familiar with addictive persons know that no addict will be motivated to do something about his/her habit until he/ she "hits bottom." In your own life, you know that something forced you to face your problem and finally get to a meeting. Whether that was loss of a relationship, a drunk-driving arrest, bankruptcy or debt problems, or just the realization that you didn't approve of your own behavior, for you, it was hitting bottom.

Step One begins there, at your first awareness of the trouble, by asking every member to admit he or she is out of control. Thus, the initial step toward hope and healing becomes acknowledging reality. Life *is* unmanageable.

How this step impedes autonomy. Once your denial is overcome (which takes time and experience), continuing to believe you are powerless over the addiction becomes counterproductive. Failure to realize your *own* growing power prevents you from achieving anything beyond arresting your addictive behavior. Taken uncritically, Step One prevents you from acknowledging the strength and power you need to overcome denial and admit your real problem.

By seeing yourself as permanently powerless over your addiction, and seeing your life as unmanageable forever, you will always feel dependent on the influence of the group to keep you from relapse, and you can never leave or grow beyond the program to autonomy, independence, and full adulthood.

Step Two
We came to believe that [only] a [Higher] Power greater than ourselves could restore us to sanity.

Why this step aids recovery. For years you struggled to control your addictive behavior and failed, until you no longer believed in your ability to control your life and restore it to sanity. Whatever it might take to control this obsession, you know it would have to be wiser and more powerful than you are. By visualizing such a power in terms of God or Inner Wisdom or the Unconscious Mind or a Higher Power and turning the problem of your destructive behavior to it, you gained the psychological support you needed to face the truth at last. This freed you of an intolerable stress and allowed you to turn your energies toward the remaining steps of recovery.

The Higher Power concept also helps to handle the overwhelming nature of problems created by your addiction and dependency: the ruined relationships, emotional pain, and financial chaos you may have caused. Once you have taken the first step and admitted the damage addiction has done, its actual extent becomes apparent, and this often leads to despair. Step Two acknowledges the impossibility of your handling it all at once, all by yourself. That's why "Let go and let God" and "Turn it over to God" are phrases heard often in self-help programs.

How this step impedes autonomy. Relying solely on an outside force to help you stop your addiction and restore you to sanity reinforces the kind of dependent behavior that made you and kept you addicted in the first place. Ultimately, it can only cause you to transfer your addictive tendencies to this Higher Power. As long as you go through life believing you are not powerful enough on your own to control your addictive behavior, you will never feel confident enough to stand freely on your own two feet. It also can become a convenient excuse for relapse: "God didn't help me, so I couldn't help drinking again."

Step Three

We made a decision to turn our will and our lives over to the care of [a Higher Power], as we understood [it].

Why this step aids recovery. The first and second steps asked you to acknowledge that you are powerless over your own addictive behavior, which you may have been denying for years and that only a new perspective (Higher Power) could help you change. As difficult as this may be, now you are asked to go a step farther in a more profound acknowledgment, and admit not only that you are unable to control your addiction but that there are other things beyond your control as well.

Like most addictive people (in reaction to the chaotic, dysfunctional, and unreliable circumstances in which dependency usually develops), you probably have been obsessed with control. You may have tried to make others act in ways you were sure would prevent trouble or pain for you, blaming them for your troubles in order to deny responsibility or avoid feelings you were unable to face. Or a dysfunctional family system may have led you to believe that you can or should control the world around you.

Your denial may have been strong, but when you face reality you realize the number of things that are beyond your control are as endless as the world is wide—the weather, accidents, other people's actions and reactions, your own feelings, and so on.

If control was important, the pain and disappointment created by your inability to control everything in your life was probably one reason you began to engage in addictive behavior, blotting out the pain of disappointment and failure. So, accepting your inability to control everything can help remove a powerful motivation to continue the addiction cycle.

Step Three also allows you to relax, and discover that acting in harmony with life, and making the best of what comes along, works better than trying to force life (and others) to be responsive to your desires.

CARLA

Carla, fifty-five, a petite, shy, and quiet lady who was battered and then deserted, says: "I was hysterical when my lover left me. My therapist suggested CoDa, but I was reluctant, until my friend Mary went, and it really helped her. So, I decided to try. Finding out that I was powerless over others was a relief. I had spent years trying to do or say the magic words that would control my lover. I prayed to God, but God didn't stop him either." Carla worked her program, and learned a lot about herself in the process. After a few months, she had a disastrous return to her former lover, where she was lied to and mistreated once again. "I see now how easily I would fall for a line. I learned a good lesson: I participate in the unhealthy relationship by being gullible, and wishing instead of paying attention." Carla then got back into meetings and worked her program, and simultaneously came into therapy. She says: "I learned how to recognize people as they are, rather than trying to make them the people I want them to be. Now, I find people I can enjoy without needing to change them." Carla is now living happily on her own, healing her relationships with her children, and developing a new, loving partnership.

How this step impedes autonomy. Letting a Higher Power handle problems in your life is, at best, a temporary expedient to assist you through a period when you have not yet developed the confidence and ability to face and solve them yourself. However, to continue to leave your sanity *completely* in the hands of a Higher Power can reinforce your old habit of depending on something outside yourself to help you cope with your life.

It is more effective (and better for your self-esteem) to consider that you have a partnership with your Higher Power. You can then cooperate with your Higher Power in an autonomous way, making decisions according to your spiritual or ethical precepts and values, but accepting responsibility for the results. To continue to leave your sanity solely in the care of your Higher Power, once you have cleared away the worst of the damage and made your life more manageable, is an abdication of your responsibility to think for yourself, and therefore it becomes denial.

After three years in AA, Jack, a thirty-five-year-old Catholic who was educated in religious schools, had an emotional crisis when some issues in his life were not solved by "turning them over to his Higher Power." He came in to therapy because he kept asking God to create a healthy, committed relationship for him, and his relationships kept turning sour and falling apart. These bitter defeats, piled on his childhood history of begging God for deliverance from a brutal father and not being rescued, brought up overwhelming rage against God and life. He began drinking again, and his drinking frightened him enough that he overcame his reluctance to getting therapy. Jack says, "The Second and Third Steps confused me. I never realized how angry and helpless I felt about God. I needed help to evaluate my own behavior, and see how I was creating my own mess. As long as I left it in God's hands, I wouldn't change. Now I have a new faith, a partnership in which I take care of my responsibilities, and trust God to take care of the rest." In order to achieve successful, independent, and autonomous living, you must learn how to evaluate your behavior, and how to place Inner Wisdom or a Higher Power in proper perspective in your life.

Step Four

We made a searching and fearless moral inventory of overselves.

Why this step aids recovery. This is probably the most difficult of the early steps, because it asks you to confront all the defects in your own character. But in order to bring the addictive cycle to a stop, it is necessary to be able to look at your own life from an objective viewpoint. Like most people in recovery, you probably had a tremendous amount of fear about facing yourself, your own negative feelings and thoughts, and unmet responsibilities, so you may have been blocking them out for most of your life. Only through facing at last the extent of the damage your addiction has done do you find the motivation to abstain.

The Fourth Step helps you take an eye-opening look at how you are *creating or perpetuating* your own pain. It begins the process of rational self-evaluation, which must be at the foundation of taking responsibility and control over your own life.

Taking a dispassionate, detached inventory is a brand-new skill if you're from a dysfunctional or abusive family, where the only options you learned for evaluating your mistakes were either to deny your defects or to mercilessly castigate yourself for having them. In a functional family, you would have received years of training in this mental skill, as your parents helped you learn to evaluate your actions and their consequnces: "Do you like it when someone hits you? How do you think Johnny would feel if you hit him? Do you like having Johnny for a friend? Do you think he would want you for a friend if you hit him? Is there a better way to settle your argument?" When childhood goes well, children are taught repeatedly, through example, experience, and explanation, that thinking ahead, evaluating future results of current behavior, and thinking of others works best in life.

How this step impedes autonomy. The main problem with this step is that having been created to help break the cycle of addiction and denial, the program often focuses exclusively on faults. If you come from a dysfunctional family, you may already carry a tendency to overemphasize your faults. When facing yourself you may tend to forget that objective review includes *both* what you do well and what you do wrong. To move beyond merely arresting destructive behavior, you must learn to include the *positive* in any self-review.

Step Five

We admitted to [a Higher Power], to ourselves, and to another human being the exact nature of our wrongs.

Why this step aids recovery. If, like most dependent people, you have been placing the responsibility for your destructive behavior outside yourself most of your life, this may be your first experience of accepting responsibility for your own actions. You may never have believed you could do this before, and doing it can make you feel stronger and less dependent.

You may also have carried an overwhelming burden of guilt (a result of what you did "under the influence"). Since most models of a Higher Power include the compassion to forgive the sincerely repentant, Step Five may also have been your first experience of the hope of forgiveness. *Twelve Steps and Twelve Traditions* says, "It was only when we resolutely tackled Step Five that we inwardly *knew* we'd be able to receive forgiveness and give it, too." Being able to accept forgiveness from a Higher Power is directly related to forgiving yourself. You may never before in your life have been ready to give up your addiction, which is one reason your earlier attempts to quit were unsuccessful. This change of attitude alone constitutes one of the main cores of recovery. Addictive behavior is often a result of the pain of being unable to forgive yourself. Taking this responsibility off your shoulders removes one more motivation to continue your addiction.

Through the time-honored catharsis of confession, you are freed from your guilt and granted permission to change. "This practice of admitting one's defects to another person is, of course, very ancient," according to *Twelve Steps and Twelve Traditions*. "It has been validated in every century. . . . Psychiatrists and psychologists point out the need . . . for discussion . . . with an understanding and trustworthy person."

How this step impedes autonomy. There is another opportunity here, as in Step Four, to overemphasize the negative. Joseph Campbell wrote in *The Power of Myth:* "Ramakrishna once said that if all you think of are your sins, then you are a sinner. And when I read that, I thought of . . . going to confession . . . meditating on all the little sins. . . . Now I think one should go and say 'Bless me, Father, for I have been great, these are the good things I have done this week.'"

Concentrating too much on the negative induces despair; too much emphasis on the positive can become denial. Independent, healthy self-evaluation requires keeping a balance.

Step Six

We were entirely ready to have [a Higher Power] remove all these defects of character.

Why this step aids recovery. At the beginning it was a big step for you just to acknowledge you couldn't handle your problems by turning them over to a Higher Power. Now, having faced the extent of those faults, taken inventory, and admitted them to another, you are finally, fully aware of the damage they have done and actively want to have them removed.

This is true forgiveness, which allows a fresh start. This is different from denial, which says, "Oh well, it can't be helped, just forget it."

How this step impedes autonomy. Being willing to stop your addiction and being willing to have someone else do it are two different things. Being willing to live without an addiction is one thing and being willing to take responsibility for your own life is another. As long as you rely on a power other than yourself to help overcome your flaws, you will remain dependent on God or the group. Remaining dependent on God or the group leads you away from learning to depend on yourself to do it instead.

Step Seven

We humbly asked [a Higher Power] to remove our shortcomings.

Why this step aids recovery. After realizing you have shortcomings and then becoming willing to change them, you are now ready to do what you have probably been fighting all along: humble yourself enough to ask for help in putting an end to your addictions. What you once denied was a problem, you now acknowledge you need to change. You have changed from being passive and defensive to taking the first active step to help you overcome addiction.

How this step impedes autonomy. You may not realize how much strength you have developed by taking this step, and thus continue to believe that it has all been the work of a Higher Power and that you do not have the power to quit on your own. As long as only God or the group can remove your addiction, you will believe you need God and the group to keep you free from your addiction.

Step Eight

We made a list of all persons we had harmed, and became willing to make amends to them all.

Why this step aids recovery. If you habitually see yourself as a helpless victim, you focus only on the pain you have suffered. You may have failed to realize the pain you inflicted on others. This step helps you reevaluate relationship problems in terms of your own responsibility for contributing to them.

Step Eight also introduces the concept of *amends,* meaning the possibility that old hurts you have inflicted can be healed. The idea that mistakes can be corrected, that you can *do something* about old problems, and that your relationships can be repaired, is essential to achieving recovery. If you can never make amends for your mistakes, then you are required to be perfect. Since it is normal to make mistakes in life, trying to be perfect makes successfully running your own life impossible. Since escaping from the pain of failing to be perfect is another reason people from dysfunctional families turn to addictive behaviors, this step removes one more motivation to continue it.

How this step impedes autonomy. As in Step Five, the danger here is that the emphasis is entirely on the harm *you've* committed. Since many twelve-step members have been victims of neglect and abuse as children, it is important for you to be able to acknowledge any harm that has been done *to you.* In order to have control of your own life, you need to be able to ask for amends when they are due you. You also need to address the harm done to you. Otherwise, as Dr. Timmon Cermak writes in *A Time to Heal,* "The irony is that when ACAs [adult children of alcoholics] fail to validate their own feelings as adults, they are guilty of *precisely* the same neglect toward themselves they received from their parents."

Step Nine
We made direct amends to such people whenever possible, except when to do so would injure them or others.

Why this step aids recovery. The Eighth and Ninth Steps separate contemplation from action, and remind you to think before acting. The Ninth Step forces you to stop running away from one kind of problem that led to dependency, and provides practice at rebuilding your damaged relationships—which often results in an experience of healing and redemption. This step gives you a chance to make amends to others for the pain your past actions caused them.

How this step impedes autonomy. By placing all the emphasis on you in the amends-making process, this step reinforces your old pattern of feeling you have to control situations. Being autonomous means learning to acknowledge the autonomy of others. Only others know how much they feel you have harmed them and how you can best make amends to them.

When Carla, whom we met in chapter 1, tried to make

amends to her grown children, their reaction was hostile and unreceptive. Carla says, "AA didn't teach me how to listen to what *others* felt. I learned from my children that I couldn't heal the relationship by telling them *my* version of my mistakes. I had to learn to hear their stories, too." Healing relationships requires emotional awareness and competence. You can begin to respect the autonomy of others by asking them if they felt harmed or offended, and find out what *they* think would make amends.

Step Ten
We continued to take personal inventory and when we were wrong promptly admitted it.

Why this step aids recovery. This step helps you incorporate the personal inventory of the Fourth Step as an ongoing part of your life. The Tenth Step can help create a daily habit of paying attention to your own behavior, attitudes, and actions in a non-judgmental, solution-oriented way. If, like most people whose lives have been ravaged by addiction, you have deliberately stayed out of touch with yourself for years, learning to take frequent inventory can help prevent your problems (particularly relapsing back into your old addictive behaviors) from getting out of hand. This is excellent groundwork for building a healthy relationship with yourself. One AA pamphlet advises that for those who have worked this step, "self-searching becomes a regular habit. . . . Admit, accept and patiently correct defects. . . . When past is settled with, present challenges can be met."

How this step impedes autonomy. Because of the twelve-step focus on destructive behaviors that must be arrested, this inventory can become another list of problems and defects. To move from recovery to health requires an equal emphasis on admitting what you do right, too. Otherwise, if you don't learn to encourage and acknowledge your positive qualities, you remain dependent on others to evaluate and validate which qualities are worthy of praise. Since only you can truly judge what is best for you, this dependency can keep you from following your own best course, unable to live according to your own ethical standards.

Step Eleven

We sought through prayer and meditation to improve our conscious contact with [a Higher Power] as we understood [it], praying only for knowledge of [its] will for us and the power to carry that out.

Why this step aids recovery. Daily focus on the wisdom available from a Higher Power helps you gain much needed support in remaining free of addictive behavior. Research has also shown that meditation is calming, and an aid to thinking clearly. Meditation can provide a process for examining your ideas from a more objective perspective, an opportunity to consider higher motives before acting, and a time of deep relaxation and/or healing—all of which can reduce the stress level that your addiction helps hide.

How this step impedes autonomy. As in other steps, the focus on the will of your Higher Power can play into your tendency to depend on the will of something or someone else rather than on your own. Alternatively, this something else can lead you to expect meditation to solve your problems without action. In either case, you never develop self-control strong enough to make decisions and achieve goals.

Step Twelve

Having had a spiritual awakening as the result of these steps, we tried to carry this message to alcoholics and to practice these principles in all our affairs.

Why this step aids recovery. The Twelfth Step helps challenge the chronic feelings of being powerless that led to your becoming

addictive. It gives you a new sense of your own worth by af-
firming that whatever problems remain for you, you are powerful enough now to help someone else. It changes your point of
view from "Who will help me?" to "How can I help you?"

With this step a member becomes a *sponsor,* begins to reach
out to help others who have suffered the same problems, and
learns the personal satisfaction that comes from helping another
halt his or her own destructive cycle of addictive behavior.
Sponsoring and spreading the word provides a powerful peer
support system to help ensure that people won't relapse by encouraging group interaction and keeping members involved
even after they have worked all the Twelve Steps.

How this step impedes autonomy. Having members who have been
in recovery keep up their involvement in the program by helping counsel and support newer members can work against the
development of autonomy in several ways. First, interaction
with persons you sponsor can replicate old, toxic family patterns, and become emotionally painful and damaging to both
you and your charge. Second, the member that you sponsor is
dysfunctional by definition, and may have severe emotional
problems beyond your knowledge and scope. This can be
damaging to your self-esteem, and impede the member's emotional progress.

Next, the sponsoring process can put the sponsor in a
powerful position, emotionally, similar to a parent's or therapist's. For addictive people, who are often controlling, it can become a way to avoid healthy peer relationships. Last, sponsoring and maintaining ongoing involvement in the program
can be a way of avoiding the challenges of life on the "outside."
You do not learn independence, time structuring, or how to
create your own sense of purpose, because all these life skills are
provided by the program.

The learning processes of all twelve steps lead you toward
independence; but they stop short of the goal. To achieve autonomy, a Thirteenth Step is needed, one that emphasizes your re-

sponsibility for yourself, emotional self-awareness, independent thinking, and functional life skills.

ADDICTION TO THE PROGRAM

This addiction to addictions is fostered by the fact that the programs as presently constituted do not address these critical issues:

- lack of healthy replacement habits
- lack of information about functional living
- lack of models for healthy relationships
- replication of dysfunctional family patterns
- dependency on the group

Indeed, because they are given no assistance in living successfully outside the group, people who leave, such as Jack, often do fail and begin to drink or exhibit other compulsive behaviors again.

JACK

Jack, a married forty-five-year-old executive, entered a treatment program when his long-term daily drinking began to interfere with his career. The six-week hospital stay ended with an introduction to AA and a strong recommendation to attend meetings. Jack did, for a few months, until he became sure he wouldn't drink any more, then he dropped out—without completing the Steps. The first time he experienced a lot of stress, from marital trouble and job pressure, he had "just one beer" at lunch, and within two weeks his problem was worse than it had been before he entered the hospital. Jack learned the hard way that he needed to complete his recovery before being on his own. He went back to AA, got a sponsor, and completed the Twelve Steps. In therapy, he learned how to negotiate and communicate with his wife, his business associates, and himself. Once he had learned to be truly autonomous and to manage his life, he could stop going to meetings and still stay sober.

Even if *you* don't try it alone, the examples of others who did and failed are numerous. Perhaps your sponsor remembers he fell off the wagon several times; or perhaps your new friend Paula went back to her destructive relationship once and got beaten up again. The *Big Book* is filled with such stories. People who leave too early get pushed back in the old patterns by the strength of their original habits, the fear that they cannot remain in recovery without the group, the isolation from friends and supportive people, and the guilt they feel for leaving the program. AA interprets these relapses to mean that leaving the group is impossible, and coming back is the only way to maintain sobriety and health. In the Real Thirteenth Step, however, achieving autonomy means learning to maintain your emotional health and support yourself effectively in living a satisfactory life.

Lack of Healthy Replacement Habits

The many current twelve-step and other self-help groups help you stop a destructive habit. They function in a spectacularly successful manner to make your life less chaotic. What they don't do is make it healthy! As the old saying goes, the absence of a negative does not create a positive.

Although your life became more manageable in the program, you are not moving forward. You no longer drink, or work, or spend, or love too much, but you don't know how to fill the time that once was consumed by your addiction. In fact, when you do find yourself with time on your hands, you probably feel the old habit reasserting itself, and are tempted to occupy yourself the way you used to—by engaging in your former addiction again. In his book *Heresies,* Dr. Thomas Szasz explains why: "Habits in personal conduct are like energy in physics; so long as we remain alive, we cannot get rid of habits by annihilating them, by making them disappear; we can only change or transform one habit into another."

To avoid relapsing into your old addiction, you probably decide to fill the time instead amid the safety and support of the group. This is certainly preferable to returning to your addiction, but it is hardly normal, healthy living as other people you know experience it.

In order for your life to be actively better, you need to do more than merely stop a bad habit. You need to develop good habits to replace it. The only real difference between people who become dependent and those who become self- or independent is that the independent people were fortunate enough to have good role models and learned healthier ways of coping with problems, stress, and feelings than the addictive people did.

As children, self-dependent people learned the healthy habits of honesty with self and others, effective thinking and problem solving, and self-reliance and self-trust. You *learned* the dependent ways of thinking and acting that led to your addiction—you weren't born with them. So it is possible both to unlearn them and to learn new, more effective ones. Another sign that twelve-step program members desperately need to learn new replacement habits can be seen in the way they hop from program to program, as new addictions arise to replace the original ones.

Recovering alcoholics will join Overeaters Anonymous, Al-Anon, CoDependents Anonymous, Narcotics Anonymous, Adult Children of Alcoholics, or Debtors Anonymous, perpetually repeating the Twelve Steps for each new replacement habit as it arises. It is very common in kicking a habit to replace it with another habit in this way. Compulsive people often move from addiction to addiction. Do you remember being surprised, as a newcomer, to walk into an AA meeting and see a heavy pall of smoke, lots of coffee being drunk, and sweets and junk food in abundance?

John Bradshaw writes of his own experience: "When I put the cork in the bottle, I still had to deal with what Vernon

Johnson calls the *ism* of alcoholism. I was still a compulsive personality. Consequently, I soon developed other addictions. I smoked, drank twelve cups of coffee a day. I became addicted to the adrenaline rush of working and making money. I struggled with sugar binges and dieting."

Why isn't successful attendance at AA enough to stop this cycle? Because it doesn't teach autonomy and self-management. The strength of the Twelve Steps is that they help stop destructive habits, but the ongoing addiction to the program demonstrates that complete healing of the inner problem has not yet occurred. As Anne Wilson Schaef explains, "The primary addictions . . . are the addictions to powerlessness and nonliving, . . . all secondary addictions lead to these two primary addictions." As we shall see, powerlessness and nonliving are the opposites of autonomy.

A few groups do attempt to address these issues, mainly by recommending literature and encouraging members to get therapy in addition to the program. Like others in these programs, you may be becoming aware that handling the root causes of addiction requires more than just achieving sobriety and serenity. The Thirteenth Step will help you confront those underlying causes, and free yourself from the underlying mental patterns behind addiction and dependency.

Lack of Information about Functional Living

Unfortunately, because programs are so tightly (and necessarily) focused on overcoming your self-destructive behavior, most of the information they provide is about maintaining your sobriety and serenity "one day at a time." Even when some of the newer programs, such as ACA and CoDA, do give reading about handling the pain of your past, most of the information is still focused on the emotional *problem* and how to overcome it. Yet without the vital living skills, you will never feel confident to face life outside the group, on your own.

If you grew up in a dysfunctional family, and you've spent many years ravaged by addictive behavior, you have probably had little opportunity to learn competent everyday living skills such as these:

- How to think clearly and rationally, evaluate people and situations, and make choices
- How to create a sense of purpose in your life free of addiction
- How to handle change and the normal upsets of life
- How to create your own ethics and guidelines for living
- How to learn to trust yourself and make commitments you can keep

Just managing your budget, deciding where and how to live, or finding a better job may feel like more than you can handle. No wonder many people fail to make it on their own, outside of the group, when the lack of these skills can keep you trapped in the recovery process and keep you unnecessarily dependent on the program by making it feel safer and easier for you to remain in your group.

Lack of Models for Healthy Relationships

Adequate relationship skills are critical for creating happiness in your life. Lack of them has been responsible for much of your current misery. Without relationship expertise you get involved with "toxic" people, overburden the ones who care, and create chaos instead of love. Failed relationships are endemic in the lives of addictive people, and numbing the pain of love lost is probably the most common excuse for addiction relapse. Since other group members come from similar backgrounds, they may provide no better role models for how to have healthy relationships than your own family did.

Yet, recovery programs teach us almost nothing about healthy relating:

- What to do about trusting people
- How to replace old, toxic relationship patterns with new, healthy ones
- How to end loneliness and create internal intimacy
- How *functional,* healthy intimacy with others works
- How to successfully deal with the *other* relationships in your life: your boss, siblings, co-workers, neighbors, friends, and so on

- How to find a healthy relationship in the first place
- How to set limits, say no, have fun, get close, create space

Without a mental picture or model of what healthy relationships look like, and the skills to build that model in your life, your chances of forming a successful relationship outside the group remain small, and your dependency on the group to supply all your relationship needs can make building an independent, autonomous, *happy* life all but impossible. When you know what healthy relating is, and you have the skills to accomplish it, your chances for complete recovery from addiction are excellent.

Replication of Dysfunctional Family Patterns

Although the "family" atmosphere created by the twelve-step and other recovery groups is of value in providing the support and reinforcement that help you stop your addiction, in many respects, the kind of family that the group will foster and re-create will have many of the damaging family patterns that led to the members' addictions.

The lack of information about healthy living and models for healthy relationships means members have no other guide for how to interact with one another than the same addictive models they learned as children. When this happens, even the good the program has already done can be undermined and the recovery group can actually drive members back to their addiction by re-creating the conditions they became addicted to escape.

John Bradshaw's experience illustrates the dynamic involved: "The group was my new family . . . my family of affiliation." Often, program members enter therapy because this "new family" has become very painful and toxic for them, and they don't know where to turn if they can't trust their recovery program. The fact is that without other strong models each of us has a tendency to re-create our original family whenever we become close to others, even though those early relationships made us very unhappy.

According to family therapist Virginia Satir, people will

usually choose the familiar over the healthy. In interacting with familiar patterns, no matter how painful they may be, we know what is expected of us and we know what the results will be. Even when we are sure the results will always be painful, they are less frightening than the unknown results of dealing in a new way with unfamiliar people. Often when in the presence of someone who evokes a parent, we feel childlike, small, power-less, and helpless—"I couldn't help it—he made me do it."

This is as true within recovery groups as it is elsewhere. In this brand new environment, because we often spend months or years with the same people in the program, by interacting in the only way we know we may reconstruct our original family without realizing it, complete with shaming, control struggles, fighting, mixed messages, and sometimes even including violence and inappropriate sex.

Because our early "family system" is imprinted on our sub-conscious, childlike mind, each of us has a tendency to interpret and respond to the world around us according to that system. Aggressive people may be perceived as and reacted to "just like" an angry father, passive people as "just like" a weak mother.

MARTHA

Martha, an overweight woman of sixty-four who had to lose weight to protect her health, attended a special program run by her OA sponsor, Bill. At first, the program went well, with Bill assigning lots of writing and homework exercises, and Martha began to find it easier to stick to her eating program and lose weight. After a couple of months, Martha's old rage at her abusive father arose, and she yelled at Bill during one of the special meetings. Because Bill had no training or ability to deal therapeutically with her rage, he got angry in return, and banished Martha from his program. Martha was so devastated that she dropped out of OA altogether. In therapy, Martha was able to express her old rage safely, and her compulsion to eat to repress the rage lessened.

We also gravitate toward people who replicate our original family members because they seem familiar. Within the group, a sponsor may take on a parental role and other group members may function like siblings, increasing the feelings of powerlessness and dependence that were familiar from childhood. To the degree that the members of your self-help group, or the Steps themselves, undercut autonomy, they are like original families—partially dysfunctional.

Child abuse expert Alice Miller explains this pattern as a search for a way to correct the old family environment: "What if a person has never had the good fortune to experience his early dependence on his parents and the accompanying separation anxiety, . . . they resort to a . . . reenactment of their dependency and obedience in early childhood. Even very brief contact with a group can give one a feeling of maternal warmth, . . . never experienced before, which makes one feel secure. . . . But . . . the group is only a substitute, the search for what is missing can never stop. . . . Every form of addiction, instead of doing away with the old longing, simply perpetuates the tragedy by repeating it. . . . Someone who was not allowed to be aware of what was being done has no way of telling about it except to repeat it."

This problem can be compounded because program members may not be recovered enough to be objective about themselves or their interaction with you. They may be projecting their early family experiences on you, as you project yours on them. Your sponsor may be wise enough to help, or may unintentionally make the problem worse. If early rage or shame erupts, an untrained person like Martha's sponsor Bill may not be competent to deal with it. Together, you can reenact the old feelings of anger, fear, hurt, rejection, and shame—and not even realize it, because those feelings are so familiar. It is both painful and enlightening to discover that you have re-created your dysfunctional family from scratch, in a brand new environment, because there's no one from your original family there. Unless you've been taught the tools to deal with painful emotions from the past, they may tempt you to slide back into old, destructive behavior.

Of course, this pattern happens in other aspects of life besides the program. People from dysfunctional families re-create their families wherever they go—at work, at school, among friends. As Dr. Sonya Friedman explains: "Not only do we become accustomed to the manner in which our parents have always treated us, but we re-create that . . . with the men we marry. . . . Most women who are unhappy in their relationships with their parents are unhappy . . . with their husbands in a remarkably similar way."

If your underlying belief is "This is how it is" or "This is what I deserve," you can continue to repeat your initial family experience without realizing it.

Twelve-step members are often enraged when the past is replayed, and seek others to blame. At first, Martha blamed her leaving the program and going off her diet on Bill, because he got angry at her, just as her father had. But by working through her rage and other underlying feelings, Martha used her experience with Bill to learn more about herself. You, too, can use difficult relationships to get a better understanding of your old beliefs and how they perpetuate the old problems. Using life experience as a mirror of your dysfunctional process is an autonomous way to gain power and understanding of healthy relationships.

Dependency on the Group
Because it is difficult for those who struggle to control an addiction to accept advice from people who do not have firsthand knowledge of the experience—even from therapists, counselors, and clergy—the fact that recovery programs surround you with the support and encouragement of others who have also suffered this adversity makes them particularly powerful and effective. But later on, the program's peer support resource, so effective in the initial stages of recovery, often becomes just another family dependency. If you have been attending as many as seven meetings a week for several years, have turned your life around with the help of the group, you may now feel that you're incapable of success *without* the group.

To stop your addiction, it was necessary to cut yourself off from the people who helped reinforce or tacitly supported your addiction. Your twelve-step friends may have become your only friends. For the first time in your life, you found yourself surrounded by others who have suffered with the same addiction as yours—and they have been able to quit. As someone with a dependent personality looking outside yourself for relief, you naturally wanted them to think well of you and wanted to feel special by quitting too. Once you have entered recovery by stopping, you naturally want to keep their approval by remaining in recovery. In a sense, what you are doing is transferring your dependency from a worse alternative to a better one. In essence, at this stage the group is still functioning as little more than a substitute addiction.

II

Completing
Recovery

CHAPTER 3

Beyond Recovery: From Dependency to Autonomy

> *The stages of human development are the same to-day as they were in the ancient times. As a child, you are brought up in a world of discipline, of obedience, and you are dependent on others. All this has to be transcended when you come to maturity, so that you can live not in dependency but with self-responsible authority. If you can't cross that threshold, you have the basis for neurosis.*
>
> JOSEPH CAMPBELL

B efore you can successfully take the Thirteenth Step, learn the healthy skills of autonomy, and move on beyond the program, you must complete your recovery by going deep within your inner self to heal the pain and *unlearn* the negative beliefs that made you and keep you dependent. Failure to address the childhood factors that created your dependency has caused all your previous efforts to stop your addictive behavior on your own (without the support of a recovery group) to end in relapses. Like anyone else who has suffered from a long illness, you must first heal completely before you attempt to build yourself back up to optimal fitness. Otherwise, you will inevitably find yourself suffering a relapse back into your old, addictive behavior.

You will always live with the possibility of relapse, even within the support of a group, until you repair the damage being raised in a dysfunctional family did to your growth as a healthy, autonomous individual and to your own confidence in your ability to meet life's difficulties, cope with setbacks, and be self-assured in your relationships with others. You can never permanently recover from the dependent behavior that has devastated your life without correcting the self-defeating thought patterns that keep you believing you are not good enough to handle problems and face painful circumstances on your own. You need to replace these with the far healthier and more positive truth that, like everyone else, you were born with all the talents, intelligence, and ability it takes to meet, surmount, or sanely coexist with whatever challenges or difficulties life might bring your way.

The good news is that once these thought patterns are replaced, successfully managing your life becomes much easier. When you are familiar and comfortable with the dynamics of autonomy, self-control feels good. It becomes a question of self-care, of doing good things for you because you deserve to be well-treated, you deserve a happy and functional life, and you enjoy doing nice things for you, including taking care of yourself. In a healthy environment, where the necessary skills that create autonomy are learned, self-control comes easily and is not forced or difficult.

In order to be free from dependence, you need to understand how the key skills that foster independence and autonomy—risk taking, problem solving, and coping with disappointment and failure—develop in healthy families and how dysfunctional families undermine your early efforts at developing these skills. Then you can begin to reverse your early negative experience by unlearning old beliefs and replacing them with positive new ones.

AUTONOMY AND THE DEPENDENT CHILD

Although we all begin life entirely dependent on the adults around us, usually our parents, in an ideal situation we would learn independence, self-reliance, and self-confidence by progressing through a series of gradual stages, until we become healthy, fully functioning adults able and eager to meet life's challenges in an autonomous fashion. Healthy, fully competent parents prepare you to become a successful, autonomous adult, sure of your own abilities, by being a constant source of encouragement during your early ventures at independent thought and action and by supporting you when these go wrong. When, as a small child, a parent makes you feel secure, you use that parent as a "home base"—venturing out and experimenting with the world for brief periods, then running back for reassurance and encouragement. This behavior can be seen in the way toddlers in a new environment grab onto a parent's legs and hide, then peek out and venture around, only to dart back to safety and hide themselves again when they feel overwhelmed or frightened by the larger world.

If you have supportive parents who feel confident of their autonomy, as you grow older your adventuring becomes more widespread and of longer duration, and your self-confidence grows: As a child of seven, you might stay overnight with a friend for the first time. As a teenager, you might get your first job working at a hamburger stand. After high school graduation, you may leave home for the first time to live on your own or attend college.

When this process fails to take place (as it so often does in dysfunctional families), you never learn that you can depend on yourself and you never feel strong enough or able enough to cope with life's challenges. Instead you feel you must depend on others to help you through them.

Autonomy

When these early ventures are supported and encouraged, a child gets the opportunity to master the three skills involved in meeting challenges or taking any autonomous action: risk taking, problem solving, and coping with failure or disappointment.

To venture forth and act on your own in any new and difficult circumstances is to take a risk. To take a risk means facing uncertainty: an outcome or consequence we cannot predict or control, with the possibility of things going wrong, of being hurt, or of failing. In a functional family, you learn to view this possibility as a challenge or an opportunity for learning from mistakes. In a dysfunctional family, you learn to see this possibility as something to be feared and situations that create it as something to be avoided. "Forbidden the risk taking and exploration essential for healthy development," writes psychologist Nathaniel Branden in *Honoring the Self*, "the child intuits that he or she is inadequate to the normal challenges of life, is inherently unfit for independent survival." With healthy parents, we learn how to handle this fear gradually, in stages, so that it never becomes overwhelming.

At first, we experience very small risks, surviving them and being praised and encouraged for taking them (whether we make mistakes or not). Thus we gain confidence in our ability to cope with risk and move on to taking larger risks. Through this trial-and-error learning, coupled with the teaching of our parents and our natural physical and mental development, we begin to develop a sense of our ability to successfully control ourselves and the challenges of our environment—we master the skill of risk taking.

Every time we take a risk and venture forth by ourselves, we are faced with the problem of deciding what actions and attitudes we might take to create a positive, productive outcome. Encouraged, most children learn the skills necessary to ensure that the majority of their encounters end successfully. Discouraged, perhaps punished, the children of dysfunctional parents never learn to solve problems on their own, and the seeds of dependency are planted.

The risk of disappointment or failure is inherent in any autonomous action. There can only be risk when we cannot be sure that our actions will result in a successful conclusion. And a situation would hardly pose a problem to us unless we felt we might be unsuccessful at solving it. Inherent in both criteria is the possibility that the outcome will be negative and that sooner or later we will make a mistake, or have to cope with failure.

Recovery expert John Bradshaw, in his book *Homecoming*,

maintains that developing a healthy, fully functioning adult mind requires making "mistakes, which are an integral part of being human. Mistakes serve as warnings from which we can learn. . . . To live in dread of making a mistake causes you to walk on eggs and live a guarded, shallow existence."

Dependency

Ideally, through positive role modeling by adults, learning from experience, and gentle encouragement, a child progresses from dependency to autonomy. But the truth is that few people grow up fully autonomous, even when they are not from dysfunctional homes.

Many people were not raised to be autonomous and independent themselves, and so cannot model it for their children, because of a strong, long-standing social bias against independent thought and behavior. Historically, in most earlier societies, especially those living in primitive or marginal conditions, independent behavior was seen as threatening the close group cooperation and fragile routines that ensured group survival. In later societies, it was often viewed as weakening or threatening a leader's control and power over the group. You can still see this bias in the way government-supported public schools focus more on robotlike "good boy and girl" behavior than on encouraging self-confidence and independent thought. In both family and school environments, a child exhibiting these autonomous qualities is often met with hostility, ridicule, and punishment. Children who challenge a teacher or parent (who has low self-esteem and a fear of autonomy) by presenting a different idea about how to solve a geometry equation, or how to make the bed, are likely to be met with ridicule of the new idea or to be told, "Do it my way because I said so." The crucial values that produce autonomy (independence and experimentation) are rarely valued or rewarded.

Our path to autonomy is blocked not only by this bias, but the development of dependency is actually encouraged by a second bias, reinforced by our schools and youth organizations, that children are not responsible for themselves. Instead, parents are responsible for their children. The parents are viewed as all-knowing, all-wise, and all-powerful, the children as ignorant, foolish, and powerless. In short, children are seen as dependent on adults and unable to make sound decisions or to take reasonable action on their own. When children are regarded and treated this way by adults they grow up seeing themselves as powerless, too.

This attitude creates a tendency to invest all power and importance in the parent, and to make the parents' feelings and reactions the focus of the child's life. "Our culture," says Dr. Susan Forward in *Toxic Parents*, "and our religions are almost unanimous in upholding the omnipotence of parental authority." Children raised this way begin to feel unimportant and powerless—which creates the roots of dependent behavior. As a result of these social biases, most parents are unable to teach autonomy to their children, because they were never taught it themselves. Instead they tend to err either on the side of protecting or restraining children too much, or pushing them forward too hard and too early, during their first childhood venturing at independence. Either extreme undermines the fledgling attempts at autonomy and prevents children from completing their growth beyond dependency.

Although we are so familiar with the idea that parents are responsible for their children that it sounds reasonable, in practice it creates dependency and prevents healthy development. We are all familiar with the example of parents who force their children to do homework or chores "because I said so," rather than help the children to understand why homework is valuable to learning. Such parents give their offspring the idea that they are to do things unquestioningly to keep their parents happy or because they're ordered to: the children never learn to perform difficult tasks on their own as a result of determining for themselves why it's a good idea for them to do it. Children who are encouraged and supported in taking the responsibility for homework, or who see the benefit of chores well done, feel proud that their efforts count and learn to be self-motivating.

Parents who try to make things perfect, or try to protect children from life's realities, or who are themselves overwhelmed by life, or who worry about how they look as parents—in other words, parents who do not feel fully autonomous—cannot model autonomy for their children, or encourage them to be independent, or help them develop beyond dependency. "ACAs often do not know what normal adults are supposed to be like," according to Dr. Timmon Cermak in *A Time to Heal*, "because their vision of mature behavior, which most people get from watching their parents, is incomplete. Their families have not provided them with all the models of healthy, or even civil, adult behavior that are needed."

If our parents are overprotective and try to hold us close to them with "smothering" love or by filling us with guilt or by doing too much for us, we grow into fearful, uncertain adults. If our parents withdraw their support and demand too much from us too early in the process of developing autonomy—holding back love as the price of our best efforts, trying to improve our behavior only by criticizing our mistakes—we are made to believe that we are not good enough or that we have to "earn" love, and thus we become stuck as adults in a futile attempt to get from others, starting with our parents, the love, acknowledgment, and support we actually need to learn to get from ourselves.

Some of us even grow up with a combination of "smothering" and criticism (one overprotective parent, one overly critical parent) which compound and multiply our reasons to feel fearful of the world and inadequate to deal with it on our own. Whichever nonautonomous family situation we had, we are left incomplete, and never develop self-confidence, independent action, and autonomy. Instead we are stuck in dependency.

DEPENDENCY AND THE DYSFUNCTIONAL FAMILY

If, in addition to this typical parental confusion about autonomy and independence, your family, like those of most people in recovery groups, was severely dysfunctional—either unpredictable, angry, or even physically dangerous; or frightened, confused, and unable to make effective independent decisions—it compounded a thousandfold the social beliefs that already inhibit autonomy. For example:

- The toddler who is severely chastised, criticized, or frightened in the experimentation stage learns to anxiously and dependently watch the adults for cues rather than venture out autonomously into the world to learn.
- The seven-year-old who has been neglected does not feel secure about proper conduct when out of the home.
- The high school student who is criticized and made to feel dependent and inadequate at home may feel discouraged and overwhelmed by school, and never make it to college at all.
- The young adult who feels his dysfunctinal parents "need" him may never leave home to try his luck in the world because he remains dependent on their approval.

Growing up in a dysfunctional family sets the stage for dependent adult behavior, as Dr. Susan Forward explains in *Toxic Parents*: "Whether adult children of toxic parents were beaten when little or left alone too much, sexually abused or treated like fools, overprotected or overburdened by guilt, they almost all suffer surprisingly similar symptoms: damaged self-esteem, leading to self-destructive behavior. In one way or another, they almost all feel worthless, unlovable, and inadequate."

As the child of dysfunctional parents, you were trapped in an emotionally dangerous situation, far too overwhelming for any child to handle—naturally, you become enraged or terrified. Since your family situation denied you any safe outlet for these devastating feelings, or possibly punished you for expressing them, you began to grasp compulsively for anything that could numb the pain of having to bear them. When you found a relationship, substance, or behavior that could block out this pain for you, you turned to it with such an insatiable craving— and with such a fear of the way this pain still remains inside you and returns every time you stop the "masking" behavior no matter how many years pass—that you are said to be *addicted* to it or *dependent* or *compulsive* about it.

Growing up with frightened, confused, or incompetent parents can also set the stage for what is called *codependent behavior*. When your parents feel inadequate and lack self-confidence, instead of being able to depend on them you are rewarded with the greatest love and approval when they are able to depend on you. In effect, the normal parent-child roles are reversed. You as a child become the parent and caretaker, with tragic results: since you only receive love when you are catering to their dependency, you become dependent or addicted to their addiction. By the time you finally grow older and leave home you are convinced that to be loved you must take care of others, and so you look for troubled people, usually those who have their own problems with dependent behavior, who will need you there so badly you are sure they will have to love you in return.

THE THREE SKILLS OF AUTONOMY

The early exploratory stage of childhood is when the foundations of autonomy or dependency are laid. It is impossible to overemphasize how important this stage is in our development as individuals. In terms of our basic approach to life, there may be no more critical passage: If our childhood circumstances enable us to make this transition successfully, we will have the confidence and skills to meet life's challenges. If they do not, we become fearful of challenge and learn only dependent, unproductive methods of reacting to it.

One reason our initial explorations in life are so important is that they represent our first real attempts to experience ourselves as independent beings, separate from our parents. When those experiences feel positive to us, they influence us to believe that independence will feel good—that it is something we will want to experience more and that we will enjoy doing again and again. We feel motivated to reach out toward autonomous living at the same time that autonomous living seems to draw us forward with its promise and excitement.

Another reason that our initial attempts at independent activity are so critical is that it is during this stage that we develop our first crude, and in most cases characteristic, skills for dealing with challenging circumstances. Learning effective skills for coping with challenge, *without being dependent* on others, means we will be able to live life as autonomous individuals. When we face new or difficult experiences, the knowledge that we have the basic abilities necessary to cope and that we can rely on ourselves to manage new situations successfully develops our self-confidence.

This trust in our ability to cope with life's challenges independently serves as the base for all our later positive attitudes toward ourselves: self-esteem, self-confidence, and self-reliance. The positive reinforcement of each success and the excitement and pleasure of autonomous learning entice us farther and farther beyond our original parental dependency—until, one day, we find we have separated from it and have become independent, autonomous individuals. In making this transition successfully, we have mastered the stages that lead to autonomy and have developed the required skills of risk taking, problem solving, and coping with disappointment and failure.

Risk Taking

Throughout life we face situations we cannot predict or guarantee in which risk is unavoidable, such as when we are forced by circumstances to change jobs or meet new people, or when we must differ with those we love. In addition, there are times when experimentation and risk taking are desirable, as when we would like to leave the job we know voluntarily, to get better conditions or a higher salary. Successful risk taking requires learning to evaluate risk before acting, weighing the advantages of success against the disadvantages of failure. In a functional home, we learn how to evaluate risk through trial and error, from watching the behavior of others, or with the guidance of healthy and supportive adults. Thus, Tommy, a typical five-year-old faced with the risk involved in making friendly contact with an unknown child, learns to weigh the possibility that he will make a new friend against the possibility that they won't get along or that the new child will be mean or selfish.

A healthy, supportive parent will help Tommy learn how to evaluate potential new playmates by suggesting positive signs (a friendly disposition, a genuine smile, ease in playing with others) and negative signs (pushing, not sharing, yelling, teasing) to watch for. Tommy weighs these possibilities as well as he can, and makes his choice. Where the encounter turns out well, Tommy's supportive parent will be pleased for him and encourage him to play with the newcomer again and to continue to meet new potential playmates. If the outcome is negative, a functional parent will sympathize while offering the encouragement needed to ensure Tommy continues to meet new people ("Perhaps he was in a bad mood" or "Maybe you will make a nice new friend at school"). Properly supported and encouraged, Tommy will soon learn how to evaluate the risks involved in meeting new people and the majority of his experiences will be positive—and he will feel emotionally secure about handling his failures. While he is mastering risk taking, he is also learning important social skills as well.

If Tommy has a dysfunctional parent, however, he or she will express their own fears about encountering someone new and emphasize the potential dangers beforehand. When, in spite of the parent's prior misgivings, the outcome is positive for Tommy, an unsupportive parent will often criticize the other child or continue to emphasize other negative possibilities ("He looks stupid" or "Be careful, he might break your toys"). If Tommy's outcome is negative they will be sure to emphasize how correct their original fears were or warn against future attempts ("I told you you can't trust other kids" or "Don't get your hopes up, a lot of kids are like that").

As Tommy grows older and able to think more abstractly and clearly, he will become better and better at evaluating the disadvantages and advantages in the risks he wants to take. Knowing how to evaluate which risks are worth taking makes any venture easier. Without this ability to calculate risk, Tommy would be either too afraid to attempt any new behavior, and dependent on others to tell him what to do, or trapped in addictive behaviors to block out and avoid his fears, which might cause Tommy to take unreasonably dangerous risks and experience disaster after disaster.

Problem Solving

Developing the second skill of autonomy is extremely crucial because it is so basic it applies to just about every aspect of life. As soon as we venture beyond the easy reach of those who advise and counsel us, we are faced with problems. Naturally we want to do our best in every new situation and bring it to a successful conclusion for ourselves and others. The moment we encounter something new to us, we are presented with the challenge of unknown and unfamiliar elements.

In order to solve problems, we need to learn the four elements of problem solving: 1) evaluating the problem, 2) considering possible solutions, 3) deciding which to try first (which calls on our skill at taking and evaluating risks), and 4) trying out the solution by taking action.

Eight-year-old Mary visits her friend Rose and stays overnight at someone else's house for the first time. When bedtime comes, Mary discovers that Rose's mother doesn't leave the light on in Rose's bedroom, as Mary's mother does at home. At first, Mary is worried, and thinks about the situation (evaluating the problem). Then she considers what she can do to make it better (considering possible solutions). Her parents told her that if she had a problem she could ask Rose or Rose's parents for help, or she could call home. Mary chooses to talk to Rose first, suggesting what she would like (deciding which to try first and taking action). Rose says that they can ask her mother, who agrees that the closet light could be left on and the door ajar. When Rose's mother says yes, Mary has solved her problem and learned an essential skill of autonomy. Without the advance support of Mary's parents, who helped her weigh the risks, acknowledged that they wouldn't criticize or overreact if she made a mistake, and prepared her for her first night away from home, Mary might have felt dependent on her unavailable parents to solve the problem, been insecure to ask for what she wanted, and remained frightened all night long. Had this happened, Mary would have been reluctant to try sleeping over at a friend's house again.

When dysfunctional parents smother or criticize our early efforts at problem solving, we are unable to properly develop the skill. Repeated failure at coping with new situations successfully by ourselves then convinces us we are inadequate to solve life's problems on our own or that the world is too complex and frightening to deal with. Either way we begin to look outside ourselves for something or someone we can depend on to help us through the new, the difficult, and the challenging, as our progress down the road toward autonomy is blocked and cut off.

Coping with Disappointment and Failure

Problem solving, whether in life or in mathematics, doesn't always lead to success on the first try. Even when we have mastered the four skills of solving problems, we are not guaranteed every attempt will prove successful. Your attempts at risk taking can still result in disappointment or failure. Otherwise, there would be no risk.

When we fail, if we have the healthy support and guidance of functional parents, we will learn how to cope with our mistake and the feelings it creates in such a way that we are not discouraged from taking future risks. Proper support helps us discover how to understand and manage the disappointment, anger, self-criticism, and frustration that can result, reassuring us that these feelings are a natural reaction when circumstances don't work out the way we hoped. With this kind of support, the disappointment and frustration quickly pass away, rather than remaining repressed inside, where they can develop into toxic shame. Then, by focusing on what we can do to correct the error or begin again, supportive parenting helps us generate hope for the next try.

Bobby, a typical twelve-year-old, might have to use this skill on his paper route. On Saturday Bobby, who delivers the papers on his bicycle, misses the steps while throwing a paper and breaks Mrs. Smith's window. First, he feels fear: "Uh-oh. I've done it now. Mrs. Smith will be really angry when she gets home. Maybe I should run away before anyone finds out I did it." Then, he feels disappointed. "I really messed that up." Next, he blames himself: "I'm too clumsy. I should have been more careful." Then, he remembers what his supportive father told him: "Everyone makes mistakes, Bobby. That's a normal part of learning. If you make a mistake, you can almost always correct it. And if you can't, at least you can learn how to avoid making the same mistake again." So, instead of giving up, running away, blaming himself, or losing his confidence, Bobby gets off his bike, goes up to Mrs. Smith's door, and admits he broke the window. He offers to pay for it and asks her to find out what it would cost. After Mrs. Smith says she will, Bobby finishes his route and goes home.

When Bobby gets home, he's still upset and tells his father what happened, and how bad he feels. Bobby's dad remains supportive, reassuring him: "Don't worry, Bobby, it was just a mistake. You didn't break the window on purpose. I know you're still upset. That's natural—I would be upset, too. But remember you've done what you can to fix your mistake, and I'm proud of how you handled it. Now, why don't you consider what you could do to prevent it from happening again, and when you've figured that out, let go of it, forgive yourself, and go on to something else." With the guidance of supportive parents, Bobby learned how to resolve his feelings, not just suppress them, and applied his problem-solving abilities to correct the problem on his own behalf. Without their support, and especially if they were overcritical and he feared punishment, Bobby might have tried running away or lying to solve his problem, adding further to his burden of guilt and shame. In contrast, if his parents had rushed right in and fixed things without allowing him to solve them himself, he would not have learned how to deal with failure at all, and his paper route experience would have become a negative memory in which he had to depend on others to help him cope and was unable to assuage his guilt.

When supportive parents give us both guidance and the information we need to understand our mistakes and work them out by ourselves, and help us handle our disappointment, we develop the third skill of autonomy. We gain the necessary confidence that we can meet most of life's challenges without having to depend on others, and that we can cope with our own failures when we don't. This is a central turning point in our development of autonomy—we are no longer afraid of the new and the challenging.

In fact, we are certain we are smart enough and skillful enough ourselves to venture forth independent of our parents and anyone or anything outside ourselves. With this certainty, we never need to become dependent on people, substances, or behaviors to help us face life's risks and problems. Since we don't experience fear and pain when we confront situations calling for autonomous action, we never develop the behaviors and attitudes that are the foundation of dependency.

THE THREE ATTITUDES OF DEPENDENCY

When dysfunctional parents prevent us from developing the skills of autonomy, blocking our growth toward independence is only one consequence. We also learn to react to the challenges of new situations in ineffectual ways that actually *increase our dependency*. When we are inhibited or perhaps even punished for our early, independent childhood venturing, we do not have an opportunity to develop the skills of autonomy. Worse yet, we may even be taught ineffective behaviors, and the foundations of dependency are laid. Lacking the ability to successfully handle new, untried circumstances on our own, we are forced to turn to something outside ourselves to help us through these challenging events, and we fail to progress. As we grow older, who or what we depend on may change—from Mommy and Daddy to a "significant other" to addictive substances or destructive behaviors.

As John Bradshaw writes in *Healing the Shame That Binds You*: "Shaming experiences . . . are recorded in a person's memory bank. Because the victim has no time or support to grieve the pain . . . his emotions are regressed and the grief is unresolved . . . imprints remain in the memory . . . of the shaming scenes . . . forming collages of shaming memories. . . . Shame as an emotion has now become frozen and embedded into the core of the person's identity. Shame is deeply internalized." When we internalize shame in this way, risks become too painful to take, problems become too overwhelming to solve, and failure too terrifying to risk, and we return to addiction to mask the pain.

Instead of learning to solve problems and gaining confidence in our ability, we believe we are not smart enough to handle them on our own and begin to panic and stop thinking when we are faced with them: we start to learn *mindlessness* and depend on the judgment of others rather than ourselves.

Instead of developing the confidence to try new experiences we begin to fear them, convinced we lack the ability to take risks safely on our own: we start to feel *helpless* and dependent on others to help us cope with them.

Instead of developing confidence in our ability to cope with failure and disappointment, we simply feel incompetent, stupid, and ashamed of our inadequacy and we begin to despair and give up: we feel *hopeless* that our own efforts will ever be good enough.

These three attitudes, or negative coping skills, made you dependent and keep you dependent. They are at the core of all your addictive behavior, obsession, and compulsion. They have prevented you from growing beyond your dependency on substances, behaviors, people, and your recovery group itself. As long as you still have these negative beliefs, you will never be able or feel able to independently cope with life's challenges and you can never perceive yourself as strong enough to stand on your own.

Mindlessness

If young children are taught that taking risks is frightening or dangerous and they are made to feel incompetent to handle new situations, they begin to avoid becoming aware of anything new—of opportunities to learn, of challenges, and of poten-tially painful situations—of anything that requires them to cope with it autonomously and on their own. It's a downward spiral: the less aware they become, the more risk they avoid; the more things go wrong, the less aware they want to be. Since most of life presents some challenge, they eventually narrow their focus to just the day-to-day or even moment-to-moment events of their lives and have to depend on others to help them through the risks of their lives.

Thus, if little Tommy has been made to feel the risk of meeting new people is too great, rather than seeking out the new boy who has moved in next door, he may ignore the child (not be aware of him). Even if he does make overtures, Tommy may be ready to break the relationship off and run home as soon as any difficulties arise between them, convinced his parents' dysfunctional fear was right. Soon Tommy may even begin to ignore most possibilities for developing new relationships, and all other challenges and risks, until the attitude has become so habitual he is no longer even aware when such possibilities arise or aware that he is ignoring them.

Helplessness

If we grow up in a dysfunctional family where our early at-tempts at problem solving are either smothered by our parents or harshly criticized, the outcome of any situation will almost always be unsuccessful. Even when the outcome is successful, we are made to feel inadequate, that we "could have done bet-ter" or that we "were just lucky this time" and that next time it will very likely turn out worse. With dysfunctional parents, no matter what the outcome our childhood efforts are made to feel like disasters. As a result, we begin to feel helpless, dependent, and unable to solve life's problems on our own. Rather than feel-ing turned on and excited by the prospect of trying new experi-ences, we become so convinced of our own helplessness that we are no longer willing to try to solve our problems and instead begin to depend on people and things other than ourselves to solve them for us.

If little Mary had come from a dysfunctional family, rather

than trying to find a solution to the problem of what to do about feeling fearful at Rose's house without a light she would have been convinced that there wasn't an answer, or that if there was, she couldn't be smart enough to find it herself, and would need to turn to someone smarter, like her parents, to fix it for her. If they were unavailable, she would be paralyzed, without a possible solution.

Hopelessness

Once dysfunctional parents make us feel our mistakes and failures can't be corrected, we have no reason to hope we can make any situation better. Our feelings of shame, or incompetence and disappointment, instead of being a natural, temporary, and resolvable reaction to failure, become so constant that they deepen into despair. We become convinced there is nothing we can do to improve or better ourselves or our efforts, and that we and our lives are both hopeless.

If Bobby's parents had been discouraging, rather than supportive, they could have made him so hopeless that he probably would not have been courageous enough to take the paper route in the first place. But if he did, and broke a window, he would have been sure nothing he could do could make it better, and most likely would run away or lie about his responsibility for the broken window. Since twelve-year-olds usually are not too good at lying, the situation would have become much more of a disaster. Both Mrs. Smith and Bobby's parents would have been angry with him. With no help or support, Bobby would be left unable to correct his error and would be convinced it was safer to just give up—not to try anything challenging in the first place.

TOXIC SHAME, MAGICAL THINKING, AND YOU

The damage dysfunctional parents do with their negative reactions to our daily risk taking toward autonomy is even more devastating because it occurs at an age when our ability to think is still imperfectly formed and we are extremely vulnerable to believing whatever they tell us. We have not yet developed the ability for abstract and rational thought (understanding non-concrete concepts such as *far away*, *next year*, *good*, *evil*, *frustrated*); the ability to evaluate ("Spilling my milk isn't *that* bad"; "mother is overreacting"); or the ability to project future likelihood from current events ("Father is very tired, and his boss gave him a difficult time today, so if I get whiny he's going to blow up").

When we are young (some experts say before age five, some before age eight), our thinking ability is only partially developed, and the world's events seem to happen magically around us. Children, wide-eyed, believe that the Tooth Fairy really left the quarter, or that Mommy's kiss heals a bumped knee, or that the Santa in the department store is really going to bring the toy they ask for down the chimney on Christmas Eve. Small children love to play peekaboo, because they believe they can't be seen when *their* eyes are covered up.

As children we cannot see the cause-and-effect connection between events (a small child cannot understand that planting a seed will produce tomatoes weeks later); we think in very concrete ways and cannot understand abstract concepts (ideas such as *near and far* and *left and right* are not understood until the later stages of development, usually ages five and up); we are the center of our universe and think everything happens because of ourself and our actions (small children interrupt conversations—they always assume you are ready to give them your attention); and we perceive our behavior to be the cause of every event (if Mommy smiles or frowns, baby feels responsible).

Connecting unrelated events and our own behavior in this way is what psychologists term *magical thinking*, the stage in a child's thinking in which we believe we are the cause of physical phenomena. In *Imaginary Crimes*, psychologists Lewis Engel and Tom Ferguson show that magical thinking is part of normal childhood development: "As children we are ignorant of the laws of cause and effect, and may at times come to irrational conclusions. . . . Magical thinking is the child's belief that she has the ability to make things happen by simply thinking about them."

In the popular film *Home Alone*, when the young hero wakes to find himself alone in the house, he (falsely, but naturally for his seven years of age) concludes it's because the night before he wished his whole family would disappear. The more prosaic truth, that he's been accidentally forgotten by his rather disorganized family amid the chaos of leaving for vacation, simply doesn't occur to him. It is this quality of childhood thinking that makes fairy tales, fables, and magical stories such as *Mary Poppins* so believable to children. In their eyes, they are as real as many other "unseen" events: Daddy's work, older brother's school, germs, "when you grow up." If a child cannot experience something with her own five senses, it is not real to her, and seems magical.

Because we are still in the magical thinking stage when we begin our first autonomous ventures into the world, we are particularly vulnerable to the damaging ways in which dysfunctional parents react. This is particularly true when it comes to the mistakes we make in the course of our initial trial-and-error efforts. Because the natural limitations of our magical childhood thinking make it impossible to evaluate situations for ourselves, we are vulnerable to whatever dysfunctional adults tell us—we simply accept, without question, that their behavior, teachings, and evaluations of us are correct. If they are overcritical and tell us, "You're bad, useless, and worthless," when we really just made a normal childlike mistake, we naively accept this overharsh evaluation of ourselves.

This childhood inability to differentiate between *doing* something wrong (making a mistake) and *being* something wrong (a bad child) eventually convinces us that we are bad, stupid, and unworthy. After a while we constantly feel ashamed of our inadequacy, as if we ought to apologize for existing and deserve to live in an environment of criticism and abuse.

This contempt for our own existence is, perhaps, the single most destructive feeling we can have about ourselves, since it makes us feel unworthy to cope, unfit to exist, and completely dependent on the effects and opinions of others. Therapists call this feeling *toxic shame* (a phrase popularized by John Bradshaw) because it is so strong and so deeply embedded that it devastates and poisons our whole life. In *Healing the Shame That Binds You*, Bradshaw explains the effect toxic shame can have on children when it is fostered during the critical period of magical thinking: "When shame has been . . . internalized, nothing about you is okay . . . you have the sense of being a failure . . . you are an object of contempt to yourself." Toxic shame forms one of the major roots of dependency, one source of the inner pain you try to subdue with addiction and compulsion. Bradshaw explains why: "When you are contemptible to yourself, . . . you turn your eyes inward, watching and scrutinizing every minute detail of behavior. This internal critical observation is excruciating."

This internal criticism or toxic shame, learned from your dysfunctional parents, is tied to every effort, activity, or thought you undertake—and always finds your efforts unsatisfactory. The belief that nothing you can do on your own is ever good enough becomes painfully embedded in your child mind, and doesn't go away. It remains locked there, where it keeps you mindless, helpless, hopeless, and dependent until you learn how to reach it and re-educate it.

In other words, if your parents treat you lovingly, if things go well, you (the child) are OK. If you, as a child, are made to believe that making mistakes is wrong, you become dependent upon others—your focus is on anxious observation of how the adults expect you to do things.

YOUR DEPENDENT INNER CHILD

As the child of dysfunctional parents, you do not outgrow your original dependent childhood personality or the negative judgments you made about your ability to cope with life autonomously. Instead, your childhood mind forms the basis of your adolescent mind and then your adult mind. And since the negative attitudes it has been taught ensure that your subsequent attempts at independence and self-control are unsuccessful, your childhood personality (which many psychologists call the *inner child* or the *subconscious*) becomes convinced, by what seems a lifetime of experience that only confirms this judgment, that you are unable to manage life on your own.

Because the attitudes and the skills that keep you dependent were formed by your childhood magical mind, and lie so deeply buried within you, they are very difficult to change or unlearn. Since they were acquired long before your earliest memories began, it is difficult for your adult mind to become aware of or communicate with this key part of your inner child. Even when you do manage to get in touch with it, you may not be able to communicate with it effectively, because it still perceives and thinks about the world magically while you tend to think and communicate as an adult.

You have probably never known why it seemed so agonizingly impossible to end your addictive behavior, why you felt so helplessly unable to control your behavior for so much of your life, or why you have always been dependent on something other than yourself to help you cope with risk and pain. But you do know, from your personal experience, just how hard it is, how much you have struggled to change, how many countless times you have failed, and how much you and those around you have suffered as a result. Yet, the problem wasn't that you were too weak or that you hadn't tried hard enough, but that you were putting your effort into the wrong places.

As an adult, you may know that your addictive behavior is destructive and that you are a worthwhile person who no longer needs to depend on others for support and guidance. But your inner child is buried so deep and thinks so differently that your message can't penetrate. This is one reason why you have heard yourself and other support group members make statements such as this: "I know I shouldn't do it, but I just can't help myself."

Unless you know that you need to communicate with your subconscious child mind in the same "language" it speaks, in a way that it can understand, you cannot work with it to change the attitudes and habits that first made you dependent. When a message from your adult mind does penetrate, your child mind doesn't understand it because you put it in adult terms. To your inner child, your attempts at communicating, though they make perfect sense to you, may seem simply like gibberish and make no sense.

In order to complete your recovery and unlearn the attitudes and skills that keep you dependent, you need to bridge the gap between your adult self and your inner child—to communicate with it in the kind of magical terms it understands. Establishing this effective connection between your rational, adult mind and your magical child mind is essential to your recovery. Only when you have your inner child's full and willing cooperation are you able to correct the damage done in your childhood.

Without a way to communicate with your child mind, you can try to overcome your dependent behavior by asserting your will power or trying to act exclusively from your adult mind. But, without the cooperation of the inner child, all you accomplish is to create an internal struggle between your child beliefs (which have the power of years of experience and repetition behind them) and your adult mind, whose ideas and knowledge are of mere recent years. So, the minute you get stressed, overloaded, or confused, your child mind reasserts itself and takes over, causing you to revert to old, familiar modes of behavior. For example, you might have decided to give up drinking because your adult mind knows it is bad for you. Logically, you know how to handle each temptation that could arise: what to say if a friend offers you a drink, how not to drink at a business lunch, how to stay out of the bars on Friday night. But, your spouse fights with you, and suddenly you're too upset to think rationally about it. Immediately, your child self reacts with dependent behavior and you find yourself drinking again, and not really understand how it happened.

A recovery group would probably tell you to go to a meeting to get help fighting the impulse. And *if you make it to a meeting,* you will probably calm down enough to maintain your sobriety. However, in either case, something *outside you* strengthens your behavior and keeps your underlying dependency controlled.

TWELVE-STEP PROGRAMS AND
CHILDHOOD DEPENDENCE

The worldwide success of the twelve-step and other self-help recovery groups is in part due to the way that the solid support of regular meetings and contact with program members provide new members with a supportive family-like atmosphere. Regular attendance supplies many of the elements necessary to overcoming dependence, elements that members never experienced while growing up in dysfunctional families. Among those elements are:

- unconditional love and support
- reliable, predictable influences you can count on, perhaps for the first time in your life
- the acceptance of being welcome, whoever you are, and whatever state you are in
- people who will listen, without arguing or interrupting, as you tell your story
- human warmth, and the support of being around others who understand your problems
- the encouragement of seeing others, who have or have had as many problems as you have, overcome addiction and make it into recovery

Thus, recovery groups provide a safe environment from which to experiment and take some risks, forgoing your addiction and facing the pain and fear that you previously screened out with addictive substances or behaviors.

However, recovery groups do not, and cannot as presently constituted, help members develop the skills that build autonomy, and can even seriously undermine any tentative growth members might make beyond their childhood dependency because of their insistence that the group is more important than the individual. Since addictive people grew up in dysfunctional families and often have long histories of being abused and/or abusive, and have been taught to discount or ignore the feelings and needs of others and the effect of their addiction on them, the twelve-step programs counter by asking members to consider the welfare of the group. By emphasizing caring about each other, they maximize the group influence and make their system of rewards more effective. Through this system of support, reward, and example, groups help people who are used to destructive behavior find a reason to control it. To make this point, one of the Twelve Traditions of AA is: "Our common welfare should come first; personal recovery depends upon AA unity."

Although this focus on group unity does help people who were alienated by uncaring, chaotic families learn to consider the welfare of others, it also has some drawbacks. Unfortunately, the emphasis on the "common welfare" can also reinforce dependent attitudes developed in dysfunctional families, where it is common for individuals to be told that they cannot do what they want because the family as a whole or the parents are more important than they are, and what they want to do (go to college, go out with friends, dress as they like) is not good for the family. Believing that others are more important than you makes you feel powerless and helpless. This powerless feeling, in turn, leads you to conclude that you are not strong enough to take action on your own.

In other words, the group, like your own dysfunctional family, reinforces a lifelong tendency to view yourself as being what psychologist Nathaniel Brandon calls a "family asset"—whose life, by right, does not belong to you, but to them, and who has no legitimate entitlement to independent action. In *Honoring the Self*, Brandon invites readers to ask themselves: "Did your parents encourage you to feel that your life belonged to you? Or were you encouraged to believe that you were merely a family asset?"

One of the important functions of healthy parents and teachers is to encourage children to realize that their lives belong to *them*, which helps them feel important enough and powerful enough to master the skills of autonomy. It also makes them feel equal to, and therefore not dependent on, the others around them. Such attitudes are discouraged in twelve-step programs, as they are in dysfunctional families and in schools, where too much independence is suspect as detrimental to the group unity and survival. If you attempt to develop autonomy within the group you may find yourself criticized for not attending meetings, or rejected by friends within the group, or even accused of relapsing. While letting go of addiction or a destructive outside relationship is encouraged, only dependent, other-oriented attitudes toward group members are rewarded and considered acceptable, and asserting your independence from within the group meets with hostility or disapproval.

One client, John, a hairdresser recovering from abusive relationships, attended CoDA fr a year and became the group secretary. After a few months, John began to feel ready to take some healthy risks, and decided to go back to school. He asked for someone else to take over his duties so he could attend a college class that met at the same time. After the meeting, members of the group warned him that he "needed them" and told him tragic stories of others who had left the group when they began feeling better and than relapsed into old behavior. No one congratulated or supported him on taking classes to improve himself.

Of course, it is important for people caught up in addictive behavior to learn to acknowledge the importance and existence of others, and to care about their welfare and regard them as important. Such people often lack socialization skills, and being an accepted member of the group enhances their self-esteem to a point where it is easier to give up their destructive behavior.

What is *not* understood by most twelve-step programs, their members, or society in general is how critically recovery from dependence rests on finding the necessary balance between caring for others and caring for self. It is difficult for most people to understand how autonomy, independence, and caring for yourself *blend with* and *enhance* caring for others. We can genuinely care for others, as opposed to being focused dependently on them, only when we care for ourselves. We are not emotionally prepared to receive anything from others or give anything worthwhile to others (close friendship, respect) if we are not familiar with feeling it toward ourselves. We cannot be emotionally willing to receive any of these unless we already feel them toward ourselves, and accept our right to deserve them.

From his unique perspective as both a minister and licensed therapist, Denton Roberts shows how autonomy and self-esteem are essential to caring for others in his book *Able and Equal*: "How I relate to myself determines what I am willing to give and receive from others. . . . *I will not let in from others that which I am not giving myself,* and *I am not adept at giving others what I am not giving myself.* The way I relate to me prepares me internally to give and receive. Until I have an appreciation of myself I will not fully receive another's appreciation."

Your relationship with you is your most intimate experience of how personal interaction feels—this internal experience is the one against which you compare all others. Whether you are aware of it or not, you measure both how you treat others and how they treat you against the criterion of *how you treat yourself.* Therefore, the more healthy and autonomous you are, the more your chances increase for having healthy relationships with others, including the members of your twelve-step program.

One reason recovery programs have only helped you stop your addiction but not your dependency is that most recovery workers have only recently become aware of the importance of the inner child and the techniques for communicating with it. Even when they have known about the inner child, they have rarely focused on issues of autonomy and the forces that undercut its development during the critical formative stages. Instead of empowering the inner child and helping it become stronger and more independent, they have focused on healing its hurts—curing the symptoms but leaving the causes untreated.

Another reason that recovery programs have not been able to correct the root causes of dependency is that once you are old enough to have entered the stage of rational thought, others can no longer directly influence your subconscious without your active participation. Once you acquire the ability to think abstractly, pass judgment, and make evaluations you no longer believe the events of the world take place in a magical way and do not believe information unless it sounds reasonable and makes sense to your adult, rational mind.

To move beyond mere surface recovery to deep inner recovery requires making a connection with your subconscious, childlike mind, bringing it into your present, everyday life, and working cooperatively with it in a way it can understand. Otherwise, it will resist any positive, healthy decisions for change your adult mind makes that run counter to its years of negative experiences and beliefs about itself. Recovery programs and therapies, unless they recognize and work with this fact, can do no more than arrest and stabilize addictive and compulsive behavior by influencing your adult thinking.

Since you are the only one who has direct access to your mind, once you learn the language of magical thinking you gain an ability no one else can ever have—to work with, influence, and change your childlike, creative, subconscious mind. Therefore, the most powerful person in your recovery, growth, and healing will always be you.

CHAPTER 4

Deep Recovery:
Learning How to Change

If you . . . study and learn the techniques, you dil-
igently follow all the instruction . . . then comes
the time for using the rules in your own way and not
being bound by them. You can actually forget the
rules because they have been assimilated. You
are . . . one . . . who has been . . . transmuted.
JOSEPH CAMPBELL

Y ou have learned how growing up in a dysfunctional family
blocks autonomy during the early vulnerable period of
magical thinking and creates dependency that becomes buried
deep in your subconscious, childlike mind. Now, it is time to
learn the special language your childlike inner mind uses so you
can communicate with it, change the dependent patterns you
were taught, and create new, autonomous patterns.

Like most languages you learn, the one your magical child
mind speaks is acquired through practice and use. First, you
learn the various words and what they mean and how to put
them together correctly in order to convey your own meaning
to someone else. Then, you practice until you become fluent.
The special language of the subconscious, childlike, magical
mind is learned in a similar fashion, but using processes rather
than words. Because of the power of these processes to create
change when properly used, and their ability to effect magical

thinking, I call them the *magical tools*. These six magical tools are:

1. The Senses: the power of experience
2. Imagery: the power to change events
3. Self-Love: the power to heal your hurts
4. Self-Image: the power to be your own hero
5. Environment: the power to create support
6. Repetition and Memorization: the power to affect your beliefs

In essence, these tools are the six basic elements that underlie all our early childhood learning. Because the early childhood mind is inaccessible through reason or abstract thinking, unless we can communicate in its "magical thinking" language we cannot change what we learned through that language—from our senses, environment, memorization, from what we see in our imagination as we are being taught, our own images of what we can be, and the way we love and are loved by others. Only through learning to "speak" to the child mind with these tools can we change that early learning as we grow throughout life. Although logical thought and reason play an important part in adult learning, the methods of these six tools are the only way the child mind can take in and learn new information.

Our focus first will be on how to use these processes to learn the language of the childlike mind and apply it to accelerate learning, change old habits, mentally practice sports or dancing, teach yourself new skills, and motivate yourself to exercise, eat healthier, relax, or learn something new. Practicing these exercises will form the foundation for the deeper work to come.

It is not our intention at this point to actually begin to change your old, dependent thinking and build autonomy, although there will be some "side effects" of changing old, dependent beliefs and learning new, autonomous skills. Instead, the purpose of doing these exercises is to become familiar with the tools and how to use them to communicate with your subconscious, childlike mind.

Learning these tools in itself enhances your autonomy because they give you the means to heal and alter your own subconscious which—by giving you the knowledge of what creates the changes, and the choice of what changes to make—makes you independent of any system of change and emotional healing, including this book. Once you master these tools, you can create and design your own system of change, without having to depend on others.

SIX MAGICAL TOOLS FOR REACHING THE CHILD MIND

To effectively reach your own childlike mind, you must find out which combination of these tools works best for you, because each of us has inborn differences in the ways we learn best and some of us tend to learn more often through one basic process than another. You must also learn how they all work and how to use them effectively. Each of these tools will help you to influence old ingrained beliefs and ideas in a different way.

An extra benefit of knowing which tools you use best is that it will help you evaluate books, workshops, therapy, meditation, or learning techniques according to the tools they incorporate, and know which ones suit you best *before* you try them. For example, if you are contemplating a new kind of meditation and you know that the sensory experience of hearing is important to you, you can choose a meditation that involves background music. If you know that physical touch or movement is important, you'll choose a meditation based on movement. If visualization works well, you'll choose a corresponding technique such as guided meditation.

The Senses: The Power of Experience

When we were very young children who had not yet developed the capacity of abstract thought, our only source of knowledge about the world around us was what we perceived directly through our senses—sight, touch, hearing, smell, and taste. Many of our earliest experiences, including those first autonomous venturings out from behind mother's skirts, occurred when we still related and responded to the world almost solely in terms of the senses. Although we develop other methods of learning about the world later, as adults we still continue to learn much of what we know about the world in this way. In a sense, this becomes the hidden foundation on which all later learning is based—information and impressions that come to us through the senses still exert a special influence over us, such as the smell of a fresh Christmas tree, hearing the song that was playing when you met your first love, or the sight of a rainbow. More important, when we did begin to develop the capability to think, we thought first in sensory images and only later learned to think in words—babies recognize Mother's face long before they know the word *Mama*.

All this suggests that the part of your mind that receives and thinks in images and impressions is more basic and its influence stronger than the part that thinks and reacts in terms of words, and that sensory impressions underlie much of the original magical thinking of childhood. The child has a "sense" of what it has experienced first, and then tries to connect events to her sensory experience with limited thinking ability. Thus, if a child has a mouthful of strained spinach when Mom and Dad have a fight, he may never eat spinach again for his whole adult life. That makes sensory impressions and memories a powerful tool for bypassing your rational conscious mind, for speaking directly to and working with your subconscious child mind, to correct the damage growing up in a dysfunctional family did to your development as an autonomous person. When you talk to your child mind in the language of the senses you contact an important aspect of your contemporary adult mind as well.

You may have experienced the power the senses have to put you in touch with your child self when some aroma or sound or flavor has suddenly recalled the memory of a long-forgotten experience. Perhaps the scent of flowers has reminded you of a favorite place, or an old song reminded you of a time when you were sad. That is why once the adult experience has covered over your child self, it can still be effectively reached through invoking the senses. A vivid "flow of thoughts you can see, hear, feel, smell, or taste" is, as oncologist Martin L. Rossman writes in *Healing Yourself,* this "interface language . . . [which] can help you solve practical problems, develop insight . . . enhance your self-confidence."

In the following exercise, you will learn and observe the powerful effect the senses can have to communicate with your own subconscious, childlike mind and to create changes mentally and physically. You will be introduced to this effect by learning how to use your imagination to invoke sensory images through building a personal "retreat." With practice, this will then become a place you can go to for actual psychological and physical relief and healing. It can also serve as a quick way of gaining access into your subconscious child mind, and an excellent setting for future mental work, as you will see when we use your personal retreat in several of the other exercises throughout this book. By practicing this exercise, you will gain valuable experience in invoking the power of your senses, one of the primary languages through which the child mind learns and communicates. You will also develop your ability to create imaginary mental images, which will become the basis for many other skills you will learn in this book, such as creative thinking.

In doing this exercise, you should take great care to imagine and develop your sensory impressions in as vivid detail as possible. You will be asked to notice how everything looks, feels, smells, sounds, and tastes. The more completely you can experience all of these sensory details, the more effective you will be in reaching and impacting your child mind. It is important to take the time to get your senses involved in the process.

When you begin practicing, don't be surprised or discouraged if you have trouble in re-creating everything in vivid sensory detail at first. As a child of a dysfunctional family, you may have learned a habit of blocking as much sensory information as possible, because it was all so powerful and negative. By now you may be out of touch with your senses and have difficulty in building a realistic sensory image that invokes all five senses.

If you worry because you feel you are not doing this perfectly, you will make it much more difficult than it needs to be and discourage yourself. Instead, just do the best you can at first, because your skill will improve as you repeat the exercise. If you can be patient and do all these exercises regularly, you will soon find that your ability to create realistic and vivid sensory impressions improves significantly. You may also find that you become more aware of your own sensory experiences in your reality. The sights, sounds, feelings, smells, and tastes of the world around you can become more vivid and begin to have more impact.

Also, even though you are being asked to picture detail and get your senses involved, you are not expected to see pictures as though you were watching a TV or movie screen. Just knowing what your scene looked like, being able to describe what you're picturing, and remembering colors, smells, feelings, and the like is sufficient. You will also realize, as you do these exercises, that your own particular way of seeing the scene works, whether you do it in words, pictures, or impressions.

Learning to use Magical Tool 1: The Senses teaches you a basic skill for affecting your subconscious magical thinking. Once you learn this method, you can use it to contact your inner childlike mind, to change unhealthy attitudes and habits into new, healthier behavior, or to heal and resolve old, painful childhood memories. Later, you will learn to use it specifically for replacing dependent thinking and skills with those of autonomy. Many of the exercises and guided meditations later in this book begin by invoking your senses as we do here.

These tools are designed to be used over and over again, as needed throughout your lifetime. However, in the beginning as you are learning them, simply do each one two or three times to familiarize yourself with it, and go on to learn the next. Because they interact and build on each other, and because they are so powerful and continuously useful, you will use them over and over until they become lifetime habits.

You may find it works best to read the instructions for this exercise and the ones that follow in this book into a tape recorder, or take turns with a friend and read them aloud for each other. Read slowly, pausing between sentences. Then you will be free to let your imagination roam, and to picture scenes in ever-increasing detail without having to stop and interrupt yourself to read each new instruction.

EXERCISE
FOR MAGICAL TOOL 1:
USING THE SENSES TO BUILD A RETREAT

1. *Choose a scene.* Pick a favorite place where you have enjoyed being alone, that feels relaxing and private enough to be yourself. It might be a beach at a vacation spot, the attic in Grandma's house when you were a child, a waterfall on a camping trip, sitting on a porch at night, a luxurious hotel suite, or even a favorite spot in your present home. Or, choose an imaginary place you would enjoy relaxing in: a restful room you have seen in a magazine, or an appealing scenic landscape from a calendar, or perhaps a place from a novel or movie—fantasy lovers might pick Middle Earth or Narnia. As you think of the scene, notice whether it feels real to you, because you'll contrast this to how it feels later. You will probably feel distant from it, and somewhat detached at this point, before you use your senses.

2. *Develop your visual image.* Get comfortably seated, relax your body, close your eyes, and use your imagination to *see the scene* you have chosen in as much detail as possible, but don't strain or struggle to see it. Just allow the scene to unfold, and add details as you think of them. Remember, it's not important to create a perfect, lifelike image. At first, just strive for a clear image of the scene. Think about what it looks like. Is it outdoors or indoors? Is it day or night? What colors are there: green grass and trees, brown carpets and flowered wallpaper? Are there flowers and rocks, furniture or decorations? Though you have

stopped consciously trying to picture the scene, you may be surprised to discover that as you invoke the remaining senses with the subsequent steps of the exercise, the scene becomes clearer seemingly by itself.

3. *Picture yourself in the scene.* Now use your imagination to see *yourself* in your scene, as a living participant, wherever you feel most comfortable and at ease with yourself. Are you standing, sitting, or lying down? What objects in the scene are near you? Which ones are at a distance? What are you wearing? What are the colors? How do you look? When you have pictured yourself as part of the scene as completely as feels comfortable, go on to the next step.

4. *Use your sense of touch.* Use your imagination to *feel the scene* around you. Are you lying on grass, sitting in a favorite chair, or standing on a city street, or perhaps dangling your bare feet in a running brook? What does the air feel like? Is it clear and rich, the way it is after a rain, or is it the close, heavy air of summer? Is a breeze moving against your skin, blowing your hair? Are you warm or cool? Are your clothes rough or smooth, tight or loose? Or are you wearing clothes at all?

5. *Use your sense of hearing.* Use your imagination to *hear the sounds.* Is there traffic noise, a radio, music, voices in another room, floors creaking, a fan whirring, birds chirping, water running, or the wind?

6. *Use your sense of smell.* Use your imagination to *smell the air* around you. Can you smell someone cooking, flowers, animals, rain on the breeze, cleaning products, pipe tobacco?

7. *Use your sense of taste.* Use your imagination to taste any flavors that may accompany the smells—the mouth-watering taste of good food cooking; the dusty taste of an old attic; the sweet, metallic flavor of rain; or the sharp, rich aroma of coffee.

8. *Reinvoke all your senses.* Take an extra few moments to use your imagination to notice the information reaching *all your senses*—sight, sound, touch, smell, and

taste. Absorb the sensory feelings of your retreat and relax fully into the scene, so you can experience your retreat in as much sensory detail as possible before going on to the next step.

9. *Modify your retreat to suit you.* Now that you have clearly established a private retreat, look around it and see how it suits you. If you can think of any improvements you'd like to make, change it to please yourself. This is your personal haven, and it is important that it be as comfortable and pleasant for you as possible. Would you prefer more privacy? Less sound? More light? More green grass and trees? A cozier place to sit? Try various combinations out; you can change them back if you don't like them. Customize your retreat until you feel it is just the way you want it before going on to the next step.

10. *Notice the difference in how you feel.* Take a few minutes and let yourself become aware of how you feel now. You will probably be surprised to discover just how much difference creating a restful scene like this has made. Do you feel more relaxed, calmer, and more secure? Have your thoughts slowed and become quieter? Do you feel emotions you have not felt for a while, such as nostalgia, peace, sadness, happiness, or love for others or yourself? You may notice that as you developed the sensory images of your retreat the sounds and sensations of your real world have receded. You may even feel more present in your mental retreat than in your actual surroundings. Relax a few moments and let these feelings sink in before moving to the next step, to get the full benefit of the calm, relaxing peace of your retreat.

11. *Preserve your retreat for future use.* Look around at your mental retreat one more time to fix it in your memory. Review all its sights, sounds, and sensations until you could describe it clearly to someone else. Select a small object from your scene, one that you can hold, touch, and see. The object you choose should be in some way symbolic of, or remind you of, your retreat, because it will become your key

to return, an object to focus on that will bring the whole scene back to your memory in full sensory detail. For example, a colored pebble from beside a brook, a key to the door of a room, a branch from a flowering bush, a doll or teddy bear from a bed, or anything else that immediately suggests the whole scene for you. Hold the object in your hand, concentrate on it, and observe every detail of it carefully enough so you will remember it later. When you have done this you have mentally preserved your retreat and completed the exercise. It is time to slowly transfer your attention back to your physical surroundings. First, wiggle your fingers and toes; then slowly and gently, because you're coming out of a dream state and you deserve a gentle re-entry, open up your eyes.

12. *Repeat to become fluent.* Now you have experienced for the first time the actual physical and mental difference that using the power of your senses to enhance mental images can make. As you become more proficient, the images you create will become clearer and more vivid and the power of their effect will grow stronger. The more you repeat this exercise, the easier and faster it will be for you to invoke your senses in imaginary settings (the basis for many of the exercises that follow in this book). In addition, you have created a mental and emotional haven to which you can retreat any time you need a break from life's stress and strains. However, you will find that this is only the beginning of what you can accomplish.

This safe haven also will become a place you use when you have inner healing work to do. When you want to return, simply choose a quiet, uninterrupted time and place, relax, close your eyes, and visualize your key object. As you picture the object, the image of your retreat will probably arise automatically in your imagination. If not, repeat the steps from Step 2 or until you have re-created the scene completely. Each time you complete the exercise, refocus on your symbolic object, to increase its usefulness as a key that can invoke the scene immediately.

Other uses for this exercise. You can use this tool to give yourself the equivalent of physical experience, and teach yourself new behaviors and skills. For example, if you tend to crave foods that are not good for you—fats, sweets, or salt—and you want to learn to eat healthier foods, use the steps above to enter your retreat, and there imagine yourself eating healthier foods such as vegetables and fresh fruits, and enjoying them. Use your sensory input to make the healthy foods look, smell, and taste wonderful. By repeatedly imagining the colors, tastes, textures, and smells of these healthy, delicious foods, you'll find that your tastes in actual eating gradually begin to change. You'll notice and be attracted to different items in the grocery store and on menus.

If you are anxious about an upcoming meeting with your boss, mentally rehearse the meeting by inviting him or her into your retreat first. In your sanctuary, you'll be the host or hostess, and you'll have the upper hand. Use all the sensory information you can: the smell of your boss's cologne, the color of his or her business suit, the sound of your voices talking. Once you've established the sensory data, picture the meeting going well. Serve coffee or a snack, and present your program, or listen to your employer praise your work. Repeat several times, until you feel calm through the entire process. You'll find that when you get to the actual meeting, you'll feel less anxious.

If you believe you are clumsy, because everyone said you were in childhood, use the exercise above to picture yourself as a child, then see yourself gracefully running and dancing until you feel confident.

Once you become fluent in using the power of your senses as a language to communicate with and change your subconscious thought patterns, you'll find you can apply it to coping successfully with many different situations.

Imagery: The Power to Change Events

One of the most powerful ways to reach back into your childlike mind and change deeply buried dysfunctional and/or destructive thoughts and attitudes is through your imagination, using what many psychologists know as *imagery* and others call *visualization* or *mental rehearsal*. Everyone is familiar with imagery to some degree: it is our mental ability to visualize or picture scenes and events without being there—what most of us call having a daydream or fantasy, something you have been doing all your life.

Here, you are going to learn how to put it to use in a powerful form of deep, inner healing. Visualization, imagery, and fantasies are powerful in their effect because the mental impressions they create are similar to the magical language of childhood thought processes. "Imagery is a window on your inner world, a way of viewing your own ideas, feelings, interpretations," writes Dr. Rossman in *Healing Yourself*, "a means of transformation and liberation." Remember how real your sanctuary came to feel as you practiced the previous exercise, and the profound physical and psychological changes it created? Experiences and activities imagined in the same amount of detail can feel as real—imagery, properly used, allows you to learn from that experience as you would from the real thing. The reason is that, coupled with the use of your senses, imagery duplicates actual, physical experience closely enough to make a similar impression on your subconscious mind. "Through imagery," writes Dr. Rossman, "you can stimulate changes in many body functions usually considered inaccessible to conscious influence. In the last twenty years, we have learned that imagery is the natural language of a major part of our nervous system."

Research shows that when we imagine an activity in complete sensory detail, nerves and muscles are electrically activated in a way that is very similar to the way they are activated when we actually perform the activity. That's why when you remember angry or happy events you reexperience your original feelings, and why remembering tastes (imagine biting into a lemon) can make your mouth water, and why the memory of something that smelled rotten and disgusting can make you feel nauseous. Athletes now routinely use imagery to practice for events because of this measurable physical effect—visualizing themselves going through the motions until they feel they have the moves "down pat"—which gives them an equivalent of actual physical practice, without overtaxing their muscles and stamina.

Once you learn how to use imagery, you have access to a way to create imaginary experiences from which to learn, and a way to learn the skills of autonomy by taking risks in your imagination without real-life consequences. Later, we will use the power of imagery to heal old, painful childhood memories and release yourself from the dependency and low self-esteem they created, and to rehearse autonomy-building experiences. These uses of imagery develop your creative ability to forecast positive options and future developments, a basic skill of autonomous thinking. In your imagination, you can create experiences that never occurred in real life. You can even return to an old scene and visualize it happening differently. Imagery has more than just a mental effect.

Although some elements of the following exercise may seem childish or silly, remember we are seeking to communicate with your childlike mind. Often, nonrational "magical" thoughts, processes, and rituals—because they are so similar to early magical thinking—will change mental patterns, and thereby heal lives where logic and conscious thought have failed.

In the previous exercise, you already used one form of imagery—visualizing a scene in order to practice using your senses to reach the subconscious. The exercise that follows will help you sharpen your skill at creating and changing vivid images easily, and show you how effective imagery can be.

The focus here is on taking a scene that is problematic and creating a positive outcome. Once you have become familiar and comfortable with using imagery in this way, your childlike mind will have a usable pattern to follow in changing deeply buried beliefs. In later chapters, we'll use this tool to rerun early scenes of your childhood in which negative experiences happened that formed the root cause of your addiction and dependency. Imagery can also be used to anticipate future events, and minimize risk taking by rehearsing the events in advance.

Again, taping this exercise or asking a friend to read it will allow you to experience it without distraction.

EXERCISE
FOR MAGICAL TOOL 2:
USING IMAGERY TO CREATE A FANTASY

1. *Choose an event or story.* Select a story you know well, where you can be the star who changes a sad ending and makes everything turn out okay. Use a story you have read or have been told by a friend, a fairy tale, a plot from a TV show or a movie, or a dramatic sports event. The story should have an unhappy ending you can change. You can be Donald Trump facing his creditors. You can be your favorite losing politician rerunning the losing campaign in your mind. Or you can be the heartbroken heroine or hero in a soap opera and win back the lover who has just left you. Did your favorite sports team bungle last Saturday's game? Be the coach or the athlete who saves the day. You can even be the princess who saves the knight by outsmarting the evil wizard, or the understudy who takes over for the star with the broken leg. When you've chosen your story, go to the next step.

2. *Involve your senses.* As you did in the first seven steps of the previous exercise, use your senses to build your retreat, relax, close your eyes, and develop all the sights, sounds, sensations, and people in the scene of your story until it is as real and vivid as possible. Again, once it is established using all five senses, imagine yourself in the scene as the main character of the story. Be sure to picture yourself dressed for the part. Take as much time as you need to develop the scene and the characters around you as fully as you can. Then, go on to the next step.

3. *Make silly changes for practice.* Once your scene is fully established, change the people and events several times, to practice using this tool and to experience how easy

it is to change a mental scene. Make your experience silly or fun, and let youself enjoy using your imagination. Redecorate the room, or change what the people are wearing. Stand people on their heads. Change maple trees to palm trees, turn everyone blue, shrink buildings into little toys, or turn the clouds green. Make at least three changes in the scene, and then change everything back to the way it was, before going on to the next step.

4. *Change the events and make a happy ending*. After you've practiced using your imagination to make small changes long enough to feel comfortable doing it, you are ready to move on to bigger things, such as creating a new positive ending for your story. Imagine you are the main character, the hero or heroine, figure out how you could do it differently, and change the ending to make it come out happy. Then visualize yourself acting out these changes until you have brought the scene to a successful conclusion. As coach, you can run different plays, or even pull in better players from other teams or from sports history, or even have Rambo play on your football team! As the soap opera character, you can have your lover storm out, then return, having realized there is no one else in the world but you. As Donald Trump, you can decide not to buy the Atlantic City casino, or conjure up a fantastically rich foreign investor who bails you out.

5. *Make changes until you are satisfied*. Stay with your story and change it any way you like until you feel you are completely satisfied with it. As you do so, you are developing your capacity to create and forecast options and alternatives, and to make choices.

6. *End the scene*. When you feel finished, find a way to end the scene—you can have all your characters take a bow and bring the curtain down, or allow your story to fade or float away—and slowly come back to your normal consciousness as you did in step 11 of the previous exercise.

7. *Repeat to become fluent*. Practice this exercise several times, using different stories and characters, until it

becomes easy for you to do. In the process, you will find you have become familiar with the techniques of imagery and visualization, and stretched the power of your imagination.

Self-Love: The Power to Heal Your Hurts

Most dependent and addictive people who grew up in dysfunctional or unstable families are confused about love. Babies learn first about love not from what they feel for their parents but from the feeling of warmth and tenderness they receive from them, so if your parents were so emotionally damaged themselves that they could not give you any of the qualities of healthy love—warmth, caring, support, or tenderness—then you cannot learn them from your adult experience.

In a society that is biased in favor of dependency, where self-love is often mistakenly thought to be selfish and uncaring, it is hard to allow yourself to be the object of your own love and caring. Because we carry toxic shame, it's hard for many of us to believe that we deserve love, even from ourselves. Many people don't even realize that such a thing as self-love is possible, much less a powerful healing tool.

Learning how to love yourself is the safest and most effective way to begin to learn how to love others. The following exercise uses a variety of love we call *friendship* to help you learn how to love yourself. It focuses on friendship because most people have healthier, clearer ideas of what it is to love a friend than to love a family member or a romantic partner. It also focuses on friendship because many of us associate the concept of love with romance and sexuality. With practice, this exercise will teach you to treat yourself as well as you treat your friends, to become your own best friend, and it will help establish a healthy pattern for all your future relationships.

This exercise uses self-awareness to learn how to become your own best friend. Once you have become familiar with it, you can create the inner security your inner child needs to complete your recovery, overcome dependency, and achieve autonomy.

You don't need to record these instructions, but you will need a pen or pencil and a notebook, journal, or writing paper.

EXERCISE
FOR MAGICAL TOOL 3:
USING SELF-LOVE TO BE YOUR OWN FRIEND

1. *What kind of friend are you?* In this step, you will learn to become aware of your patterns of giving friendship, and begin to develop a description of them. Take a moment to consider what kind of a friend you are. Think about how you treat your friends, especially those in your self-help group, because they are probably people you met while in recovery, when you were beginning to develop somewhat healthier behavior patterns. Without being critical of yourself, just seek to discover what you can about how you treat others. Chances are, you will find that you treat them with as much respect, kindness, and caring as you can manage. If a friend needs you, you probably try your best to do what you can to help. Most likely, you also care about whether your friends are happy, and you try not to hurt their feelings or upset them. Probably, you even attempt to be polite and considerate, when at all possible.

To get a detailed idea of what kind of friend you are, make a list of the ways you treat your friends. Title the list "My Friendship Style." You can use your answers to the following questions to get started; others may occur to you as you go along. Are you a casual or more formal person? Are you affectionate, or would you prefer a good conversation to a hug? Do you like to send greeting cards and letters? Would you prefer to talk on the phone or meet for coffee? Do you like to be with several friends at once, or do you prefer one at a time? Try to be as specific as you can. "I want them to be nice to me" is not as informative or useful in the later steps as "I want them to listen to me, and not criticize me." Add as many other details as possible to your list about how you act with friends. This list will describe how you offer friendship.

2. *How would you like your friends to treat you?* In this step, you will learn to become aware of your patterns of receiving friendship, and further develop your description. Now consider how you would like your friends to relate to you. Don't be concerned if it differs from what you do for your friends, or even if it's different from what you do for yourself. Make another list, called "How I Want My Friends to Treat Me," and again try to be specific. Keeping your uncritical attitude, write down in as much detail as possible how you like to be treated, using the following questions to guide you. What would you like from your friends: To be listened to? To be invited to go places? To have quiet times together? To be hugged? Do you want them to respect you and keep their agreements? Do you like to get presents, cards, and letters, or are hugs and being listened to more important? This will tell you how you would like to receive friendship. When your list is long enough to satisfy you, go to the next step.

3. *Determine what friendship means to you.* Review the first two lists, comparing the way you treat your friends and the way you want your friends to treat you. Place the lists side by side, and see what is similar and what is different. Again, *do not criticize yourself.* Your objective here is to learn more about friendship, and what it means to you. Take some time to consider what the items on your lists mean, how the way you want to be a friend is similar to or different from the way you want your friends to treat you. Many people give differently than they would like to receive: some send lots of cards and letters, but prefer receiving phone calls. Some people would rather listen to others, and are not so concerned about being listened to. Knowing whether your giving and receiving are similar or different will help you understand how you want to love and be loved. At this point, you have already learned some things about your ideas of friendship, and you may find that you want to add

to or change either one of your lists. For example, if receiving phone calls is on your second list, you may realize that you like to make them, too, so add it to your first list. Make as many changes as you like. When you feel your lists are ready, and you understand the similarities and differences, you are ready to go on to the next step.

4. *Develop your definition of friendship.* Draw up a third list, called "My Ideal Definition of Friendship." If your examination of the other lists tells you that you like having deep conversations with your friends, and you like them to call you up on the phone, you know that conversation is an important sign of caring to you. If you like to play golf or tennis or football with friends, then sharing athletic activities, challenge, and competition are probably an important expression of caring for you. If you like hugging and lots of caring attention, then warmth and affection are important to you. Or, you may like friendship to be more formal and have enough distance that you don't feel smothered. Make this list as complete a description of friendship in its ideal state as you can, based on what you've learned, and realizing that no one will do this perfectly all the time. Then, read it and ask yourself, "If my best friend treated me like this, would I feel cared about, loved, and happy?" If not, make the necessary adjustments. If your answer is yes, go on to the next step.

5. *Determine how you treat yourself.* Now, consider how you treat yourself. Do you treat yourself the way you would like to treat others? Do you treat yourself the way you would like your friends to treat you? How does it compare with your definition of friendship? Make a list called "How I Treat Myself," containing statements such as "I'm critical of myself" or "I break agreements with myself" or "I like being alone with me."

6. *What kind of friend are you to yourself?* Now compare your definition of friendship with your list about how you actually treat yourself. You may be dismayed to find out how very different the way you treat yourself is from your

ideas of friendship. You might not keep your promises to yourself as you would to a friend. You might not treat yourself with kindness and respect. Perhaps you mentally nag or criticize yourself. You may never break a date with a friend, but keep putting off your time with yourself or caring for yourself with exercise or relaxation. The best test of your friendship with yourself is this: If someone else treated you the way you treat yourself, would you want to be their friend?

7. *Becoming a friend to yourself.* Now that you have discovered the kind of friendship you enjoy, and compared that with how you treat yourself and how friends should treat one another, you have some more thinking to do and some choices to make. First, decide how you want to improve the way you treat yourself. Develop three simple ways you can be a better friend to yourself. One way to do this, if you have a friend you feel good about, is to treat yourself as you would treat the other person. Ask yourself, "What would I do or say to Maggie if she were in my shoes?" Chances are, you will find you are usually kinder to her than to yourself. How would you speak to your friend if you thought she forgot to do something? Now, do you treat yourself more harshly? By comparing the way you treat yourself with the way you treat your friends you will begin to develop clear guidelines about how to change the way you treat yourself. Write down your ideas about befriending yourself.

8. *To develop trust, be consistent.* Once you begin changing the way you treat yourself, you must be consistent in order to develop a habit of being nice to yourself. Just as you learn to become friends with others because they consistently treat you well, you can build a friendship with yourself by consistently treating yourself as you would a friend. Once you develop your ideas about how to be a better friend to yourself, post your list of guidelines somewhere where you can see it often. Renew your plan for being a better friend to yourself every week for at least six weeks. At the end of that time, you'll find that treating yourself well becomes much easier and feels more comfortable.

Self-Image: The Power to Be Your Own Hero

One of the first things children begin to learn is an inner self-image. Self-image is the way we imagine ourselves to be: attractive, unattractive, competent, incompetent, happy, scared, angry, friendly, lucky, unlucky, lovable, unlovable, and so on. This self-image is made of their abilities; what they have done and their emotional reactions to it; bits and pieces of characters from television, movies, stories; and the examples of adults they observe outside the family. But a very large part of this image is absorbed from the parents, composed of what they see in their parents' character and the attitudes that the parents have given the child about her- or himself.

When parents are healthy and functional, the self-image children learn is primarily positive and promising. They feel that they will be able to learn or do whatever they need to and that they will possess many good qualities like kindness, honesty, and courage when they grow up. Visualizing themselves in this way encourages children to aim high in life and not to be afraid of challenge—because it is what they expect of the person they see themselves as being.

When parents are dysfunctional, the self-image children learn is basically negative and dysfunctional, too. This means their sense of their own abilities and potential is negative and stunted. They may feel that they are stupid, or a loser, or will become a victim like Mom was or macho and abusive like Dad. Visualizing themselves in this way limits their expectations of what they might be and can accomplish—and so they learn to give up in many areas before they even try and in others simply to adopt that behavior they expect of themselves without really trying to accomplish anything else.

By using imagery to access your child mind and help it learn a new self-image, you can replace the damaged, dysfunctional elements in your self-image with positive healthy ones. Picturing yourself this way can provide you with self-confidence, the motivation to venture forth into life, and enthusiasm for living. This then also provides powerful images that access your subconscious magical thinking and permit healing and change to take place. At the same time, you are acquiring magical tools that can be used to heal the dependency and damaged self-esteem of your early childhood.

In the following exercise, you will learn how to use the power of self-image to visualize yourself as the heroine or hero of your own life. Creating this image will help generate the courage and provide the model you need to confront the issues of your life more effectively.

One classic heroic image you might want to develop is that of a warrior who challenges the old patterns and ventures forth into an unknown new way of living. Others include the magician, the saint, and the good witch. Danaan Parry, in an article about his work with war veterans who suffer from post-traumatic stress syndrome called "Peace and the Warrior," defines the warrior image in aiding healthy growth: "Warriors . . . are . . . able to embrace the unknown . . . a pretty scary place. Not just the physical unknown. . . . It's going into their own psyches . . . those dark places . . . the ability to face the darkness . . . [that] puts them in the class of warrior." You can learn how it feels to have personal power through using imagery to visualize your own heroic image of a warrior. You can become a "warrior," writes Lucia Cappacchione in *The Picture of Health,* "in the psychological sense of one who battles with his or her own destructive patterns and tendencies . . . to confront anything that blocks our creativity and growth . . . [with the] vigilance, discipline and courage . . . to face the negative habits that keep . . . us from fulfilling our goals and dreams."

Thinking of yourself as a warrior, whatever your portrayal, provides a new concept within which you can redefine your "self" in your subconscious thinking. For example, Fred, who feels stupid and inept, can imagine he is James Bond, agent 007, to experience being a man of intelligence and action.

Psychologists know that "acting-as-if" something is true often makes it true. Here is an example:

MARGUERITE

Marguerite, a pretty, twenty-seven-year-old client of mine who had a mother who was afraid to go out in the evenings, found herself similarly afraid and unable to "reasonably" talk herself into going out socially. I suggested she pretend she was the glamorous, self-confident Loretta Young (a former TV personality). She tried it the next time she wanted to go out, and it worked. By pretending to be Loretta Young, she felt much more enthusiastic about going out, and handled the situation the way her heroine would have. A few days later, she called me, laughing "This is 'Loretta'— Dahling, it worked! I had a marvelous time." The "heroic" image of Loretta's behavior provided a role model for confidence in social situations, and replaced the timid, insecure model of Marguerite's mother. Having a more self-confident image to emulate was the tool that Marguerite used to overcome her subconscious fear. After a few times of pretending to be Loretta, Marguerite began to feel strong and capable enough to go out as herself.

This exercise will show you how to use the power of self-image to rehearse and develop desirable character traits you don't believe you now possess.

For best results, read these instructions onto tape, or have a friend read them for you.

EXERCISE
FOR MAGICAL TOOL 4:
USING SELF-IMAGE TO CREATE
YOUR INNER WARRIOR

1. *Choose a model.* From current life, history, or fiction, find characters you admire. You can use friends or public figures; comic-book or movie heroes or heroines; storybook characters; figures from Greek, Roman, Native American, Celtic, or other legends; mythic figures; saints; angels; or any other powerful model.

2. *Determine what you find heroic.* Study these ideal persons and try to determine what it is about them that

makes them heroic to you. Is it kindness in the face of difficulty? A high moral character? Serenity and inner peace?
Physical courage? Special intelligence? Questing for knowledge? Helping the needy and/or helpless? Write a definition of heroism that incorporates that aspect of your heroines or heroes. For example, "My heroine is a strong, wise
woman who uses her intelligence and awareness to take
care of herself, who is caring and generous to those who
need help, but who also knows how to say no so she does
not get used or taken advantage of." Or, "My hero is a
clever man who outsmarts his enemies and uses his wits to
succeed at his goals." Or, "My heroine is a warm, nurturing, motherly woman who is strong enough to protect herself and her children from violence and danger." Chances
are your definition will also include independence, self-
confidence, and self-reliance—in short, autonomy.

3. *Create an image of your warrior.* Using these
qualities, put together a composite mental picture of your
hero or heroine. Give your heroic figure a name you like,
either a regular name you've always liked such as Rebecca
or Harrison, or a descriptive name such as Power Woman
or Loving Man. By doing this, you separate the heroic
qualities from the original stories, and make them more flexible and usable in your own life. For example, if your heroic
figure is James Bond, you can make a new character called
Jason who has all Bond's intelligence and savoir faire but
omits the violence. Use sensory imagery to develop a mental picture of your heroine or hero, including clothing, facial
features, body type, life-style, and living space. For example, Jason might be blond where James Bond is dark, and
Jason might have a different car, clothing, and apartment,
all of which are more to your taste.

4. *Imagine the effect of your heroic image on your
daily life.* Once your mental picture of your heroic image is
complete, picture your hero or heroine living *your* life. (Picturing someone else, who feels more powerful than you do,
will give you a new perspective on how the challenges of

your life might be met differently from your usual habits and ingrained ideas.) What would it be like if your heroine or hero image showed up at your work disguised as you? How would she or he get along with your friends? What would change about the look of your home? How you wear your clothing? Begin by imagining your heroine or hero waking up in your bed, having her or him look around your room, and developing the sensory details: sights, sounds, and sensations. Then move your heroic image through an average day, seeing what he or she would eat, wear, say, and do, in each activity of your normal day. Notice how others react to and treat your heroine or hero. Make corrections as you like. If your heroine or hero is too overpowering, make him or her a little more gentle. If he or she is too perfect, give her or him a few minor flaws, less beauty, or allow him or her to make a few mistakes, to make your heroic figure more real. Play with the scenario until you are comfortable enough with your heroic image to aspire to be like that.

5. *Bring your heroic image into real life.* Now that you've imagined how this powerful, courageous heroic image would live your life, try adopting some of her or his attitudes and actions for yourself. Practice living your life as your ideal hero or heroine would live it. This may seem difficult or scary at first, but if you take it one small change at a time, you can improve the quality of your life and your interaction with people a lot. To begin, just try adopting some of your hero or heroine's attitudes. For example, you could be more cheerful in the morning, or more confident at work. Use your heroic image as a model. You can try out the changes before you actually act on them by using imagery. When the need to make decisions arises, imagine how your heroic image would handle it. When problems occur, what solutions would your warrior consider?

6. *Develop a habit of consulting your heroic image.* Once you have developed a clear picture of your heroine or hero, you can also invoke her or him at any time as a counselor. If you're facing a problem or dilemma, you can

meet your hero or heroine in your mental retreat (that you developed in the first exercise) and talk about the problem before making a decision. You'll find the discussions give you a clearer picture of the problem, because you have to present it in such a way that someone else can understand. You will also be surprised at how effective your heroic image's advice will be. Often we possess insight in our subconscious, childlike mind that can only be reached through the aid of a magical tool, such as talking to an inner warrior, hero, or heroine.

Environment: The Power to Create Support

You learned many of your dependent, destructive attitudes from the dysfunctional role models your parents provided you. All children learn some of their behaviors from mimicking those around them. You can easily see this in young children as they play house or play teacher and imitate exactly the adults they know.

You can put the power of role models to work to help you change many of your own behavior patterns and replace them with more healthy ways of relating with others by using Magical Tool 5: The Environment to create your own group of people who interact in healthy ways providing positive role models for one another. Being in the company of those who provide healthy, functional models of your new beliefs and attitudes in action can be a powerful support in your attempt to develop these positive new attitudes. Oncologist Bernie Siegel, a medical expert who also understands the magical aspects of healing, describes the value of surrounding ourselves with such a group in *Peace, Love and Healing*: "Through our pain we can find others to love and to heal. That's what groups like Alcoholics Anonymous and Exceptional Cancer Patients (ECaP) are all about. In fact, I always say that if you're fortunate enough to be an alcoholic or drug addict or have a disease, you can find a group to be part of, and you'll have lots of people to love and be loved by. We need to start groups for people who just enjoy living." Thus, the role models in support groups can be very beneficial in your healing process. However, to the degree that these new role models are dysfunctional, it can set back or block your healing.

A network of friends is what Bernie Siegel might call a group "for people who just enjoy living." It consists of people who care about you, treating you with kindness and respect, and for whom you also care and who you treat with the same regard. The exercise that follows shows you a controlled, gradual process that you can continue to build on and develop lifelong as you become increasingly autonomous, eventually building your own network of friends. In such an environment, you can experience the new attitudes with all your senses—seeing, hearing, feeling, smelling, and tasting the atmosphere as the people around you interact. The ability to find, choose, and establish friends of your own will provide you with the support and encouragement you need to grow and change. The sensory experiences of being surrounded by healthy, loving, supportive friends will also support your childlike mind in maintaining healthy, new ways of thinking.

The following exercise will show you how to build on your recovery group experience and learn to create your own individual group of mutually supportive role models. Once you have learned how to form a support group and keep it going, use it as a prototype for all your future networks. By following these steps, you can change dysfunctional, dependent patterns of relating to others and begin to develop a healthy pattern in their place, which will help you move from dependency on the group toward more autonomous group activities.

EXERCISE
FOR MAGICAL TOOL 5:
USING ENVIRONMENT TO BUILD
A SUPPORT NETWORK

1. *Identify others who have similar goals.* Select a goal you want to implement that, ideally, would be easier if done as part of a support group. Find several people who share

these goals. Perhaps your common interest is looking for new jobs, learning a foreign language, creative writing, or even an interest in a craft or hobby you can enjoy together. To find them, you can talk to friends and family, or put an announcement up on a bulletin board at work or school, at your recovery group, a community center, the laundromat, or the market. You can even place a small ad in a local paper. (Note: if you are contacting strangers, don't give your address, and arrange to meet in a group in public places until you know each other a little more.) When you have found at least three or four others who express interest in your project, go on to the next step. You may not believe you can find anyone who is interested in your project at the start, but if you discuss your interest with others, you may be surprised to discover just how many are enthusiastic.

2. *Agree to meet.* Arrange a time and place to meet, *specifically to support each other in achieving your goals.* At your first meeting, discuss your purpose as a group and work up guidelines. What is the intention of the group, and what are the responsibilities of each member to be? Set an agenda, a schedule of what you want to accomplish, for the first few meetings. This agenda is just a beginning guideline; the group will alter it to suit its needs as the meetings go on. Determine how often and how long your meetings will be. Ask members of the group to make a commitment to meet together on a regular basis (for example, once a week for two months), any frequency as long as the meetings are regular and reinforce the habit of meeting as a group.

3. *Work together toward your goal.* If your group was formed as a support for those who want to find better jobs, you can get together to discuss career possibilities, read and share job-search articles and books, look for job openings for yourself and each other, work on résumés together, role-play job interviews, encourage each other when things are not going well, and celebrate when one of you is successful. If it was formed because you share an interest in needlework or art, you can share ideas, work together on your projects for a specified time each week, and pool re-

sources to get supplies or special equipment (buy a quilting frame, hire a model) you need. To work on developing your autonomy with this book (or to accomplish the goals of any other how-to book), you could read and discuss a chapter at each meeting, and do the exercises all together or in smaller groups.

4. *Live what you are attempting to learn.* Use your meetings as an opportunity to practice what you are learning. If you are learning French together, make an agreement to speak only French for at least part of your group time. If you're learning to be more autonomous, agree to practice saying what you want and what you think in group, and to support each other in taking risks and solving problems by noticing and encouraging each other's moves toward independence. Whatever your goal, make it a practice in the group to be as positive and encouraging as possible.

5. *Discuss your satisfaction with the group.* Set aside ten minutes of each meeting to discuss how well your group is working, whether the meetings go the way each member wants them to, how well you're meeting your goals as a group, and what can be done to make it more effective. If you like, you can do a round: each person, in turn, says a sentence or two about how well the group is meeting his or her needs, and what, if anything, should be changed. To encourage attendance and build closeness, make feeling good and having fun together one of your group priorities. Strive for balance in giving and getting support. Are you as supportive to yourself as you are to the others? Remember, the most effective network, the one that lasts, is one where giving and receiving feels balanced for everyone involved. Don't allow the group atmosphere to degenerate into dysfunctional patterns such as pressure to perform, criticism, and power struggles. You can support and encourage each other's optimum learning (and autonomy) much better with praise, information, and caring. As an individual, observe each member's behavior and attitude. Seek to discover which make the best support team for you.

6. *Develop problem-solving guidelines.* One way to

avoid re-creating old, toxic family systems is to agree in advance on a method your group will use to handle problems when they arise. All group interaction eventually requires some problem solving, so pick a system that all members of the group can agree feels productive to them. It doesn't matter if you work out a system by yourselves, or decide to solve any problems that arise by taking a vote, or use *Robert's Rules of Order*, or try discussion and agreement, or any other method all members agree to abide by. Having this worked out in advance will prepare you for coping with problems as soon as they do arise, and provide a healthy model of interaction, so members can avoid slipping into old, unconscious, and dependent patterns. Follow your group agenda and use its problem-solving process as necessary, until the group completes its goal.

7. *Review your experiment as a group.* When the group goal has been achieved (most of you have gotten new jobs, or learned belly dancing) or if it is beginning to feel successful, have a meeting and review the whole experience together. This can be done as a celebration of your accomplishments. Ask each person to say what he or she learned as you worked together, and have each person make suggestions about what, if anything, should be done differently next time. In what ways was it supportive? What were the problems? How did it feel to have a support network that met regularly? What would you do differently next time? This will help the group decide if they would like to continue getting together, and help you as an individual understand the interaction from everyone else's point of view. Since there are bound to be different opinions, some in exact opposition, about what went well and what didn't, you'll all have an excellent opportunity to learn about how differently people's perceptions of group interaction are, which will give you practice in dealing with diverse attitudes and solving interpersonal problems.

8. *Review the process for yourself.* Before you continue or repeat your group experience and go on to build a net-

work, be sure you understand the personal value of your experience. Review how well the group worked for you, and how you relate to the others. Can you say no if the group wants to do something you don't want to do? Who is easiest for you to talk to? Why? Who is the most difficult? Why? Did you enjoy working with these people? Who did you enjoy most? Why? Was there someone you had trouble with? Why? What kind of influence did interacting with the group have on your attitudes and ideas? If you did it again, what would you do differently? Is there anyone in the group you'd like to maintain contact with? If so, let them know and ask them if they're interested in exploring a personal friendship.

9. *Repeat to develop a network.* If the group decides to continue, the odds are good that you will begin to become an ongoing network. To do this, just begin at step 2 again. If the group disbands, you can continue to enjoy any friendships you made on an individual basis, or you can build another group, repeating this exercise from step 1. By doing this several times, you can eventually build a permanent support network with the people you enjoy most from these single-purpose groups. Also, you can begin to look for new friends everywhere you go, using the relationship skills you learn here to help maintain those relationships and begin to build a more informal group of friends.

Repetition and Memorization: The Power to Affect Your Beliefs

One of the first ways children learn ideas and behaviors, and a way we still learn much of the new ability we acquire as adults, is through practicing them repeatedly until they are locked in our memory—whether we're learning about riding a bicycle, writing our first alphabet, or beliefs such as "I am stupid." Memorization and repetition influence the childlike, subconscious mind because they are based in our original way of learning. As children, we learn by repetition of ideas and activities, and by hearing what is said to us over and over. As an adult, if you repeat a statement or paragraph enough to memorize it, it becomes a part of your automatic thinking—the thoughts that arise, unbidden, into your awareness.

When we have repeated a thought enough for it to take effect on our child mind, it becomes part of our subconscious belief system. These repetitions suddenly produce a cumulative effect where new awareness and abilities seem to "click in" in a particular moment, and at that point we make a quantum leap from being new and awkward at the task or idea to doing or believing it as though we had done it forever. That moment is visible on the outside as measurable change. This magical quantum leap of change takes a long-term commitment to practice, but is eventually realized in an instant.

As children, we often learned negative ideas about ourselves because our dysfunctional parents told them to us repeatedly: "You're a bad boy"; "Girls aren't smart"; "You're a problem child"; "You'll never get what you want." Reinforced by repetition, these negative ideas become part of a litany, a series of programmed instructions that, repeated in our subconscious child mind, still affects our attitudes and behaviors as adults.

You can use the same process by which you learned the negative beliefs to replace them with healthier, more positive beliefs. As simplistic as it may seem, repeating a positive phrase over and over until it lodges deep in your child mind and takes effect can counteract this subconscious negative programming. Although the effectiveness of repetition as an aid to learning has probably long been known to you, you may never before have realized that it might be applied to changing your own inner programming. Using affirmations, prayers, poetry, proverbs, wise sayings, quotations from literature, and other positive statements, and making them a part of your mind through repetition and memorization, you can confront your internal negative thinking.

You may find, as you begin to repeat a positive statement, that the old programming in your subconscious child mind reacts quickly and that your first impulse is to argue with the positive statement. If your statement is "I am lovable," as you begin to repeat it, your inner child mind may react with internal comments such as "Oh yeah? Then why did Harry leave?" Such arguments are an indication that the statement is beginning to have an effect, because it's reaching deeply enough to raise an argument. Just keep repeating your positive statement, and you'll find that the negative arguments subside after a while.

The exercise that follows will help you change negative thoughts such as "I'm not lucky, nothing good ever happens to me" or "No one will ever love me" to positive, self-supporting statements. It will show you a simple way to use the power of repetition, which is one of the earliest ways we learn—by doing or hearing something over and over, until it becomes automatic. You have already used the power of repetition in every exercise you have done so far, and you have seen how you become more capable and confident of your ability each time you repeat an exercise. This exercise will help you learn a method of verbal repetition that you can use to counteract and change the dysfunctional messages you received in early childhood, which are buried deep in your mind.

EXERCISE
FOR MAGICAL TOOL 6:
USING REPETITION AND MEMORIZATION TO
PLANT NEW SEEDS OF CONSCIOUSNESS

1. *Choose a positive statement.* Choose a one-sentence statement, preferably just a few words, that would help you to feel better about yourself or your life. Select a quote that feels positive, encouraging, and supportive to you. Simple lines such as "I am OK today" or "I am smart and capable" or "Today is my lucky day" are sufficient. Or, find a positive quotation from poetry or literature, a quote from the *Daily Word* or other meditation guide, a biblical quote (for example, from the twenty-third Psalm), a song lyric, or a quote from philosophical writings. Other good sources are Shakti Gawain's *Creative Visualization* and Sondra Ray's *I Deserve Love.*

2. *Copy your statement.* Copy the statement you have selected several times onto file cards or pieces of paper. You can make these decorative or simple, but try to make them easy to read.

3. *Post your statement.* Place these copies of your positive idea where you will be sure to see them: at your desk at work, in your wallet, on the refrigerator door, over your kitchen sink, on your bathroom mirror, beside your bed, on the dashboard of your car, in your gym or school locker. By doing this you will be reminded often of this positive thought.

4. *Repeat your statement.* Each time you see your positive thought, read it to yourself to become familiar with it and memorize it. The more you repeat this statement, the more effect it will have on your childlike, subconscious mind. If it's a longer quote, consisting of several sentences, read the whole thing over each time. Then, focus on one sentence per day until that phrase is memorized. You can make it a point to commit it to memory immediately if you wish, but it's not essential. Simply repeating it by reading it daily will do the trick after a while. (*Note:* Repeating the statement may create some internal agitation. Your old, negative thinking may become very clear to you. This is actually good; it means the positive message is getting in. Just keep repeating your statement, and allow the negative thoughts or feelings to pass.)

5. *Change your statement when it is memorized.* Once memorized, this new positive statement will become part of your natural attitude and thinking process. After a while, you will find that your statement begins to repeat itself, like a chant, in your mind whenever you're bored, tired, or overloaded. You will begin to make all your decisions from the basis of this new attitude, rather than your old, negative thoughts. Shortly after you notice this, you will also notice that things you do are beginning to change "all by themselves." This is repetition and memorization at work.

You now have six powerful tools with which you can gain access to your own subconscious thinking, reeducate your childlike magical thinking, and heal old toxic shame. The magical tools of the senses, imagery, self-love, self-image, environment, and repetition and memorization are the keys to your subconscious. By practicing these tools until they are familiar and easy to use, and by using them in the exercises of this book, you can create a model of autonomy and health for yourself that transcends your toxic past. Mastery of the magical tools gives you the power to face your inner fears, establish contact with your inner self, and develop autonomy.

CHAPTER 5

Completing Recovery: Facing the Self

As Freud discovered, and as Jung, Rank, and later Rollo May elaborated and refined, when the conscious and the subconscious become acquainted with each other, a new persona is born. A whole, awake, compassionate person steps forward from the one who was previously fractured, incomplete and at war within himself or herself. Those early analysts observed, as do therapists in general, a sudden burst of enthusiasm for living in such cases, a quickening of the senses, an acceptance of the self as it is and the world as it is.

PETER LONDON

O nce you have learned how to use the tools that speak directly to your subconscious child mind, you are ready to complete the process of recovery through facing and changing your deepest self. By replacing the attitudes of dependency—mindlessness, helplessness, and hopelessness—you can move on to achieve autonomy through learning the skills of risk taking, problem solving, and handling failure and disappointment.

These two processes don't happen separately; they happen simultaneously. You don't really *unlearn* something such as an incorrect address or idea or way of performing a task. Instead, you *replace* it with new knowledge that corrects it or takes its place—such as learning the right address or a new scientific view or a better way of doing a job. You may remember the old idea or behavior for a long time, though most likely you will eventually forget it from disuse. You just don't act on it or think much about it because it seems so silly and wrong now. Completing recovery involves laying the foundations of autonomy, which simultaneously replaces and heals the last vestiges of dependency.

If four-year-old Sally is severely punished for spilling her milk, she feels flawed—she believes she was "bad" to spill the milk (actually normal behavior for a child her age) and she is also frightened and pained by the punishment. If this happens often enough to Sally, she will begin to change: She may become distrustful of herself, her environment, and the people around her. She will become afraid to try anything she is not certain she can do perfectly, to avoid punishment. She will probably learn to look to others anxiously for constant approval and reassurance that they are not going to punish her.

To correct this problem, to help Sally overcome her fear and return to her normal, self-confident state, a more competent adult would have to intervene and teach Sally what to do about spilt milk: Get a sponge and clean up; get another glass of milk; fill it less full; and hold it more carefully when she drinks. In addition, to lessen her fear, Sally would need to be reassured that she would not be punished in the future, that you believe the best way for her to learn is to correct her mistakes. In treating Sally this way, you would have both healed her emotional hurt and taught her how to behave differently in the future. Sally will soon forget the spilt milk, although she will probably remember how to handle milk properly.

If no one intervenes, even years later as an adult Sally's experience will be active in her subconscious childlike mind, undermining her self-esteem and hampering her risk taking, even though she spilt the milk and learned to think of herself as "bad" years ago. As an adult, she must correct the learning that occurred in childhood before she will be free of the dependency created there.

Being aware of your subconscious child mind and how magical thinking works gives you the ability to face yourself in new and powerful ways. For the first time, you can confront the hidden motivations and conflicts that recovery programs don't cover. In this chapter, you will learn how to use the magical tools you developed in the previous chapter to simultaneously resolve and correct the childhood emotions at the root of your dependency. You will build a new foundation of attitudes and behaviors upon which autonomy can grow. In addition, you will learn how to create the inner safety your child self needs to let go of old, hurtful experiences and forgive yourself and others.

Awareness, learning, and forgiveness are adult, corrective versions of the three skills that build autonomy: risk taking, problem solving, and coping with failure and disappointment. They combine the experience and learning you would have gotten as a child from successful autonomous experiences with a focus on helping your child self begin to accept and develop more autonomous attitudes and behaviors—and with a supportive, caring attitude. Replacing your dependency with autonomy requires taking these three steps. Now that you have the tools for replacing dependent attitudes with the skills necessary for autonomous living, your old addictive behavior might seem easily conquered. But often it isn't.

THE INTERNAL WAR:
RESISTANCE AGAINST AUTONOMY

As you apply the tools of autonomy to completing the work of recovery you may find yourself encountering inner fighting and resistance, as your deepest self attempts to defend what's familiar (dependency). In a dysfunctional family, you learned in childhood that dependency was safer than autonomy because the adults around you viewed your childish attempts at autonomy as rebellious or dangerous. Without support, many of your childhood attempts at risk taking failed, which confirmed the adults' fears and your own.

You may feel your resistance as emotional symptoms—such as fear, panic, shame, hysteria—and even physical ones—such as headache, nausea, or sleeplessness. Change naturally creates some resistance, because it requires extra thought and work. For example, we all groan at the thought of moving house, even if we're excited about the new home, because we know we'll have to pack, move, and then get used to a new place. Change involves taking risks—it presents us with a lot of new situations that we will have to find new solutions for (such as how to get to work from a new home). Emotional change is risk taking, too. No matter how difficult your old, dependent behavior is, it is familiar to you, and you know how it feels. At the mention of change, your child self, who like any little one is easily frightened and hurt and who feels helpless and hopeless because he or she tried many times and has had many failures, will balk, stall, and go into hiding. No matter how enthusiastic you are about completing recovery and gaining autonomous control over your own life, you will still encounter some internal resistance to the necessary changes.

Although most formerly addictive people discover they have a lot of resistance to overcome on the path to self-awareness, if they persevere they find that there are many rewards for overcoming that resistance. It truly takes the self-image of a warrior, at times, to continue the hero's journey toward healing.

Your Internal War

Because of the difference between your subconscious childlike thought patterns (also called your *intuitive, feeling aspect* or *right brain thinking*) and your rational, adult, reasoning thought patterns (also known as your *thinking aspect* or *left brain thinking*), you may feel there are two (or more) "voices" in your mind—each with a different attitude and opinion. As the child of dysfunctional parents, your subconscious (and still dependent) side—which is still locked in addictive thought patterns—is often in conflict with your rational adult side—which knows it is in your best interest to learn.

When you begin to work to actually change your inner child's thinking, this struggle can escalate and you may find yourself caught in an internal "war" between these parts of your inner self.

Being at war within yourself may sound absurd, but it is common. Psychologists are very familiar with this phenomenon. M. Scott Peck, author of *The Road Less Traveled,* describes how common this resistance is: "It may sound strange to laymen, but psychotherapists are familiar with the fact that people are routinely terrified by mental health. A major part of the task of psychotherapy is not only to bring patients to the experience of mental health but also, through a mixture of consolation, reassurance and sternness, to prevent them from running away from that experience once they have arrived at it." Signs of this internal struggle or warfare are:

- feeling obsessive, compulsive, or addictive
- procrastinating
- fighting and arguing with others
- depression
- dissatisfaction
- irritability
- exhaustion
- anxiety
- tension

Depression and exhaustion are two very common symptoms of this internal struggle. Just as in a fight with someone else, the arguing, turmoil, and destructive negative interchanges of an internal war damage your sense of a healthy, unified, whole self and absorb almost all your energy. It is as depressing and exhausting to fight with yourself as it is to constantly bicker and argue with someone else.

This inner warfare also produces a constant noise in your mind, as the voices of these two sides of your mind become locked in never-ending argument, which makes clear thinking almost impossible. As long as the war continues, you will continue to use poor judgment in the important decisions of your life, because a substantial part of your thinking ability is hampered by the war. Just imagine trying to think in a room where two people are arguing about everything, most of the time! Not being able to think clearly means you are not aware of the information you are receiving that could tell you who is trustworthy and who is unreliable; or are not able to evaluate all the options available to you and make clear decisions; or cannot sort out the difference between a practical and realistic evaluation of a situation and evaluations that are too negative and pessimistic or too positive and optimistic to serve as the basis of a good decision. In addition, the exhaustion resulting from constant turmoil causes you to "forget" or feel unable to think clearly about your circumstances and your actions, which leads you to be dependent on others to do your thinking for you.

This internal war is unwinnable, since both sides feel equally right, and equally powerful. Even if one side *could* win, *you'd* lose, since either your childlike feeling, creative, expressive, and intuitive (subconscious) side would be defeated, or your logical, thinking, result-oriented adult (rational) side would. Either way, you'd be operating at half power, unable to think clearly, or unable to feel feelings—which is what happens to many people. Just as in wars in the external world, both sides inevitably pay a heavy price.

JUDY

Judy, a fifty-five-year-old attractive woman who was battered by her husband for over twenty years, and whose children were also battered, tells why she remained in the marriage after being close to death from battering several times. "I couldn't think. Every time I tried to decide what to do, my mind would jump around from 'This is awful—I have to get myself and the kids out of here' to 'How would I live without him earning the money?' to 'This is what I deserve anyway.' I could never think clearly enough to figure out what to do. After a while, I would get tired of trying to think about it, and not do anything.

However, when you can get both sides to negotiate and work together, then everyone wins—you create a problem-solving team that is both intuitive and rational, creative and practical. Only when your internal war is settled, and the two sides form a working partnership, do you attain the capacity to use the full power of your thinking ability.

This resistance can be overcome, because it's only a result of your old magical thinking. To overcome your resistance, take small steps in the beginning. When feelings of embarrassment, unworthiness, shame, or fear arise, just slow down, and remind yourself that your resistance is built-in to your subconscious, dependent thought. Pause whenever you feel resistant, to give yourself a chance to relax. Don't push yourself, or criticize yourself, but use your magical tool of self-love to reassure and encourage yourself past the problem.

Discussing issues with yourself, asking yourself questions, and comforting yourself are hard concepts for a dependent, childlike mind to understand, because being dependent means being focused on *others,* not on yourself. Even once you understand how to confront your inner feelings, you may resist at first, because you feel confused, ashamed, or embarrassed. The old, ingrained subconscious beliefs that your feelings are frightening and that you're unworthy of attention are fighting with your new, rational adult knowledge that you are important to you.

Most people with addictive and dependency problems encounter this resistance when they attempt to change their behavior, as the following story illustrates:

BARBARA

Barbara is thirty-eight, intelligent, educated, attractive, and frustrated. She sits in my office, saying, "Why can't I do what I know I need to do? I know when I'm doing something self-destructive, like overeating, and I know when I'm *not* doing something good for me, like looking for a better job—but I just can't seem to make myself do what's right."

I SUGGEST: Barbara, have you asked yourself what the problem is?

BARBARA: I don't know, I get confused when I think about it.

ME: Will you try something right now? Will you ask Barbara inside you what's going on?

BARBARA: You mean, talk to myself?

ME: That's right, go to the source of the confusion and ask.

BARBARA: Oh, I couldn't do that—that's crazy.

Barbara's embarrassment, confusion, and objections are all versions of resistance, which takes understanding, patience, and effort to overcome. After some work on her inner confusion and the belief that she didn't deserve the attention she was asked to give herself, Barbara did get into the dialogue, using *Barbara 1* and *Barbara 2* as names for the two voices at war inside her (the dialogue actually took about twenty minutes and is condensed here to save space):

BARBARA 1: Why won't you do what's good for you? Why do you eat the wrong foods? Why don't you exercise like you should?

BARBARA 2: Why should I? It's no fun, you make me eat weird food and do boring exercises and you'll just make me do more crummy stuff after I do that.

BARBARA 1: Wow! I didn't know you were so angry at me about it. I'm only wanting you to do what's good for you. I know the food is weird, but that's how diet food is. And exercise is boring.

BARBARA 2: Well, Susie is thin, and she eats regular food, and I'd rather walk or dance than go to a smelly, boring old gym.

BARBARA 1: I guess you're right. I haven't been thinking much about this. I think we can find a way to eat regular food that's more fun. I guess we don't have to diet like my mother did. Nowadays, there's nonfat frozen yogurt, and we can eat fresh salads, fruits, and vegetables. I guess if I feel like munching while watching TV, I could make plain popcorn, and eat fresh fruit, graham crackers, or carrot sticks. Do you think we could do that?

BARBARA 2: Yeah, that doesn't sound too bad—as long as we can have a special treat sometimes.

BARBARA 1: Now, what about exercise? What can we do if we don't go to the gym?

BARBARA 2: Some of those dance exercise classes are OK, and I like the jacuzzi at the gym, but I hate the machines. I want to go for a walk, or roller skating with friends, or take some dance classes.

BARBARA 1: Gee, that not only sounds like it might work, but like it might be fun for a long time.

BARBARA 2: OK, let's do it, but let's make it be about fun more than about losing weight. I don't care about what I weigh, I care about feeling good. And don't get crabby with me. I won't do even the fun things if you yell at me.

BARBARA 1: OK, you're right, I do get crabby at you, and that's not fair. How about if we make a deal? You help me figure out how to make being healthier fun, and I'll be more encouraging and praise you more often.

BARBARA 2: OK, you've got a deal. I'll let you know if you get crabby.

Like Barbara, you may have old, toxic childhood beliefs that you're not worthy of attention, that confronting your inner turmoil is confusing, and that your feelings don't count, which make it impossible for you to think clearly enough to see the inner struggles that hamper you. Like Barbara, you may have been taught that talking to yourself is crazy.

You can overcome this resistance by doing internal dialogue exercises, such as those that follow in this and later chapters. Try "Finding Your Trouble Spot" (p. 146) to begin. Once you negotiate an internal truce, you can become a new kind of person within whom both the intuitive, feeling part and the rational, acting part work together for the common good, without a "good guy" and "bad guy" or winner and loser, and seek to solve problems so that both sides are satisfied. Negotiation, communication, and partnership become an integral part of your relationship with yourself, producing a sense of wholeness and power that gives you the confidence to take risks and to be autonomous.

AWARENESS, LEARNING, AND FORGIVENESS

To complete your recovery, and build the self-confident base needed to move into autonomous thinking and behavior, you must master three essential elements: awareness, learning, and forgiveness.

All internal change requires these three elements, and when they are present, and you are proficient at all three, you'll find that making permanent changes in your old dependent attitudes and behaviors, learning to take autonomous care of yourself in an unpredictable and not always reliable world, and freeing yourself from the tyranny of your past behavior and

circumstances is not only possible to do but also very rewarding. By making these changes, you can discover true inner peace
(freedom from your internal war and turmoil), satisfaction, and
a sense of competent teamwork with yourself.

Through awareness of your internal turmoil, confusion,
and dependent thinking you will learn about how your inner
struggle operates and what triggers it, which will let you know
what you need to change. Then you must learn what you need
to do to make the changes you believe are necessary. Forgiveness is a way to make sure those changes are effective and solid
enough that you can let go of the pain, suffering, and struggle
your addictive and dependent behavior (and the out-of-control
behavior of others) has caused you.

Awareness

Change must begin with awareness, because you cannot effectively change something that you do not know about. Until you
become fully aware of your subconscious inner beliefs and the
patterns that keep you dependent, you cannot bring them out of
the past, into the present where you can work to correct them.

Becoming aware of these beliefs and patterns at first may be
difficult, because if you grew up in a dysfunctional family you
probably spent years trying not to be aware of how you felt and
what you wanted. Because every effort at risk taking ended in
pain or humiliation, you stopped being aware of your desire to
learn new things, to have new experiences, and to take risks. Potential risks were everywhere: in being aware of your thinking,
you risked thinking independently; in being aware of your feelings, you risked feeling stifled, outraged, and explosive; and in
being aware of thinking and feeling, you risked having to take
action. Eventually, to avoid risk, you stopped being aware of
anything, and began to focus instead on others, who became
your central guides in life.

In stifling your natural urge to risk being aware you suffered
some consequences, because lack of awareness kept you from
developing positive skills:

- paying attention to clues from people, your environment, and yourself that problems were coming
- seeing opportunities that presented themselves through similar clues from you, your environment, and the people around you
- thinking clearly and learning to solve problems
- working out problems in relationships, because you could see them arising, and were aware of what caused them
- making choices and decisions that would be easy if you were aware of all the options available to you
- being objectively aware enough to be able to evaluate others for reliability, safety, and their own internal health

Awareness of self is normally a natural attribute of a healthy personality. As children, we go through a time of fascination with ourselves, including our fingers, toes, bowel movements, and other body functions, and eventually our thought and feeling processes. To a young child, the idea of self is fascinating— we are eager to learn what our feelings mean, and how they are similar and different from those of other people. This natural self-awareness (which, in a healthy environment, will eventually lead to curiosity, risk taking, and eventually autonomy) has to be interfered with (through criticism, ridicule, and shaming, as it often is in the dysfunctional family) in order to be stifled. If we are allowed to grow in a supportive environment, we gradually develop awareness of the world outside ourselves, of others, and of ourselves as separate from our sensations and feelings.

In a dysfunctional family, however, we are taught to be suspicious and ashamed of our feelings, reactions, and inner impulses (in short, the basic elements on which our definition of self is based), because the adults around us are often unable to manage or express their own feelings. When as a child you expressed strong emotion, your parents probably felt helpless and frightened. They viewed your childish feelings as evidence that they were not parenting correctly.

As children, with magical thinking, we interpret our parents' negative reaction to our feelings to mean that our feelings are bad. Therefore we block them out, turn off our awareness, and treat feelings as something to be avoided and afraid of. Later, when we try to become aware, this childhood habit of avoiding feelings is so strong we accept it as the truth, and believe that awareness of our feelings is terrifying and dangerous. This fear forms the basis of our reluctance to become self-aware. It becomes what we call *resistance*.

This damage is particularly acute when it comes to emotion. To act or think, we have to face emotions of which we are terrified, so we avoid them. Most clients in therapy encounter these fears as they begin to look at their inner mental process. John, an M.D. who had never in his forty-five years been aware of what he was feeling, began to sweat and tremble when he did the "Trouble Spot" exercise. Judy, the battered wife quoted earlier, cried from fear for several days in a row before she was able to begin facing her inner feelings. Both John and Judy, as they eventually became self-aware, found that their initial fear was far worse than any of the repressed emotions.

When you are unaware of your own emotions, you become dependent on others to tell you how you feel, or on substances and behaviors to keep your own feelings submerged, as your internal stress and the pressure from repressed feelings grow constantly stronger. Most people from dysfunctional families have had their feelings squelched as children by the following statements:

- Don't cry, I can't stand it when you cry.
- Shut up, or I'll give you something to cry about.
- Don't you get angry at me, young man (lady), I'm still the parent in this house.
- Don't tell your father (mother), it will just upset him (her).
- Don't get so upset over nothing.
- Don't raise your voice in this house.

- Don't get too excited—you'll just be disappointed.
- If you get too happy, something bad will happen.

The result of all this denial and fear of emotions is that you become *emotion phobic*—deeply afraid of your own feelings, for the reasons mentioned, and even of others' feelings, for fear they will tempt your own tightly held feelings to burst forth. Though you have been aware of your emotions until now, they are still there. The evidence that you are feeling them, and that they are acting in your life, is your addictive and dependent behavior, the internal stress and tension you probably feel, the mental turmoil of your inner war, and probably occasional uncontrollable outbursts of rage, hysteria, or ongoing depression. Being unaware of your feelings can cause you to be destructive and out of control; and the pain of suppressing them is a major reason for addictive behavior.

There are many reasons people commonly give for not allowing themselves to feel their feelings. However, every one of these reasons, some of which seem rational or sensible, represents the fear of self-awareness. Yet the good news is that fears and concerns about feelings are groundless. Handled appropriately, your feelings, when you become aware of them, not only won't hurt you but can also help you heal old problems:

You will be able to stop crying. The worst that can happen is you'll cry yourself to sleep, perhaps for several days in a row. By allowing this to be OK and crying all the old tears that were held in, you can eliminate depression, making it easier to think clearly, heal old pain and hurt, and achieve a sense of inner peace. Research shows that crying reduces stress and boosts the immune system. Once you have cried out all the old backlog of inner tears, you will find that you react more appropriately to sad and tender situations, and you are effectively able to respond to others who are sad.

Acknowledging your grief and disappointment when you suffer loss will not damage you. Grieving a lost opportunity, or allowing yourself to feel disappointed at a failure, allows you to acknowledge the loss and move on. Without expression, your grief and disappointment can keep you stuck and unable to let go. Faced and accepted, it can become an opportunity to change direction, and give yourself a new opportunity.

You won't become more impulsive or violent if you express your anger. Allowing themselves to express old, repressed anger and learning to manage it in effective ways has helped many people change from unemployable to successful, move from isolation to warm, loving friendships, and lose mysterious and debilitating aches and pains. Releasing these old feelings also makes the expression of your current anger at small irritations more appropriate, since they're no longer the excuse to vent old, forbidden rage.

Expressing feelings reduces pain; it does not increase it. You are far more likely to be pushed into old, addictive behavior if you *don't* express your feelings, because repressed feelings are so painful, than if you do release them, which removes the internal pressure that causes you to seek relief in old, addictive behaviors.

Feeling positive feelings will not get you in trouble, or get you hurt. Love doesn't get you into emotional trouble; dependency (based on old, toxic shame) does. Excitement is not dangerous; it is motivating. Feeling positive feelings makes life feel worth living, because it's more fun. Remember, feeling your feelings is not the same as *doing* anything. You can still choose your actions wisely, even when you're happy, excited, or in love.

Because you were taught to deny and repress your feelings, internal awareness becomes a form of risk taking. If you grew up in a dysfunctional family, becoming fully aware of your self and your feelings as an adult will feel like risk taking for two reasons. First, as a child in an unpredictable, toxic environment, you learned (like young Sally) to focus all your attention on pleasing and placating the adults around you. Surviving amid an overcritical or overprotective family teaches you to be anxious and vigilant, constantly looking to others for approval and reassurance that you're doing OK. You learn to ignore and suppress awareness of your own needs, feelings, and wants, because they are viewed as disruptive by parents, teachers, and others. In dysfunctional families, caring about yourself is believed to be selfish and cold, and people who are selfish are believed to be unworthy of love.

Second, the internal pain of toxic shame makes self-awareness seem frightening because children who have internalized shame are convinced they're going to do badly at whatever they do, including handling their feelings. In addition, your toxic shame created a backlog of stored up "unacceptable" feelings—rage, grief, despair, and terror—which have never been acknowledged or expressed. These repressed feelings and the shame connected with them are painful, and avoiding them is often the driving force behind the need to escape self through addictive or dependent behavior. Because these feelings were held in and not properly expressed, managed, or faced in childhood, when we become adults they seem painful, overwhelming, and unmanageable.

Not knowing how to manage feelings safely and appropriately keeps you in helpless bondage. Until you face your inner pain, the best you can do is to remain in recovery, because your inner pain is too great to leave the safety of a recovery group. To move beyond recovery means making a heroic journey to self-awareness. This journey is heroic because, as you begin to challenge your old, dysfunctional beliefs about your feelings and desires, you will probably encounter all the pent-up and suppressed emotion. Your embarrassment, procrastination, reluctance, and fear can become intense. Facing your inner feelings means heroically encountering and overcoming your resistance.

The exercises in this section will help you discover and develop self-awareness of your internal voices, and of the struggle inside. Each exercise uses a combination of magical tools—particularly the senses, imagery, self-love, and repetition—to help you end this conflict by directly influencing your subconscious and simultaneously healing old, dependency-creating beliefs while building new, autonomous skills. The "Finding Your Trouble Spot" exercise will help you zero-in on your inner conflict and establish clear communication with your subconscious, child self. When you experience tension, depression, or other signs of the inner war, the "Negotiating Table" exercise uses visualization to help you turn your internal war into an inner partnership.

When you begin to become aware of yourself and your feelings, the first thing you may discover is your own inner tension, anxiety, or troubled feelings. The energy it takes to stifle or repress your feelings, and the resulting stress, are usually experienced in your body as muscle tension. This tension can be felt as a headache, a stiff neck, tight upper shoulders, lower back pain, an upset or queasy stomach, a clenched jaw, or tenseness, tightness, or pain anywhere in your body. The majority of people in recovery have had a sensitive or tense area in the stomach or chest, along the breastbone.

Barbara, the young woman who was reluctant to talk to herself, whom we met earlier, came into a session and said, "I feel anxious and uptight, and I don't know what's wrong." I asked her to focus on her body, and tell me where the tension seemed to be. After a few minutes' thought, she said, "My chest feels tight."

Barbara then did the "Finding Your Trouble Spot" exercise that follows to find out what was creating the tension. The first thing Barbara's spot "said" was: "I'm angry at Fred because he reminds me of Dad." Barbara's response was, "Oh, Fred's not so bad. Maybe he didn't mean it," which discounted her inner feelings, as expressed by the spot. Barbara was amazed to realize that she had this argument with herself about Fred frequently, but she had never noticed before. She realized, as she became more aware of her feelings, that she was feeling frustrated in her present relationship because she wasn't being treated well, and as she allowed her inner feelings to come out, she found they went all the way back to her childhood, to early experiences with her father, from whom she couldn't get time or attention or any expression of caring, no matter how hard she tried.

Once these feelings were out in the open, and Barbara knew what they were, we were able to clear up her early childhood issues through adult/child dialogue, and as Barbara began to feel less upset, more in control of her own life, and better about herself, she began to see her current relationship more clearly. She realized that Fred was mildly neglectful, and somewhat thoughtless, but not as cold and cut off as her father, and she began to learn how to ask Fred for what she wanted. Not only did her relationship with Fred improve, but Barbara's relationships with other men, such as her boss and her brother, got better also. Through getting in touch with her "spot" Barbara learned what caused her tension, dealt with the feelings, learned some new skills, and became able to think more clearly and better able to satisfy her own needs independently. Her relationships became more satisfying, because she felt less needy and dependent on men. The men she dated could relax and enjoy her company, without feeling pressured, so they viewed Barbara as more attractive.

Doing this focusing exercise accomplished three things for her: (1) It helped her to separate Fred's mildly forgetful behavior from the serious neglect of her father. (2) She saw the importance of working on her issues with her father. (3) It helped her clear up her confusion about whom she could trust and with whom she could be friends.

Like Barbara, you can become in touch with the specific causes of your inner conflicts by tuning in on your trouble spot. When you're no longer struggling with it, but learning to cooperate and be partners, it will become a source of valuable subconscious information, because it is a place where the tension from unexpressed feelings collects. If getting your trouble spot to open up and let your feelings out goes slowly at first, remember you may have repressed those feelings a long time and must allow some time for them to be released. Before long, you will understand things about yourself that are new to you, such as why you overreact to certain people and situations, or what is causing your depression. You can use this "Trouble Spot" exercise any time you feel body tension or internal stress, to locate the causes of the conflict, resolve them, and thus ease your stress or tension.

For most people, the problems that this exercise will bring to your attention will be quite easy to handle by following the instructions. If, as you try contacting your trouble spot, you become concerned about what you're finding—such as a history of incest and child abuse, or overwhelming rage—talking with a counselor may be helpful. Remember that even with tough inner problems the worst part is already in your past. There is nothing inside you now that can harm you, if you learn how to cope with it in a healthy functional fashion. "Finding Your Trouble Spot," once mastered, will become a way to create quick and easy communication with your subconscious, which means you will be instantly aware of your intuitive feelings about people, events, and situations. It will help you learn to evaluate new situations *before* you enter them, because your intuitive feelings about people and events will be available to you, making your emotional risk taking more apt to be successful.

Have a friend read this to you, or record it on tape, so you can do the exercise uninterrupted.

EXERCISE
FINDING YOUR TROUBLE SPOT

1. *Find your tension spot.* Sit in a comfortable place, where you won't be interrupted. Close your eyes, and take a few moments to focus on your body. Mentally go over your body to find the place where tension or upset seems to be

most strongly concentrated. You may discover tension or tightness in your chest, stomach area, head, neck and shoulders, arms, legs, or back. When you have found this spot, put your awareness on that part of your body. If you discover several tension spots, choose the one that feels the worst and begin there. If you discover none, try focusing on your chest area. Focus your attention there and use your power of imagery (Magical Tool 2) to visualize soothing, relaxing warmth beginning to surround and penetrate it and ease the discomfort. After a few moments you will probably feel the tension let go a little. To help yourself feel the warmth better, gently place your hand there.

2. *Be a good listener.* Say gently to your spot (to increase the chances that your emotional attitude is helpful and caring): "I'm ready to hear what you have to tell me." And listen, for a while, to what your subconscious inner self has to say, holding your attention on the spot. Your spot will communicate to you in words, images, or physical feelings, whichever comes naturally to your subconscious. For the purpose of this exercise, whatever method your spot uses to communicate we will call *talking*. Do not censor or reject any thought that comes into your mind now. Just pay gentle attention, and allow whatever images, ideas, physical sensations, or thoughts you may have to surface into your awareness.

3. *Allow plenty of time.* Allow enough time (about ten minutes, in the beginning) for the images and/or sensations to emerge from within you. If you get restless, remember that it's just resistance, caused by your old self trying to avoid change and to convince you that your feelings don't count. Remind yourself that you care about you, and be patient with the delay. When you begin to get images and sensations, don't argue with them or agree with them, just let them come. If your inner voice says "I don't know" or "I don't want to tell," say something like "I'd really like to hear, I know I've neglected you, but now I realize you're there, and I'd like to hear what you have to say." Or, just sit quietly

and patiently for a while, to show your inner self, who may be used to being ignored, that you are willing to listen. Accept whatever information you get, however meaningless or silly it seems. You probably have an old childhood belief that your feelings aren't important, so counteract that by assuming that what you get is meaningful, even if you don't understand it yet.

You may get physical sensations: warmth, cold, your pulse beating, a tightening, or a relaxing. You may receive symbolic images: a wall, a knot, fire, whimsical creatures, dragons, teddy bears, little boys or girls, religious or fictional characters, or wise teachers. You may remember early scenes from your own history. You may just "hear" your inner self talk in a matter-of-fact way. Whatever you receive, maintain a "this is interesting—tell me more" attitude, as you would if a friend were telling you about his or her inner secrets. This friendly interest will help the information flow faster, and prevent the blockage caused by criticism or argument.

You are creating a new awareness of your self and your feelings as you do this, so allow yourself enough time for this new attitude and method, and be as open to learning new things from your inner self as you can.

4. *Begin a mutual dialogue.* After receiving whatever your inner voice has to share with you, you can begin a dialogue. Offer suggestions ("I will ask Fred to listen more carefully, if you like") and ask questions ("Why do you think Fred is scary?"), but don't argue right or wrong. Your objective is to become aware of and understand the issue that your inner self is trying to bring to your attention. If your inner self says something you don't like, such as "You like Fred more than you like me," you may have trouble listening to it. Try not to attack or discount what you learn ("How could you say that?"), but strive for understanding ("Why do you think I love him more?"). Your magical mind, the subconscious, speaks in its own language, the language of your

dreams and intuition. It may take you a while to understand it. Keep in mind that this is a part of you "talking," and you already know everything you need to understand what your inner self is saying. Learning to listen to your inner voice is much like prayer or meditation—an open mind, focused here on your tension spot, instead of on your Higher Power. Once you become proficient at this, you can bring up specific issues to discuss with your inner voice, and give and receive counsel as you would with a friend. This makes you less dependent on others to help you "talk things out" when you're contemplating a new move, or beginning a new relationship, or meeting new friends. Knowing your inner self's intuitive and emotional reactions to new people and situations gives you needed information to help you take risks more successfully, and cope with the feelings that come up when you do, which are skills useful in attaining autonomy.

5. *Repeat for proficiency.* The more you make contact with your spot (the place in your body where you tend to store tension and repressed feelings) and practice becoming aware and inner communication, the easier this exercise will get. After doing it four or five times, you will find that you can "check in" with your spot more easily, and after twenty times, you'll be able to do it on a moment's notice, without closing your eyes, and even while you're doing other things. This ability to instantly know your inner child mind's reactions gives you the autonomous power to take care of your own feelings on the spot.

Once you have established communication with your spot, you have a technique that can be expanded to end your internal war. In addition to communicating with one inner voice, as in the previous exercise, you may find that on some issues there seem to be two or three voices taking different positions on the issue. The following exercise will teach you how to handle them all together. At one time, hearing voices in your head was thought to mean you were crazy, but several decades ago many modes of psychotherapy—including psychosynthesis, transactional analysis, and Gestalt and Jungian therapy—recognized that inner voices are normal, and that everyone has some kind of mental commentary going on most of the time. These therapies began to focus on these "arguing aspects" of our minds and developed methods for dialogue, which create inner harmony by resolving the conflicting ideas into cooperating parts of a mental team, as you will see here. This exercise uses similar techniques and is especially effective in resolving your internal war, which shows its presence by the signs mentioned earlier, such as tension, depression, and irritability.

EXERCISE
THE NEGOTIATING TABLE

1. *Listen for the voices.* Whenever you feel anxious or tempted to return to addictive behavior, or you're having trouble making a decision, assume there *is* an inner struggle between various parts of your self, an internal war. Arrange some uninterrupted time to sit quietly, close your eyes to help you concentrate, and listen to your inner self. Chances are you will become aware of several voices that are arguing in your mind. At first, you may hear nothing, or a confusing babble of several inner voices talking at once, but if you allow some time and patiently wait, as you did with your tension spot, what they say will begin to come clear. You may have inner voices saying "I want to take the new job, I need a change" or "I'm scared. Everything will be new and unpredictable" or "I better stay where I am. If I try it, I'll fail" or "I'm too stupid to make this decision myself."

2. *Name your voices.* To most people, these voices usually begin to feel as though they have personality characteristics or attitudes, such as grown-up and child (grown-up: "You have to get a job"; child: "I don't want to"), or dreamer and pragmatist (dreamer: "Wouldn't it be nice if

we won the lotto and didn't have to work?"; pragmatist: "We'll never win, and we need the ticket money."), or male and female, or procrastinator and nagger, or memories of the voices and attitudes of your actual parents. When you have distinguished two or more voices, give each one a name to help you keep them clear. The names can be people's names (Joe, Mary), or descriptive (like those above). One of my clients has two main arguing voices he calls the Rebel and the Visionary. Another woman has a whole crowd, with whimsical names such as Hysterical Harriet, Angry Amy, Pleasing Pauline, Critical Carl, Depressed Debra, and Rusty Resistance. Choose whatever names you like, or ask the voices if they can tell you their names. Having names will help you keep track of who's talking, and therefore more control over the "conference."

3. *Seat everyone at a table.* Visualize the characters your voices represent seated at a conference table. Give each one a turn to talk, and listen to that point of view. Becoming aware of what issue your internal voices or characters are arguing about makes it possible for you to mediate, and come up with solutions that satisfy all parties.

4. *Take charge of the conference.* In order to take charge of the confusion, and end the internal war, you must be a moderator and not get drawn into the argument. If bedlam breaks out and all your internal voices begin talking at once, call your imaginary meeting to order just as a moderator does. Ask questions of each voice, just as you would at an actual meeting. Try to get them to make useful suggestions about how they could solve the problem at hand. Keep focused on your goal of getting your internal warring voices to cooperate with each other. Your attitude here, as moderator, should be much more active and directive than in the previous exercise.

5. *If you get confused, write it down.* If you have too many voices arguing over a particular issue, keep them separate. If doing this strictly in your imagination feels difficult, try writing the different points of view on paper, where

you can become aware of them in an orderly fashion. Make a column or a page for each voice, and briefly write down that voice's opinion on the issue in question. After you get all the voices written down, go back into your conference and again work toward a cooperative solution to the problem, using the written paper as reference. For example, you might write as follows:

REBEL: I won't work. You can't make me.

DREAMER: I know my prince will come and rescue me from drudgery.

TASKMASTER: You have to look harder! You're not doing enough.

PESSIMIST: It's no use, I won't find a job anyway.

6. *Be aware of should's.* While sorting out the struggle look for *should, ought,* and *have-to* on one side and *won't, can't,* and *you can't make me* on the other. They are the keys to your internal struggle, because those words polarize and antagonize a discussion. Direct the voices who are saying *should* to use *could* and to explain their reasons for wanting it that way. Direct the ones who are saying *won't* and *can't* to say what they want, and why. This will establish a more cooperative, less antagonistic feeling. Make it clear, as moderator, that the committee's job is to reach a mutual agreement, not to just fight. Insist that each voice offer *solutions,* and don't allow them to just complain. In the examples above you could instruct the Rebel to say, "Instead of working, I want to play my music," and the Taskmaster to say, "We could find a job if we looked more."

7. *Reach agreement.* Continue the session until you reach an acceptable agreement that feels like it satisfies everyone. If there are too many problems to be dealt with at one meeting, create an agenda (a list of topics for discussion), write it down so you won't forget, and have several

sessions until you solve each item on the agenda. If your committee began working on a job issue, but then issues about money, the kind of work you do, car repairs, and your expensive shopping habit came up, you need to have a separate meeting for each issue at another time and stay focused on the job issue for now.

8. *Repeat to build cooperation.* By doing this exercise several times, you will become more comfortable with your inner voices, know how to handle them better, and therefore be more in charge of your committee. Each time you repeat these steps, your inner voices will follow the negotiation routine more easily, until soon you've re-trained them to behave more cooperatively, and you can negotiate internal problems very quickly. After repeated use, this exercise will virtually eliminate the internal noise and anxiety that these voices can create. With this constant din gone from your mind, you will be able to think much more clearly, weigh the pros and cons of various solutions, and make decisions a lot more easily.

After doing these exercises, you have probably realized that attaining self-awareness doesn't have to be mysterious or difficult. Awareness brings inner problems out into the open, and helps you resolve inner conflicts, but awareness by itself is not enough. Without new information you would lack anything but the old, ineffective solutions.

Learning

To move from this awareness to change, you must learn new options. Learning changes people, because once you learn something new, your perception of yourself and your environment is different—sometimes profoundly different, as when you first learn that you can stop drinking by following your recovery program; and sometimes slightly different, as when you learn a new way to cook a meal. Learning your six magical tools in the previous chapter, even though we have not really begun to apply them to your inner dependency, has already changed you. You know how to use your senses, your mental power of imagery, and self-love to make changes within your mind; and you are beginning to understand the power of self-image, environment, and repetition, which means that you view the world about you and your own mind differently. You have more information about, more understanding of, and therefore more control over these aspects of your life. Awareness increases your motiviation to learn, and through learning, you obtain new options and solutions to old problems.

Self-awareness is an emotional form of risk taking, because you are risking learning new things about yourself, and learning is the equivalent of problem solving, because in learning you develop new answers to new questions. In childhood, at the stage that you were attempting to develop autonomy, your risk taking and self awareness were blocked, so you never got the opportunity to learn problem-solving skills, especially in regard to your feelings. Solving problems in connection with your inner awareness and your feelings requires that you learn new attitudes, because the old attitudes created the problems to begin with.

Surprisingly, a large portion of helping people to heal their lives and develop autonomy is simply helping them to *learn* practical techniques for living. If you grew up in a dysfunctional family, you were prevented from learning many practical living skills and techniques. If, for example, you were discouraged from taking risks and making new childhood friends, you will lack social skills.

Denton Roberts explains the importance of learning new options: "Psychotherapies tend to focus primarily on pathology, illness and the restoration of healthy functioning. Once we have corrected any historic mistakes we still need a method to assist us in maintaining health and staying on our side."

Being able to learn new autonomous modes of behavior and thought is essential to maintaining new attitudes, because the success you gain by using new skills reinforces your new beliefs. Like many addictive and dependent people, you may be convinced you cannot learn, because your dysfunctional family discouraged risk taking and problem solving, encouraged dependency, and did not help you acquire learning skills. Learning new skills now will free you from your dependency on the people who have them.

What most of us don't realize is that we *learned* everything we do. As a newborn baby, you weren't habitually afraid, angry, discouraged, or hopeless. The helplessness and dependency you had at that time was a *real* limitation of abilities, not a set of beliefs. As an adult, if you are hopeless, afraid, angry, discouraged, helpless, or dependent, all those attitudes were learned because of *environmental influences* (Magical Tool 4). Understanding this should encourage your progress away from dependency.

If you've read this far in the book, and done the completing recovery exercises as they were presented, you have already learned a great deal. Learning involves risk taking and when you opened the covers of this book (even if you weren't aware of it) you were taking a risk that you'd have a new experience that would change things about your life. Your old attitudes and beliefs are being challenged and changed by new information, by the experience gained from doing the exercises, and by the realizations you have had as a result of this experience. By now you have already learned to use your imagination to practice new skills, and may already be exploring some new hobby or skill you first tried out in your imagination. Or, you may be using your private retreat from the very first exercise to relax you on a daily basis. Every exercise and paragraph in this book is a learning opportunity.

If you have ever held a job, driven a car, gone to school, played a sport or a game, or ever found your way to a new friend's home, you have proved yourself capable of learning. If you ever made a change from using a dial phone to using push-buttons, or used a computer, or a VCR, you are indeed capable of learning, and of changing long-standing behavior patterns.

Because you have conclusively proved you can learn, and indeed have already learned a lot in this book, the question is not to teach you *how* to learn but to help you discover how you *naturally* learn—what I call your *learning style.*

Learning How You Learn

Learning becomes easier and more effective when you become aware of *how* you learn. People receive information in different ways—we are auditory, visual, tactile, and imaginative in different proportions. That is, words (sounds), pictures (sight), touching, and imagination are more or less important to you depending on your learning style. Your learning style consists of two parts: *sensory preference* and *attitude.* Sensory preference is merely a description of which senses you naturally use more than others. Attitude is a more complex description of how your personality traits, learning history, and prejudices affect your approach to learning. Together, they create your learning style.

Sensory preference refers to the senses you learn through most easily and with the deepest understanding.

If you are mostly verbal and auditory, you are not a visual person. In visualization exercises, you will be more likely to think in words than in pictures, and you know you have learned a new idea when you can explain it clearly. It would be most effective for you to talk, hear, or read about new ideas, and lectures and audio tapes may be a good way for you to learn. You may enjoy listening to the radio. You'll probably use phrases such as "I hear what you're saying" or "It sounds like . . ." to mean you understand someone.

If you are more visual, and tend to picture things rather than capture them in words, you probably know you've learned something only when you can visualize the steps or imagine yourself using it effectively. Then visualization techniques, videos, watching someone else, or seeing diagrams and pictures are probably the most effective way for you to learn. You may say visual things such as "I see," meaning I understand, or "See that?" meaning do you understand?

If you lean toward the physical, and you are a tactile (touching) person, you learn best by doing, tinkering with things, and you know you've learned it when you "feel" it more than see or hear it. "Walking through" a new skill or habit, acting it out physically, could work well for you. For you, "I feel it" or "I've got it" are ways to say you understand.

If you are an imaginative person, you are able to *see* in your mind's eye things you have never seen in reality. When you read fiction or fantasy, the landscapes are real to you, and you can daydream vividly. Visualization and imagery will be powerful techniques for you, and "I can picture it" or "I can imagine" are ways to say you understand.

No matter what kind of learning style suits you best, if you take advantage of your sensory preference, learning will be easier for you. You will not have to struggle against or translate the method you're learning from into your own preference before you can absorb the information.

Attitude is the other part of your learning style. Your attitude is heavily influenced by your early environment and experience, and refers to the preset ideas you have before you encounter new information.

Some people are enthusiastic about learning, because their experiences in the past were rewarding; some people are more cautious; and some people are resistant, because to them, in the past, learning meant failure (such as from a bad school experience). Your learning attitude also includes preferences (whether you like to learn quickly or slowly, alone or with others) and prejudices (such as "Book learning is more prestigious than learning a trade"). These attitude differences can be incorporated in your learning just as your sensory preferences are. For example, if you like to learn with others, and you think "book learning" is best, you can form a book study group. If you like to learn alone, and you value "practical" learning (skills you use), you'll enjoy video or audio tapes or books with titles that begin with "How to . . ."

Some learning attitudes can create problems. If you come from a family where education is positively emphasized, your attitude toward organized learning will be positive. You'll be proud of formal, organized learning (schools, courses), anticipate it with excitement, and seek it out. However, your family's emphasis may cause you to miss the fact that there are many kinds of learning, and to value academics above sports, current events, mechanics, and the arts.

In contrast, if you come from a family where education is laughed at, or where you're told you're stupid, then book learning is negatively emphasized, and you'll fear it. But, you may be much better and more relaxed at other things, such as auto mechanics or dance, and not realize they're kinds of learning, too.

Your attitude determines whether you approach learning new things with enthusiasm or procrastination, calm or anxiety. Positive attitudes toward particular kinds of learning make those kinds easier: "I love school, and it's fun and easy" or "I love to work with my hands." Negative attitudes toward particular kinds make them more difficult: "I hate getting my hands dirty," "I'm afraid of hurting myself," "I'm no good at anything mechanical," or "I hate books and teachers, I was never good at school."

If a dysfunctional family made you feel too pressured about school grades or that learning was for sissies, you may try to avoid it. (It's impossible to avoid learning, but if you have a rigid definition of what learning is, you can believe you avoid it.) If you attempt to avoid learning, you may wind up learning many new things the hard way, through being forced to by negative experiences. That is, if you don't learn about your car because it's "dirty work," you may be cheated by mechanics or find yourself stranded on the highway until you learn enough to know the danger signs of a failing car. If this is the case, you can use the tools you are learning in this book to change attitudes that are getting in your way.

The following two quizzes are intended to help you discover your learning style—the first is about sensory preference, and the second is about attitude. After taking them, you'll combine them both to form a complete learning profile, which you can then use to make all future learning easier.

These questions are designed to help you understand your

learning process. There are no right or wrong answers. You may have more than one choice per question, or a more appropriate, original answer. No one is 100 percent auditory, visual, tactile, or imaginative. We do all four, but we have preferences.

To discover your sensory preference for learning, take a sheet of paper and make four headings across the top. Down the left margin, write the numbers 1 through 5 (see accompanying chart).

AUDITORY (A)	VISUAL (V)	TACTILE (T)	IMAGINATIVE (I)
1.			
2.			
3.			
4.			
5.			

Make a checkmark in the proper category for each answer to the following questions; when you're done, tally up your totals. The category with the most checkmarks will indicate the sensory mode through which you learn most easily. The columns with the highest number of checkmarks indicate your natural learning modes (the ones through which you learn readily), and those with the least checks indicate modes that are less easy for you to use. By using these results, you can see what your most natural, habitual, and effective learning styles are, and tailor your own learning to take the best advantage of them.

QUIZ
YOUR SENSORY PREFERENCE

1. *When you think, do you*
   hear words in your head? (A)

draw or visualize pictures? (V)

write things down or touch related objects? (T)

daydream fantasies and visions? (I)

2. *When you are or were in school, did you learn better from teachers who*

talked interestingly? (A)

wrote or drew diagrams on the board or showed movies and pictures? (V)

gave you hands-on experiments or homework? (T)

asked you to imagine or guess what the situation was like? (I)

3. *When you want to learn something new (for example, operating a computer, cooking Chinese, dieting, a new game or sport) do you*

take a class or read a book? (A)

watch someone else do it first? (V)

experiment and learn as you go? (T)

dream about knowing how to do it? (I)

4. *You feel confident you've learned something when you*

can explain it to someone. (A)

can see the results or watch yourself do well in a mirror or video. (V)

can do it with your own hands or when it feels easy. (T)

can see yourself doing it well in your imagination. (I)

5. *You do a lot of*

reading and writing. (A)

watching TV, movies, and people. (V)

physical activity. (T)

daydreaming and fantasizing. (I)

Discovering your attitude is more ambiguous than finding your sensory preference and does not lend itself to columns of checkmarks. Heading a piece of paper "How I Learn," rephrasing each question as a statement, and writing each answer out completely will give you a more useful, narrative description of your attitude. For example, if your answer to question 1 is the first answer, write it out as: "I approach learning something new with an 'Oh, boy' comment." When you've written out all the questions and answers, you'll have a paragraph that describes your learning attitude. A sample paragraph and instructions will tell you how to use it at the end of the quiz.

QUIZ
YOUR LEARNING ATTITUDE

1. *You approach learning something new with which of these comments?*

   Oh, boy!

   Oh, dear!

   So what?

2. *In reading this book, do you feel*

   skepticism?

   acceptance?

   resistance?

   enthusiasm?

3. *When you first encountered this exercise, did you*

   read the whole thing through without doing it (so you knew what you were getting into)?

plunge right in and do it as you went along?

share it with a friend first, to see his or her reaction?

4. *Do you feel learning is*

   work?

   helpful?

   fun?

   like solving a puzzle?

5. *Do you often*

   get lost in learning something new and forget what time it is?

   learn something new just to make life more fun and interesting?

   have to have a logical reason to learn something?

   resist or procrastinate about learning?

6. *In learning new things , are you most motivated to*

   prove you can do it?

   compete with someone?

   beat your own previous effort?

7. *When you face a brand-new task, do you prefer*

   to be left alone until you figure it out?

   to be led step-by-step through it until you know it?

   a combination of guidance and hands-on practice?

8. *The things that seem most valuable to you are*

   things people learn from books, teachers, and/or school.

things people learn that are called *trades*, such as mechanics or carpentry.

things people learn in office jobs.

practical skills, such as driving or cooking.

fun skills, such as sports, the arts, or hobbies.

9. *Rank the options in question 8 in order of their value or importance to you as follows:*

most important

very important

somewhat important

not very important

least important

10. *Now rank the same five options in question 8 in order of their usefulness as follows:*

most useful

very useful

somewhat useful

not very useful

least useful

11. *You know you have learned enough for a session when you*

feel overwhelmed and confused by the new information.

have mastered the new task or skill.

are told it's time to take a break.

get bored and restless.

feel _____ (fill in the blank).

At the end of your paragraph, add the information from the sensory preference quiz. (This will give you your learning profile.) Here's an example of Mary's result from the two tests:

HOW I LEARN

I approach learning something new with an "oh dear" comment. Even in reading this book I feel resistance. When I first encountered this exercise, I read the whole thing through without doing it, because I was nervous about it. I feel learning is helpful, but I often resist or procrastinate about learning. In learning new things, I am most motivated to beat my own previous effort. When I face a brand-new task, I prefer to be led step-by-step through it until I know it. The most valuable things to me are things people learn from teachers and school. The most important things to me are things people learn in school; the least important are things people learn that are called *trades*. The most useful things are things people learn in office jobs, and practical skills like cooking and driving. The least useful are trades. I know when I have learned enough when I feel overwhelmed and confused by the new information. My learning style is mostly visual, somewhat imaginative, and not auditory at all.

Here's where you begin to use your sensory preference. If you found out you're auditory, read your paragraph aloud to yourself, or discuss it with a friend. If you are visual or imaginative, read your paragraph onto a tape, and as it plays back close your eyes and make a mental picture of your profile. If you're tactile, act it out. If you have more than one strong preference, use more than one method. When you've got a clear idea of what parts of your learning style are positive and helpful, incorporate them into your learning in the rest of this book. For the parts that you find problematic, that might get in your way, use your magical tools and other exercises to change them.

If you find that your learning style is making you avoid learning, or making learning hard on you, you can change it by using the "Finding Your Trouble Spot" or "Negotiating Table" exercises to reach your subconscious child mind and counteract the dysfunctional information that's in there with new, more correct ideas. When you do this, make learning, and specifically how it feels, the topic of discussion. Your objective is to correct old, negative attitudes your childhood experience taught you (such as, "I'm stupid, and learning is hard for me") with new, positive information (such as, "I have been learning all my life, without knowing it; I am smart, and I can learn whatever I want to know"). Using Magical Tool 6: Repetition and Memorization is another excellent way to replace negative attitudes and beliefs about your learning abilities.

After reviewing her paragraph and picturing in her imagination how her learning style would look in action, Mary realized she was visual, very tentative and hesitant in learning, would do best with a guide or teacher, and most respected institutional (school) learning, although she used practical things more. Thinking about this for a while, Mary decided that using a support group or learning with a friend (Magical Tool 4: Environment) or taking classes were the easiest ways for her to learn, and that she should take the time to visualize the subject she was learning or watch someone else or use pictures, such as videos or a picture cookbook, to make learning easier. She also decided to encourage herself more about being able to learn by using the exercises for Magical Tool 3: Self-Love and Magical Tool 6: Repetition.

Becoming comfortable with and understanding your style of learning can renew your early pleasure at seeing old things in new ways. Once you begin to replace your old skills of dependency with the creative skills of self-awareness (risk taking) and learning (problem solving), there is only one thing that can keep you tied to your past: the need for forgiveness, which can correct the childhood circumstances that prevented you from learning how to cope with mistakes and failure.

Forgiveness

Now that you feel reassured about your ability to learn and know how to best apply your innate learning abilities, it's time to learn how to handle failures and mistakes. Learning to handle mistakes means learning to understand that mistakes are natural and normal, and even helpful, rather than disasters or signs that you are hopeless and stupid, as you came to believe in childhood, and discovering how to forgive yourself for making them.

Learning forgiveness begins with learning to forgive yourself for the damage you did to yourself and others with your old destructive habits and for allowing others (beginning with your dysfunctional family, and including later adult relationships) to be abusive to you or take advantage of or undercut you in the past.

My definition of forgiveness is a bit different than the one you may have been taught. The dictionary defines *to forgive* as "to give up resentment of," which I have found is nearly impossible for people who grew up in dysfunctional families—often there are too many real injuries to forgive. It can also be unwise, because resentment is like a reminder to yourself to "watch out—this hurt me before." Ignoring the past and forgiving others who may still be abusing you now ("He didn't mean to beat me up, he was just drunk") gets you hurt or mistreated over and over again. Dependency is often perpetuated by forgiving and forgetting that someone has hurt you, and by not confronting the person or ending the relationship.

Forgiving yourself for past destructive behavior, if not based on a real, inner change of attitudes ("It wasn't my fault, I had a rough childhood"; "I can't help it, my anger just takes over"), becomes dysfunctional permissiveness and self-pity. Forgiving yourself without learning from your destructive behavior, and without determining how to change, is aptly termed *denial* by recovery programs. If you don't recognize the consequences of your destructive behavior and accept responsibility for it, you have no incentive to change.

However, simply hanging on to resentment will not really protect you, or allow you to let go of the past and move on in your life. As long as you hold on to the resentment, you will feel like a helpless, hopeless, dependent victim of your past history. You do need to learn to forgive, but just giving up resentment is not sufficient. You need a new model of what forgiveness is.

As a person from a dysfunctional background, and one who has been controlled by addictive and dependent attitudes and behaviors, there are a number of things you may need to forgive:

- You may need to forgive yourself for doing emotional, mental, or physical damage to others.
- You may need to forgive yourself for doing emotional, mental, or physical damage to yourself.
- You may need to forgive yourself for letting others damage you in those ways.
- You may need to forgive others (parents, children, spouses, friends) for hurting themselves in all the above ways.
- You may need to forgive others for doing emotional, mental, or physical damage to you.

Safely and honestly forgiving all these past hurts is not accomplished by simply giving up resentment. First you must find a way to be safe from future damage and abuse. Once you have learned how to create safety you can rely on, and you know you have the autonomous ability to protect yourself from damage and to prevent yourself from causing damage, forgiving past destructive behavior (your own and others') becomes easy, because you are no longer threatened. When you have real reasons for resentment, both against others and against yourself, only the assurance that you can take care of yourself so that you won't be hurt or that you can be sure you won't get destructive makes true forgiveness possible.

Recognizing the consequences of your own destructive behavior and taking responsibility for it does not mean punishing yourself; it means becoming aware of the dependent ideas and feelings that are behind your behavior, and learning how to change them. It is possible to love and approve of yourself now and still be aware that you have allowed yourself to be damaged by yourself and others, and that those experiences have been painful and destructive. If you've caused yourself pain in the past by being involved with abusive people, you can learn to understand your inner reasons for feeling dependent on such abusive people. By using your inner awareness exercises and your magical tools, you can change the beliefs that keep you helpless in such relationships.

If your own behavior has been damaging to yourself or others, you don't have to continually blame and punish yourself in order to remember the consequences of destructive behavior. Instead, you can use your inner awareness exercises and magical tools to find the deep inner feelings and beliefs underlying your behavior and make the necessary changes.

Although it is often not possible to prevent others from hurting themselves or attempting to hurt you, you can take steps to see that their rage and destructive behavior does not threaten or damage you. Remembering who hurt you is not the same as condemning them. You don't have to condemn others as bad people to be wary of their out-of-control or problematic behavior. You can recognize that they are fallible human beings, too, and often more damaged by childhood experience than you were, and that until they repair their own damage, as you are repairing yours, you must keep a safe distance. In fact, the possibility that they might lose you, or that you will keep a safe distance because of their destructive behavior, is often the only type of confrontation that will make them look at their own behavior.

The following exercise will help you learn new ways to cope with situations in which you were hurt by others, beginning in your childhood. Through the power of imagery (Magical Tool 2), you can learn to protect yourself from others by rehearsing and changing old painful scenes as many times as you need to make sure you know how to take care of yourself.

It is not easy to be sure an old behavior problem (your own or someone else's) is gone forever. Even when you or the other person has done inner work to correct the problem, in a situation of enough stress it may still return. This exercise will help you learn how to take care of yourself in difficult and painful situations, and will give you a chance to practice various solutions and responses until you find the ones that work, without risking any real-life consequences. This is learning to care for yourself in very realistic terms, and it begins with healing old, painful scenes from early childhood.

The fear of recurring destructive behavior, on their own part or from others, is a great problem for many addictive and dependent people as they complete their recovery. This exercise is a way to reassure that fear, by assuming control of events in your subconscious past and unlearning some of your old, dependent decisions about life, replacing them with new, more autonomous ideas. It is also a wonderful way to learn the skills of early risk taking, problem solving, and handling disappointment or failure. I believe "Time Travel" is the single most powerful exercise you can do to clear out old traumas, remove the roots of dependency, and build autonomous skills, including the ones that keep you safe from emotional, mental, or physical harm. "Time Travel" helps you develop the self-protection needed to achieve forgiveness and let go of damaging behavior, situations, and people.

Through consistent use and practice of this exercise and the ones that follow, you will no longer need your resentment to protect you, because you will have learned how to ensure your safety. You will be able to release and forgive old hurts, recognizing that the people who caused them (yourself included) didn't know any better ways of behaving at the time. As you learn how to stop the dysfunctional adults in your past from hurting your child self, and to protect and care for yourself, you will also learn how to recognize when people in your life today are uncaring, and what to do about it.

In the form shown here, this exercise is most effective whenever a memory of emotional, physical, or psychological pain from your childhood is troubling you. But, with minor changes, you can use it for other inner work, too. For example, if you're having a recurring dream that troubles you, you can use this exercise to replay the dream, and it won't bother you any more. By using scenes from times other than your childhood (a quarrel with your current mate, or an encounter that you're afraid will happen with someone who's angry at you), you can use "Time Travel" to practice risk taking (rehearse in advance social events where you'll meet new people, or talk to someone you've been shy around).

To allow yourself the full impact of the exercise, without interruption, read the following steps into a tape recorder and play them back.

EXERCISE
TIME TRAVEL

1. *Invoke a childhood scene.* To begin, sit quietly by yourself and close your eyes. Visualize yourself as a small child (Magical Tool 2: Imagery) in a scene from childhood that was painful. You will learn how to correct the scene, take care of yourself, and then forgive whoever created the problem—and forgive yourself for your own participation. Allow the troubling scene from your memory to appear around your child self. You may get a mental picture, or if not, just imagine the scene as you remember it. Remember to use Magical Tool 1, your senses, to establish your scene clearly, unless this is a scene of childhood abuse or incest. In that case, you may find it too painful or stressful to use all the senses, so allow yourself to keep your distance by just thinking of the scene and not developing as much sensory information. If your scene is very painful, or frightening, view the scene as objectively as you can, as though it is a story about someone else.

2. *Enter the scene as an adult.* Like a time traveler from the future, visualize yourself in the scene as the grown-up you are today. There will be two of you present—the small child you were, and your modern, adult self.

When Tom, twenty-nine, a talented musician and owner of his own business, did "Time Travel," he went back to a birthday party he had attended at age five. His parents had dropped him there and he had felt abandoned. The other children made fun of him, and he had been afraid at parties and gatherings ever since, convinced that he was socially inept, and that no one would like him if he went to a party. He visualized the scene of the party as vividly as he could, and then imagined sitting down by little Tommy.

3. *Take charge of the scene.* Now it's time to take over the story—as you did in the Magical Tool 4 exercise (self-image)—and protect your child self. Do whatever is needed to stop the adults or other children from upsetting, hurting, or neglecting your child self. If the other children or adults are too badly behaved, you can make them leave if you want to—you have total power here, in your imagination. Use that power to make a safe environment and to provide protection for your child self. If you like, you can also surround your child self with loving people.

Tom helped young Tommy in two ways. He realized Tommy was dressed much more formally than the other kids, so he helped him take off his tie and suit jacket and roll up his sleeves. Tommy was too shy to join the other kids, and the grown-ups there were too busy to notice, so Tom helped Tommy find a game to play. Soon other kids joined them.

4. *Take care of your child.* This small version of you may be frightened, angry, confused, feeling helpless, or overwhelmed with grief—the "adult you" can use Magical Tool 3: Self-Love to be rational, effective, competent, and reassuring. You may encounter some resistance to doing

this, in the form of feeling incapable of taking care of your child self. But remember, you can do this over and over in your mind until you get it right. You can try to fix the situation in several different ways, before you decide which is best. Visualize removing your child self from danger; comfort and reassure; correct any lies your child self was told (that he was stupid, or it was her fault) by telling your child the (positive) truth (he is intelligent, or no child causes her own abuse); and take time to begin to establish a friendship with your child self. If you see that your child self needs some information or help, provide it. Promise that your child will never be left at the mercy of ignorant, malicious, incompetent, or uncomprehending people again.

When another child began teasing Tommy, Tom imagined intervening. He comforted Tommy, gently corrected the other child, and got the other child involved in the game. He told Tommy, "I love you, you're OK, that little boy is just teasing."

5. *When your child self feels safe, discuss forgiveness.* When you have corrected the scene enough that your child self is out of danger and feeling safe, talk with your child about what happened. Discuss what went wrong and who made mistakes, and decide how to avoid being the victim of those same mistakes again. Once you and your child both know he or she will not be hurt again (because you'll do what it takes to protect him or her), you'll find that your child will be ready to forgive the people who hurt him or her, and will understand that they just don't know how to behave. Help your child see that whatever happened was not his or her fault, and your child self doesn't have to make the same mistakes the others made, or repeat the mistakes he or she made.

Tom and Tommy talked about the party, and decided that Tommy's parents should have gotten more information before the party about how Tommy should dress, and they should not have dropped him off, but stayed with him until they knew he would be OK. The grown-ups at the party should have watched what was happening with the children more, and Tommy himself could have been less afraid and not taken things so seriously when he was teased. Tom promised he would check out social situations in advance from now on, and not leave Tommy stranded among strangers without Tom there.

6. *Take your child to a safe place.* Close the scene by visualizing your child self in a safe, secure place, completely out of danger. Reassure him or her that you'll be there when you're needed, and tell him or her how to get your attention when he or she feels in danger. This means that your adult, rational self will not leave your emotional, child self alone, dependent, and at the mercy of people who are hurtful. Do not leave the scene until your child self feels calm and secure.

After their discussion about the party, Tom visualized taking Tommy back home, where Tommy felt safe, and tucked him in. He hugged Tommy, told him "Good night," and said Tommy could call him whenever he needed him for protection.

7. *Repeat regularly.* After you have done "Time Travel" the first time, you can keep your promise to keep your child self safe (and build self-trust) by time traveling back to your child self as often as needed, until it becomes an unconscious habit (Magical Tool 6: Repetition). Once you've done this many times and become proficient, you will not need to close your eyes to be in instant contact with your child self; you will be able to imagine being with your child self at any time. Doing this exercise repeatedly, whenever old, painful memories arise, will eventually clear out your childhood traumas and correct the damage done within your dysfunctional family, while helping you practice the autonomous skills needed to take care of yourself. You'll find that you

instinctively know when someone or something is hurtful to you, and when you're being hurtful to others. You'll also know what to do to correct the situation (don't be alone with violent or emotionally hurtful people; don't allow yourself to be in tempting situations; and so on) and you'll feel safe enough to forgive those who are confused and behave in hurtful ways, because their behavior will not be dangerous to you.

With practice, and by going back to other scenes where Tommy was uncomfortable around people, and helping him cope, Tom found that he was much more comfortable in crowds and at parties. He had new ideas of what he needed to do to have a good time, and how to take care of himself if something began to go wrong. Tom found that he saw other people differently, too. He could keep his distance from people who didn't treat others well, and he could recognize easily the people who were safe and healthy for him. Once little Tommy, his child self, knew when and how to join in appropriately, Tom could have fun, be playful, and feel more relaxed.

Once you have overcome your resistance and made the journey within, facing yourself and becoming aware of your inner feelings and beliefs, and have begun to learn how to care for yourself effectively, releasing the hold the past has on you, you have completed recovery and entered autonomy. The more adept you become at self-awareness, learning, and forgiveness, the more autonomous you can be. The hurts of the past can be healed, and the dependent beliefs you learned as a child no longer have the power to prevent you from feeling capable of taking care of yourself. The old hopelessness and helplessness fade away, and you are ready to live independently in the world, in charge of your own life.

III

Achieving Autonomy

CHAPTER 6

Autonomous Thinking: Weighing Choices in Everyday Life

Autonomy can be described as the power we possess, used or unused, to direct our energy to create our individual lives. The question of whether we will take advantage of it, claim it as our own, is the most persistent and recurring issue we face. Claiming this power is both a difficult and rewarding task.

DENTON ROBERTS

U p to this point, all the work you have been doing has been focused on learning how to complete recovery from the dependent attitudes you learned in childhood by changing old negative subconscious thought patterns and old negative perceptions and interactions with yourself. This in itself is a life-changing experience, because as your perceptions of yourself and your reactions to situations change and become more effective, your life automatically begins to feel freer, healthier, and more hopeful.

Now it's time to concentrate on developing the skills of autonomy by shifting your focus from your internal world to your outer world. Now you will learn to apply your new skills and ways of thinking to help you cope effectively with the problems and challenges of everyday life.

THE MOST IMPORTANT CHOICE OF YOUR LIFE

The biggest challenge of autonomy is giving up the dependent dream that someone else out there will take care of you or that someone else can make it better, and accepting responsibility for running or governing your own life. "Ever since we relied on our mothers to make a bruised knee better with a Band-Aid and a kiss," writes Ellen Langer, learning researcher, in *Mindfulness,* "we have held on to the assumption that someone out there, somewhere, can make us better."

Not accepting the responsibility to take care of ourselves is dependency. Accepting the responsibility, and taking care of our own lives, is autonomy.

The truth is that no one else can or will take care of you, because each person has all he or she can do to run his or her own life properly. We can give love and caring to one another, but it is impossible to effectively take responsibility for someone else. No one else can make it better for you, because another person cannot know your needs, wants, thoughts, and circumstances intimately enough to make effective choices for you.

The truth is that you are responsible for your life already, whether you accept it or not, because even avoiding a decision is a decision. You alone will bear the consequences of making or not making this choice as you bear the consequences of all your decisions. There is no choice you make or avoid, and no action you take or postpone, that does not produce some effect in your life.

The consequences of your choices, decisions, and actions will be yours, like it or not, *even if you choose to remain dependent.* Accepting this fact, and learning how to make those choices effectively rather than relying on others who cannot pursue your best interests or blindly avoiding them altogether and leaving your life open to chaos and turmoil, is the key to successful, autonomous living.

Relying blindly on others, keeping you dependent on their reactions and decisions, is what results in codependent relationships with inappropriate partners. If we are dependent on the other person and we feel helpless and hopeless, then we cannot choose an appropriate partner, or firmly reject a partner's abusive or irresponsible behavior.

That's why deciding to make your own choices and to take responsibility for them is so critical: before you can do anything, you first have to *choose* to do it. Choice and decision making precede everything you do and every action you take, every course you set, every relationship and interaction. Before you can begin to take healthy, effective action, you need to learn to make effective choices.

This is the most vital decision of your life, the most important choice you will ever make or avoid, because in deciding whether or not to choose autonomy you are also deciding whether or not your life will still be chaos and pain or whether you will move on to achieve satisfaction and success.

Relinquishing the hope that others will take care of you and assuming responsibility for yourself and your life is a choice only you can make; no recovery program, therapist, workshop, exercise, or book like this can make it for you.

It is a *vital* decision you have to make for yourself, by yourself. And it is *not* a decision you can put off if you wish to move beyond the dysfunctional need to depend on recovery groups to keep you in the bondage of recovery. It is a decision you must make if you want to be in charge of your own tomorrows. There is no doubt that making your own choices and taking responsibility for your life requires dedication, commitment, and effort, but when you consider the alternatives, it is easy to see that autonomy is by far the least painful choice. If you choose to remain in dependency, you can be certain of these consequences:

- You will repeatedly find yourself at the mercy of people who attempt to control you, smother you, or abuse you.
- You will often feel out of control, and in danger of relapse.
- You will have difficulty making decisions, and be troubled with procrastination and bad choices.

- You will not feel good about yourself, your life, or your actions.
- You will not be able to distinguish healthy people from addictive/dependent people, or healthy love from code-pendency, and will repeatedly find yourself in destructive relationships.
- You will never be able to achieve your full potential in life, or set and accomplish your deepest personal goals.
- You will never know the true joy, happiness, and freedom from fear that are a result of learning to make your own autonomous choices, or the self-confidence that results when you know you can successfully rely on yourself.

When you finally accept that only you can make life better for you, and only you are responsible for your choices, you encounter the world from a new perspective: your view of yourself and everything around you completely changes. Instead of expecting others to take care of you, which keeps you powerless and dependent on them, you meet them as someone who expects to take care of yourself and who expects others to take care of themselves.

In a relationship, each of you remains independent and has the right to ask for what you want, the power to say yes or no, and the responsibility to make good decisions on your own behalf. This may sound less romantic than being taken care of, but it actually gives each of you the room you need to be fully yourselves, and makes your sharing free of painful, damaging *strings* or the weight of hidden dependency. This produces support and caring on a new level where neither of you is drained or deprived by the unmet dependent needs of the other. Instead, you look forward to sharing the pleasures and solving the problems of life together, as equals.

When you are fully autonomous and equal, you also gain the security of knowing that you are loved for yourself, for the unique person you are, with your talents, skills, feelings, successes, and shortcomings—not for how needy you are, or how much you can give, but because you are a delight and a joy to your lover, and your lover is an equal delight to you. The result is a *sustainable* relationship, with constantly renewable joy, sexual pleasure, satisfaction, and mutual regard.

The way that you relate to situations is also changed. You no longer see yourself as a helpless, hopeless victim of circumstances, but as a capable individual who encounters challenges and problems confident of your ability to meet them and make effective choices. You know you can rely on yourself to think clearly, and respond effectively and creatively to unforeseen circumstances.

THE SIX ELEMENTS OF EFFECTIVE CHOICE

To become fully autonomous, you must be capable of taking care of yourself effectively. Caring for yourself, and learning responsibility for managing your life, require making constant choices, some large, some small. The more effective your choices are, the more success, confidence, and self-respect you will experience.

There are six elements that constitute effective choice: 1) paying attention, 2) being creative, 3) evaluating options, 4) making a choice, 5) committing to your choice, and 6) adapting to the unexpected.

Paying attention means deliberately and consciously choosing to focus your awareness on what is going on inside and outside of you that can tell you when making a choice is necessary. Being creative means using a combination of your intuitive and practical thinking to develop options and solutions for handling your problems from which you can choose. Evaluating options means considering both short- and long-term probable results of each selection, and weighing them for effectiveness and possible drawbacks.

Based on these three preliminary steps, you then make the best choice you can. But, your work is not finished. Once a choice is made, you must commit to your choice and follow through on it. Then, even after commitment, your choice may not work out as you thought, because of circumstances beyond your control or events you did not foresee. So you must be capable of adapting to the unexpected, which includes coping with your surprise and disappointment and then overcoming any resistance this creates to making another choice.

HARRY

Harry, an autonomous person who pays attention, begins to notice (internal awareness) that he feels cramped and uncomfortable in his apartment, that (external awareness) he's making more money and can afford to move, and that his landlord is advertising the building for sale. So, he begins to search (being creative) for options: First, he does the "Reality/Fantasy" exercise (later in this chapter) to find out exactly how he wants to live; then, he looks in the right neighborhoods and the papers and lets friends know he wants to move. When he has enough options to choose from, he compares them against (evaluating options) what he wants, what he can afford, how close to work they are, and so on, until he knows which is his best bet. At this point the choice is obvious, and Harry decides (making a choice) he's going to put a deposit on the new place.

Now comes an unusual and crucial step. Harry talks it over with himself one last time: "Is this choice OK with me? Have I checked it out thoroughly enough? Do I understand the probable advantages and disadvantages? EVEN IF IT TURNS OUT I'M WRONG, CAN I ACCEPT THAT I MADE THE BEST DECISION I COULD? OK, I'LL STICK WITH MY DECISION." From this point on, all the possibilities have been discussed and agreed on, and Harry makes sure he doesn't allow himself to waffle, procrastinate, second-guess himself, scare himself, or doubt the move. He is committed to his choice. However, life is not predictable, and two months after Harry gets into his new apartment, he finds out that the city has declared his block to be a new civic center, and all residential buildings are being torn down. Harry is angry, life feels unfair, and he thinks he did all that work for nothing. He allows himself a while to feel this frustration and disappointment, releasing them in a healthy way by complaining to friends and calling the city to object.

Then he tells himself: "I still made a good decision, and there was no way I could have foreseen this. It's upsetting and unfair, but I have six months to enjoy this apartment before I have to move, and that's plenty of time to find an even better one. Besides, I may even get some compensation from the city for my inconvenience." He adapts to disappointment and is ready to make a new choice.

Paying Attention

In order to make effective choices, you have to pay attention to yourself and the world around you. By paying attention you will notice when stiuations calling for choice arise. Also, by paying attention you will notice the elements of the situation you need to know about to make an effective choice. Paying attention is a conscious choice in itself, a commitment to find a *new, more effective way* to think about events and ideas.

Think of any small child you know: whether their faces are dirty or they are upset, whether asleep, cuddly, playful, noisy, or angry, they are still lovable. When children are small, they have not yet completely learned to be self-conscious, ashamed, and wary of others. If you look at a photograph of yourself as a baby or a child of two or three, you will probably see an open, wide-eyed, curious person, who has not yet been frightened or damaged by the world, and your heart will go out to that child. You'll want to keep him or her safe and secure. A parent who wants to be responsible deliberately and consciously keeps his attention focused on the actions of his small child, anticipating her needs and her developing problems in order to take care of her and ensure her well-being. Similarly, if you want to take responsibility for yourself, you need to deliberately and consciously keep some of your attention focused on your actions in order to anticipate your needs and your developing problems.

This does not mean you must be perfectly aware and alert 100 percent of the time. No one can do that, because as human beings we get mentally fatigued and our minds need frequent rest. Also, when we're under stress, extra tired, anxious, or otherwise overloaded, our thinking ability is hampered. That's why we need to take breaks from paying attention—little breaks, such as meditation, naps, reading, television, or recreation, or larger breaks, such as vacations and days off—when we don't have to maintain as high a level of awareness. When you're relaxing on the beach, at home, or with friends, and there is nothing you need to accomplish at the moment and no problems facing you, mindlessness is fine, even healthy. It gives you a vacation from thinking, and refreshes your mental powers.

As long as you know how to pay attention when it's needed, you're OK. At times when you definitely do need to make important choices (when your health, safety, emotional well-being, financial security, or happiness are involved), when you are handling problems and setting goals, paying attention to both your internal feelings about what's going on and to the external conditions and factors that affect your decision allows you to be prepared with the most effective choice when the time to make it arrives.

In *Mindfulness,* Ellen Langer writes: "Mindful awareness of different options gives us greater control. This feeling of greater control, in turn, encourages us to be more mindful. Rather than being a chore, mindfulness engages us in a continuing momentum." In other words, mindfulness produces its own excitement. In fact, the human mind *thrives* on alertness. Langer reports that in experiments in which elderly people were asked to perform tasks that reminded them to pay attention and think, they actually stayed healthier and showed fewer signs of aging than other seniors.

Paying attention is to your mind what physical exercise is to your body. As you choose to pay attention more and more often, it becomes an easier and easier habit to maintain. Eventually, you find you pay attention to the world around you, and your inner world as well, almost all the time: you notice circumstances and situations that call for choices when they arise as well as the elements you need to base your choices upon.

Being Creative

To make effective choices you need to consider and imagine as many options for yourself as you can. This challenges your ability to be imaginative. Every new invention or idea is a result of rejecting the old, proven, conventional ways and taking a risk by trying something new. Creativity is connected to your ability to think *non*rationally, to fantasize, daydream, and envision, and is therefore more like play. Creativity, or being childlike, is often silly or nonsensical, and it can be irrepressible. You can block out your awareness of it, but you cannot stop doing it.

The exercises and magical tools you have been working with, by reactivating your ability to fantasize and use imagery, have already begun to release the pressure to be creative and remove the blockage. Through "playing" with these fantasies and images, and through using scenarios from your actual life in fantasies that you can alter at will, you can become aware of your creative thinking. You'll find that this familiarity with creative, nonrational thinking will be a powerful help when you need to come up with new ideas. With practice, you will be able to come up with at least five solutions or options whenever you are faced with any problem or choice.

No one needs to tell you precisely *how* to be creative, because creativity comes naturally to your childlike, subconscious mind. Small children do more creative thinking than any other kind, because everything in their environment is new and must be figured out through experimentation and guessing. They use fantasy and imagination much as you did in the magical tool exercises—to try out new ideas without having to take risks.

Evaluating Options

Once you have developed a number of options, it is time to evaluate them and to know which seems likely to be the most effective. For example, you may want to live in a $500,000 house, on a $30,000-per-year income. There are several possible ways to resolve the disparity, from finding a way to change your income to choosing a cheaper house. What usually works best, however, is to examine all the options you have been able to imagine and decide what is important for you.

You may want that house for status, because it's lovely to look at, because it's big enough for all your projects and friends, or because it overlooks the ocean. If you only require some of the components of the house—the ocean view, a front porch with columns, or more room than you have now—you may be able to get them elsewhere in your price range. If you want the prestige, maybe you can get some of that by being active in your community. If it has to be *that* house, in *that* area, maybe you can start your own business, or become a real estate agent, and find a way to afford it. In Harry's case, he checked his options against a list of requirements: Is it quiet enough, light and airy enough, close enough to work, within my price range, and so on.

Evaluating the options is not difficult if you are supportive of yourself in the process. As long as you remind yourself that you are smart enough to figure it out, and you deserve to have what you want, you'll be able to think clearly enough to do a proper evaluation. As the child of dysfunctional parents, you never learned how to evaluate options effectively and were taught you weren't smart enough or it was too difficult. As a result, you may be uncertain about what criteria to use in evaluating options. The following list of considerations might make it easier for you to feel confident that the evaluations you make are sound and healthy:

- Is it practical?
- If it doesn't seem practical, is there some part that is practical, or is there a way you could make it practical?
- What are the benefits?
- What are the drawbacks?
- Do you know the steps you have to follow to bring it about?
- How do the rewards if it is successful compare with the penalties if it goes wrong?
- Do you presently feel good about it?
- How does your inner child self feel about it?

- Does it make sense? Can you explain what you're doing clearly to someone else or on paper?
- Would you advise a friend to do it?

Making a Choice

Surprisingly enough, when you have covered the first three elements of effective choice making, actually making the choice becomes simple. Because you have sufficient information, and you've evaluated the realistic aspects of your options, one or two best choices will stand out. Only if you have a rigid, dependent definition of the "right" way to do things and are not open to considering new and different solutions will your choice seem limited or blocked (for example, if it's cheaper, faster, and less stressful to take the new rapid transit system to work, but you insist that, for prestige reasons, you have to drive in your Mercedes, your prejudice will prevent you from making the soundest, most effective choice).

Committing to Your Choice

After you've made your choice, you must commit to acting on it. No choice is really made until the commitment is made to it. Not making a commitment to your choice gives you the loopholes of procrastinating, wavering back and forth, or criticizing yourself endlessly about your choice. It is possible to focus endlessly on the potential what if's of making choices—"What if the roof falls in?" "What if I haven't thought of everything?" "What if I'm wrong?"—and never get to making any choice at all. If you do that, each decision becomes an invitation to an internal war of self-recrimination, argument, and doubt.

If you are from a dysfunctional family, committing to your decisions may be difficult at first because you were taught to fear mistakes and were led to believe your early decisions were disasters. In a dysfunctional environment, you get used to blame because when a decision goes wrong everyone accuses everyone else. Dysfunctional families focus more on who's at fault than on how to fix the problem.

When in the past you have made a decision, you probably have been unable to commit to it and wavered back and forth. You may have given yourself excuses ("I'm too stupid to make this decision by myself" or "I'll think about that tomorrow") to avoid the commitment. But you don't need to fear making a poor choice or one that doesn't work out as well as you hoped. Making mistakes is natural, and everybody does it. No one can know every factor before making a decision, sometimes you don't do all the preliminary research perfectly, or perhaps your mind loses focus and you don't make as effective a choice as you might. Yet once you have generated and researched options and evaluated them sensibly, there is no reason to be afraid of taking responsibility for your decision. Committing to your choice becomes easier when you have the confidence that you have thought it out as best you could, and that your choice was made as well as you could make it.

In order to commit to your choice, first check with yourself, as Harry did, to make sure "all of you" is in agreement with the decision, with no reservations. Using the "Negotiating Table" exercise from the previous chapter is a very effective way to make sure you are ready to commit to your decision without second-guessing yourself after the fact.

Committing to your choice means you can choose not to argue with yourself over it, not to doubt your judgment, and not to put off acting any longer. It means not blaming or accusing yourself if things go wrong, but rather focusing on how to fix the problem. Committing to your choice is the point at which you choose to stop focusing on solving the problem, and begin focusing on implementing your solution.

Adapting to the Unexpected

No matter how carefully you evaluated your options, or how satisfied and pleased you are with your choice at first, sometimes things don't work out—or you can even outgrow your old choices. If you find you've made a mistake, or an earlier choice no longer suits you, to effectively run your life you must be able to begin the whole process over again and make a new healthy choice in its stead.

None of us has total control over what happens in our lives. Other people can let you down, move away, or fall ill, or circumstances can change unexpectedly: your employer might lay you off because of a recession, or you might come into unexpected money, become ill, fall in love, or be offered a job opportunity you couldn't have anticipated. Often life thrusts choice on you when you are not expecting it, and you are forced to make choices you didn't anticipate.

Adaptability is the willingness to handle change, and choose again when our choices do not work out, without wasting a lot of time and energy in resistance or resentment. Once you have made a commitment to a choice you like, being faced with the need to change it is disappointing. In addition, sudden, unanticipated change that you did not initiate through your own choosing (particularly if the change is unpleasant or creates difficulty) can produce some resistance and resentment. These feelings can be coped with, using much the same techniques as you have learned to help you cope with the disappointment of failure at risk taking.

When failed or forced choices make you feel frustrated, angry, resentful, or disappointed, simply let your inner self discharge the feeling (use the "Finding the Trouble Spot" exercise to handle your feelings), acknowledge it, and agree that it makes sense to have that reaction. Do this until the feeling subsides or feels satisfied. If your disappointment is great (such as a death or major tragedy), you can use the "Discharging Your Feelings" technique in chapter 7 to help you cope.

Once you have fully acknowledged the feeling, remind yourself that you believed in the choice when you made it, and that you are capable of making another choice. Now, look for any "silver linings" in the change, such as Harry seeing the possibility that he would be reimbursed by the city, or that he would find an even better apartment.

The combination of acknowledging your feelings, supporting yourself unconditionally, and looking for silver linings will help you feel more hopeful, and generate the energy you need to begin the process of making another, more effective choice.

THE IMPORTANCE OF MAKING CHOICES

Accepting full responsibility for your life means learning to make careful, effective choices. When you make your own choices, you are saying that you are important enough to you to care what happens. Every thoughtful choice you make betters your life and affirms that you feel your worth, and demonstrates that you care enough to think carefully about what affects you. In taking responsibility for your life, by your willingness to pay attention to the need to make choices, by creating and evaluating options, by making the choice, by committing to it, and by adapting to the unexpected, you develop the skills to take care of yourself in any and all circumstances—you no longer need to depend on anyone else to help but *you*.

You now have the tool to enable you to take charge of your own life and circumstances. This makes being responsible for yourself possible, and also gives you the opportunity to arrange your life and circumstances to suit your individual, unique needs. You can now choose, perhaps for the first time in your life, how your life will be.

No longer do you have to do things you don't want to do because your dependency on someone or something else demands it. Instead, you are able to do what pleases you, and you will find that you feel more generous toward others. You will give to them or do things for them because you *want* to, because it makes you happy to make them happy. You will be able to choose to be around people who treat you with respect and kindness, and who are enthusiastic about you. You will begin to have an autonomous life, designed and planned to enhance your own well-being and satisfaction, as well as to enjoy the friendship of others.

This autonomy produces its own dilemmas, poetically described by Rev. Virginia Greeley:

Choices

The choice comes not one time—or two
but every day, in all I do.
Every day when I awake

I choose the prize—and what's at stake.
Then every moment through the day
I choose again, what games I'll play.
No choice is really a wrong turn
it might just bring me more to learn.
Voices speaking at each ear
which one will I choose to hear?
First one speaks and then the next
I could choose to be perplexed!
But inbetween is not much fun
besides, it leaves nowhere to run.
Will I stick with pain and fear
and stagger through each passing year?
Or will I dare to make the choice
and listen to the other voice?
I'm the one who must decide
that's one choice I cannot hide.
No one else can choose for me
what I do and who I'll be.
So every moment every day
I must choose again my way.
Will I stay with fear and doubt
or will I take the other route?
The route which says that I'm OK
the I can do great things today.
Great things for me may be no more
than going out my own front door!
But day by day, and choice by choice
I strengthen the supportive voice.
It really is a daily chore
to get up, and choose once more.

By making effective choices in your daily life, you can learn new skills and new ways of being. When you're open to learning—not criticizing yourself for the old methods, but making corrections where necessary—a world of new ideas opens up. Friends, books, workshops, and classes can provide new ideas about functioning successfully in business, relationships, and everyday life. All these sources can provide options (a better way to save money, a new recipe, a new way of evaluating your options), but *you* are the one who gets to make the final choices.

One of the problems with facing the unlimited new options that your effective choice making and autonomous thinking will open up is that some of these new alternatives will be good, and some will be bad, for you.

In order to know what new options are good for you, you apply your system for effective choice: experiment to find new options, think and evaluate, and choose. Whose ideas suit you best? Which methods, if applied in your own life, will be most effective?

The ability to choose well is perhaps the most important difference between dependency and autonomy. Being able to make self-aware and effective choices also frees you from the limits of "What will people think?" and makes what *you* think more important. Because you have learned to pay attention, you no longer need to depend on what others think to know your decisions are as sound as they can be.

Being able to think for yourself in this way is one of the great gifts of autonomy. It means that your life becomes undeniably *yours*—you are the one responsible force behind it. Creative thinking is one of the most enjoyable talents of your magical, childlike mind. It's fun! As Peter, a twenty-two-year-old who learned autonomous thinking, said, "This is playing 'like the big kids'—I experience great glee in challenging popular views of 'the way it is' and reexamining the facts for myself. Finally, I feel competent and grown up."

MEETING YOUR RESISTANCE TO INNER CHANGE

You may find yourself resisting your own autonomous thinking because it creates an enormous change and disruption in your belief system and life-style. When you are operating your life from dependency, everything you do—your work, family, friends, and intimate relationships—is based on the old helpless, hopeless addictive feelings. Making the inner change to autonomy and high self-esteem changes the basis of these same things. Family relationships that were based on guilt and duty begin to change, and after everyone is reassured that they can be loved for who they really are, become more open and honest. Social relationships that were based on superficial facades or false images crumble, and you begin to let your real self show, which gives you a stronger, more independent image. Intimate relationships based on dishonesty and withholding, with both partners struggling for control, become based on mutual respect, love, and negotiation.

These changes are uncomfortable because they are unfamiliar. They are somewhat frightening because each change represents a risk: you cannot predict the outcome, and you will be presented with new situations about which you must then make effective choices. Sometimes you will fail, or be disappointed.

If you grew up in a dysfunctional family and were prevented from learning risk-taking skills, your child self will find these changes scary, because he or she will not yet trust that you can solve all the problems that may arise, make effective choices, or handle failure and disappointment. Your child self is still afraid, and dependent on you now, and wants someone to "make it better" and to tell it what to do. However, you, as an adult, *are* capable of taking risks, solving problems, correcting mistakes, and handling your feelings. You can use all the skills and exercises you are learning to handle problems as they arise, and also calm, comfort, and reassure your child self.

Change requires us all to take risks; there is no way to guarantee that the outcome will be what we want it to be. However, as you learn to think more autonomously, you'll see that this new way of thinking allows you to evaluate the risks and anticipate the outcome with a high degree of accuracy. Autonomous thinking actually makes risk taking far less risky because you make far more effective choices than when you avoid them or look to others to tell you what to choose.

If you frighten yourself or discourage yourself in advance,

by telling yourself you can't handle change, or won't like it, or if you forget to care for your child self, your adaptation to the change will be much harder. The truth is, that you have been facing change all your life, no matter how hard you tried to resist it or block it out with addictive behavior. Resisting change is what creates chaos, because when you resist it you cannot be aware of it enough to make effective decisions about your changes; so you wind up having things change on you without your control or participation.

Change is a basic fact of life. We grow older, seasons come and go, people move away, change their minds, or die, and the circumstances we live in are constantly in flux. Once your resistance to autonomous thinking is resolved, you'll find the experience of change becomes exciting and exhilarating, and you'll look forward to it.

MEETING CHALLENGES FROM OTHERS

Once you have broken through your own internal resistance to autonomous thought and begin to express your individuality, you will probably encounter some external resistance from some of those around you. People with sufficient self-esteem of their own will realize how positive your changes are, and encourage and applaud you; but dysfunctional, dependent people will often challenge, test, or even attack those they see as more independent or stronger.

People who are close to you form a type of "family system." That is, close friends, lovers, and sometimes even business associates (if you work very closely together, or have been working together for a long time, or work for a small company) act somewhat like family members and duplicate old family patterns, even if you are not related. Dependent people are threatened by independent behavior because it jeopardizes the entire family system, where each person depends on the other's dependence to keep the family together. In other words, such a family is based on the belief that if you don't *need* one another to function in life, why would you stay together? Anything that threatens this neediness feels dangerous, so sometimes they will escalate their needy, critical, and/or abusive behavior to try to eliminate the threat that you will become independent and abandon them. Thus, dysfunctional family members create and maintain dependency by attacking behaviors that appear to be independent. As you become more autonomous and learn to think for yourself you come into conflict with those who _depend on your dependency,_ and also with society's prejudices.

Most people, especially if they have dependency problems, are upset by change, and try to resist it. People who are insecure and believe they are unworthy of being loved unless it's based on dependency become fearful when someone they care about becomes independent. As you change your behavior, your friends, family, and co-workers may react with criticism or fear, because at first all they can see is that you're different. It will take them a while to see that the difference is an improvement. When you get negative reactions from your friends and others, they may invoke old, childhood memories of being criticized, attacked, abused, or rejected by your dysfunctional family.

SUZANNE

Suzanne, a twenty-seven-year-old legal secretary who was recovering from bulimia and compulsive overeating, used to take her father (a Fundamentalist Christian alcoholic who had neglected her as a child) out to lunch every week. At one lunch, when he was complaining about how big a problem he had with drinking, she suggested that the same therapy that had helped her might help him. He shocked her by replying, "If therapy turned me into an unloving person, like you are, I don't want any part of it." Suzanne was understandably upset and hurt by this remark. In her therapy session, she was able to see that her father was just frightened at the thought of facing his problems, and since he knew being loving was important to her, he attacked what he instinctively knew was a tender spot to distract her from his problem. Using Magical Tool 3: Self-Love, Suzanne evaluated her own behavior, decided that she was a loving, caring person, and was able to recover her inner calm. By the next time she saw her father, she knew that if he was mean, she would tell him he wasn't allowed to talk to her like that. But in his irresponsible way, he had forgotten his earlier remark.

As a person who grew up in a dysfunctional family, you've been dependent on the approval of others, so you may find these negative reactions frightening or upsetting. Keep in mind that no matter how hard you try, your choices and actions can never be approved of by everyone, all the time. Wanting constant approval from everyone is just a sign that you are experiencing some last vestiges of dependent behavior. The price you pay for trying to please everyone is tremendous—a loss of self-esteem, being out of control, emotional pain, uncertainty, and, eventually, return to dependent, destructive behavior.

One of the tasks you undertake when you accept responsibility for yourself and choose autonomus, independent living is to nurture and protect your new attitudes and abilities until you grow strong enough to withstand a more confrontive environment. By reinforcing and supporting your autonomous thinking in this way, you become your own sponsor (parent, adult, guardian) and no longer remain dependent on a group, friend, lover, recovery sponsor, or relative to support and encourage you. You are still free to discuss events and ideas with others, but evaluating them yourself ensures that you can listen to advice autonomously and choose to use it or ignore it.

Healthy human beings have to learn to live with the disapproval of others. In order to be fully yourself, to operate at your full potential, you must learn to be comfortable with occasionally being the center of both positive and negative attention from others. If your self-esteem doesn't feel strong enough to withstand the negative reaction of those who are threatened by specialness, you may be tempted to give in and try to stifle your individuality.

However, through the work you did in the previous chapters, you've already begun to handle this problem. By using your Magical Tool 5: Environment, you can choose to surround yourself with people who will support your autonomy, individuality, effective choices, and autonomous thinking. Also, because you have worked to resolve your internal war, and learned to use the Magical Tool 3: Self-Love, like Suzanne, you have created internal safety for yourself from those who do attack or criticize or disapprove of you. Because you are your own friend, and know how to support and comfort yourself, you can recover from others' disapproval if they criticize you. With sufficient internal support, and an independent group of friends who will help you encourage yourself, you will easily be able to withstand the occasional frightened, dependent person you encounter who attempts to criticize or devalue you.

Don't get upset over these attacks, or let them divert you or drop your commitment to your choices. *You* are the one who is responsible for your life, and the one who has to live it. Don't take attacks personally either, because they are based on the subconscious fears and childlike magical thinking of people who have not yet taken control of their inner, dependent beliefs and fears.

CHALLENGING YOUR RECOVERY GROUP

As you complete these final chapters and move into fuller autonomy, you may find you no longer need to depend on your recovery group to be your support system. Although you may still *choose* to maintain friendships you began in your group, or choose to sponsor others or continue to be involved at your discretion (going back once in a while as you want to), you'll find that you possess all the skills and abilities necessary to make clear, effective choices about your own life, and about what behaviors are right for you, independent of the opinions of the group or its members. Instead of relying on the group or a sponsor to be responsible for, think for, and take care of you, you are now able to rely on yourself.

When this happens, you may find your perceptions of and reactions to your recovery group and its members changing significantly, and theirs to you. In the beginning, you needed them to model healthier, nonaddictive behavior, and many of them were much farther along in recovery than you were. Now, you may begin to see flaws and weaknesses you never noticed before. You may discover that many, though they have stopped their addiction and been able to remain in recovery, are still caught up in dependent attitudes and addictive behavior. At first, you may feel critical of them, or upset that your relationships are changing, but instead of focusing on the negative possibilities, you can also use this as evidence that you are growing and changing, and increasing your own possibilities for satisfaction and happiness by learning to take care of yourself.

Dependent, fearful members may also react negatively toward you, and perceive your ability to remain recovered and free of addictive behavior without the group as a threat because the program has taught them to perceive it so. You'll find that if you don't react negatively, but stay calm and reassure them that you're doing well, most of them will relax.

PAM

Pam B., a successful businesswoman in her thirties who had been in sobriety for several years and had done her work on her feelings and learned autonomy in therapy, stopped calling her sponsor very often and only attended meetings occasionally, as she wanted to. One day, her sponsor called her up, and, in an angry manner, began giving her orders: "You're risking a relapse. You must attend at least three meetings a week. You must call me every day." Pam calmly said, "I'm sorry, you've helped me a lot as my sponsor, and I should have told you how well I am doing. My life is going well, I have no temptation to drink, my job is great, and I feel fine. What works for me is going to an occasional meeting, but I don't need such regular attendance." Pam got no more trouble from her sponsor, and a few months later, at a meeting, her sponsor hugged her and congratulated her on her success.

You may also find some group members looking up to you to model autonomous, healthy behavior for them. As this is probably your first experience at being viewed as a role model, you may find it surprisingly uncomfortable. Being in the spotlight can be scary for people who grew up dependent, because in a dysfunctional family environment being the focus of attention often means being criticized, made to feel guilty, belittled, or punished. But don't be afraid; it's good for you and you deserve it.

AUTONOMOUS THINKING AND INDIVIDUALITY

When we take responsibility for ourselves and begin to think for ourselves, we begin to discover our own individuality. Once your child self is reassured, and trusts you to care for him or her as your parents did not, and once you gain the necessary practice of your effective choice skills, and make the commitment to being responsible for your own life, an interesting thing happens. By taking care of yourself completely, and creating internal and external support for yourself and your individuality, you will provide your child self with the secure base he or she needs to blossom and grow, and to express what he or she has been longing to express all your life—your own special, inner, individual self.

As you get to know this previously hidden part of yourself,

the part that does not depend on others for approval or acceptance, what you will discover is your true individuality. As this response rises from within you, you will begin to look around with a new sparkle in your eye, a creative individual approach, a way of looking at the world, life, and other people that you've never seen before. Both your secure and loved inner child self and your competent and effective adult self will be facing life together, as a team. The adult you, by using clear thinking and effective choice, provides the safety the child in you needs to take risks, experiment, and express himself. Your child self will keep the adult open to creative, new ideas, and aware of your feelings and reactions. The combination of this team—and the cooperation between the child's fantastic, magical thinking and the adult's rational, practical thinking—will allow your individuality to begin to express itself, in a way that is attractive to others and productive for you.

PERRY

Perry, a forty-five-year-old computer programmer, was faced with the need to make some career changes. He felt paralyzed—although he knew what he should do, he was unable to begin. Perry was terribly afraid of any new, untried situations. When his fear and the resulting helplessness were examined in therapy, a memory arose: At eleven years old, he took ballroom dancing and deportment lessons, which he usually enjoyed. One day, proper introductions were taught. The boys were to say: "Hi, my name is _____, would you like to dance?" When his turn came, he said "Hello, my name is Perry . . ." and the eighty children in the hall broke out in derisive laughter because he did not say "Hi." Perry was humiliated. Although he admitted he enjoyed the classes when he got there, he resisted going, and eventually stopped. The possibility that he might be laughed at was too terrifying. Perry realized it was this terror that was stopping him from searching for a new job. Using

"Time Travel," Perry went back to that scene, and adult Perry told child Perry (and the whole class) that saying "Hello" was not only acceptable, it was admirable, because little Perry had taken the lesson and individualized it. Once that early scene was resolved, Perry's resistance to meeting new people and trying new situations faded, and he was able to make his career change.

You are displaying your individuality when you take an idea or event and place your own unique stamp on it. You are making your own choices and displaying your individuality when you have satisfying relationships that are quite different in form from your parents' marriage, or from those of your friends. You may, for example, prefer to live separately, although you are in a committed, monogamous partnership, or you may be more conservative and traditional in your relationship than your friends are.

You are being an individual when your work is satisfying, even though it may be different from what your parents and friends think you should do. You might give up a job they approve of for something you love doing. You are an individual when you have friends who enhance your life, and to whom you can say no if they tempt you to do something you think is not good for you. Your friends might be an unusual mix of people, different from your family.

You are expressing your true individuality when you eat, wear, and do what is right for you, regardless of the fads and trends of the day. When your home suits you well, and you enjoy being there, its decor reflects your own individual taste (perhaps combined with that of a partner). As an individual, you get to express yourself as you wish. If you have a talent (such as art, acting, sports, writing, public speaking, caring for pets, crafts, or cooking) you make room for it in your life.

To stimulate your individual thinking, try this mini-exercise:

EXERCISE
TAPPING YOUR INDIVIDUALITY

1. *Ask your own opinion.* At frequent intervals (about five times a day) during your regular work day, ask yourself: "What do *I* think about this? Do I like it? Does it make sense to me? Do I agree or disagree with the others? If I had unlimited power, what would I do?" By doing this, you'll get used to asking *your own opinion* of ideas and events.

2. *Listen to the answer.* Listen to your opinions as you would to the ideas of a respected friend. Consider them, weigh them, and even discuss them with yourself from time to time. Allow them to influence your daily thought. If you feel, for example, that your work is not satisfying enough, just accept and allow that feeling to be there, and it will eventually create a need to act, and many exciting ideas for how to act. There is no need to act on your ideas yet, for now you're just practicing the thinking.

3. *Repeat to make decision making easier.* After you practice asking your own opinion faithfully for a few weeks, it will become automatic to have personal opinions about everything around you. If you don't pressure yourself about your ideas, but let them incubate at their own pace, after a while knowing your own opinion will have a profound but gradual effect on what you do and how you act. Activating your individual thinking ability will gradually increase your options and choices, and make decision making faster and easier.

When you're faced with a choice you have to make, or you have a new idea you'd like to try, you can use two different types of thinking—subconscious, creative, childlike fantasy, and rational, practical adult evaluation—together, to develop creative and effective choices. Your child, magical mind has feelings, intuition, and the creative ability to fantasize about options. Your adult, rational mind has life experience, wisdom, and the ability to evaluate your ideas for practicality. Using them both in coop-eration will make sure you're being as creative as possible, imag-ing the largest number of options, yet make sure they are con-sidered in a logical, practical manner.

As an illustration of this, recall the example of Harry, who was trying to decide if he wanted to move.

EXERCISE
REALITY-FANTASY DIALOGUE

1. *Use your favorite method of dialogue.* Select a fa-vorite form of adult/child or rational/subconscious dialogue (time travel, trouble spot, adult-child dialogue, inner voices) to use for discussing a problem or new idea with yourself. *Harry used an adult-child dialogue.*

2. *Fantasize.* Your subconscious, childlike mind is cre-ative and fantastic—new ideas abound, without constraint. Let yourself freely fantasize about what you would like to have happen. Be sure you don't get practical at this point, because that cuts off the creative flow—it's OK if your fan-tasies aren't possible, they'll still contain usable ideas, and some new things your practical side wouldn't think of. Allow your creative self to be as silly, whimsical, impractical, or fantastic as it wants to be. *Harry's child, when asked to think about where he wanted to live, came up with the following ideas: Moving is scary, I want to stay here. I want to live in a castle. I want to live in Paris. I want to go live in the woods.*

3. *Begin a dialogue about the fantasy.* Begin a di-alogue between your creative, child mind, and the more rational, adult mind. Remember, this is not a fight, an argu-ment, or a contest. It is a brainstorming and problem-solving session. Make sure both aspects of your thinking show inter-est in the other's ideas, and keep the dialogue focused on solutions. If you don't understand an idea, ask a question—don't criticize. For instance, if you're facing a decision about moving, your dialogue might sound something like this:

HARRY: What do you want to do about moving?

CHILD: I don't want to move. I want to stay here forever.

HARRY: Well, I thought you wanted more room, and a place for a cat.

CHILD: You're right! I do. Let's move to a castle.

HARRY: What do you like about a castle? Aren't they cold and drafty?

CHILD: A warm castle. I want lots of space, and a place to be alone. Like in a tower room.

HARRY: Oh, I see. How about an extra bedroom with windows and maybe lots of cupboards and closets?

CHILD: Yeah! That's it. And a moat.

HARRY: A moat?

CHILD: Yeah, water for me to play in.

HARRY: Oh, I see. How about a hot tub or a big bathtub?

CHILD: Yeah! And I want to live in the woods.

HARRY: In the woods? Why?

CHILD: Cuz I want trees and grass and maybe even a dog.

HARRY: Oh, I see. Would a place near work with lots of trees and grass be okay? And can we try having a cat, before we decide about the dog?

CHILD: Okay, if we can see about a dog later.

This dialogue may sound a little trivial, but Harry is really uncovering longings he has had for more space, contact with water, more green surroundings, and a cat, all of which are possible to realize in practical terms if not in the child's fantastic ideal. With information such as this, flowing uncensored from the child and translated into practical terms by the adult, Harry can know what kind of home would really feel like his "castle."

4. *Translate child dialogue into adult terms.* After you have discussed the idea for a while, use your adult, rational thinking ability to translate from childlike magical thinking into real-world terms, remembering that your child mind sees everything in magical, exaggerated, and fantastic ways. To Harry's child mind, a home with a whole extra room *would* seem as big as a castle, and a nice, big bathtub or a hot tub *could* become a moat. Harry could also check with his child mind and see if living by a beach or a lake would meet his wish to play in water.

5. *Write down translated ideas, and review.* When you have some ideas both your creative side and your practical side can agree on, summarize them in writing and let them sit for a few moments, or even a day, to get some perspective and then review them. Use "Playing Chess" (next exercise) or the considerations in the Evaluating Options section to help make your decision. You'll like your final decision better if both sides of you have participated, and you'll feel more certain you made the right move. *When Harry went apartment hunting he kept his inner child wishes in mind, and he recognized the light, airy, large apartment, in a garden complex, with a pool and a big Jacuzzi bathtub, the minute he saw it. Since the rent was within his budget, he took it right away.*

6. *For big decisions, repeat several times.* If you're facing a momentous decision, such as health issues, a big job move, or a relationship commitment, doing this exercise several times will help reassure you that your decision is sound, and will build self-confidence.

The next exercise will help you further evaluate options by teaching you how to look ahead for possible consequences and outcomes. Like a chess master, you can use foresight in your own life to evaluate the results of decisions before you make them. The great masters of chess are masters because they, too, have developed this ability to look at the chessboard, work out in advance every possible move that might be made, and then consider all the possible consequences.

EXERCISE
PLAYING CHESS

1. *Think creatively and fantasize.* Visualize yourself (Magical Tool 4: Self-Image) as a chess master, using your life as the board. Whenever you're facing a choice or decision, take the time to visualize (Magical Tool 2) about each option available. Suppose you have two job offers. Before deciding, take the time to gather as much information as you can about each job, then try to picture what the work and the job environment would be like. Imagine getting up in the morning, going to work, interacting with the people there, being in the work environment, doing your assigned tasks. Imagine the pluses of the job. Imagine the drawbacks. Do this with each possible choice, creating as complete an image as you can. Remember to consider the long-term possibilities as well as the immediate ones.

2. *Evaluate the possible choices.* As if you were a friend whose well-being and happiness you care about, ask yourself questions to learn how you feel about each choice (Magical Tool 3: Self-Love). If it's a new job, your questions might be: Is the drive too long? How about your potential co-workers, the company atmosphere, the work itself? Is this a job you could do for a long time, or is this one that would be difficult to sustain?

3. *Sort and evaluate your choices.* If the choices you have to make are many or complicated, use what you know about your learning style to help you: If you're auditory, try discussing it with a friend, talking out loud to yourself about it, or writing a page about each option and reading them out loud. If you're visual, you might find that arranging your

list of pros and cons into two columns on a page makes seeing which one is better much easier. If you're tactile, try acting out going to work, and doing the job, to see how it feels.

4. *Get expert advice.* To verify the reality of your ideal images, and provide environmental support (Magical Tool 5) for your search, locate some real experts who have first-hand knowledge about the information you are seeking. If it's a job search, find people who worked for that company, or in that field, and ask them what you should look for. When you go in for an interview, instead of just letting the interviewer question you, have some questions ready that will help you make your choice. You might ask: Is there smoking in the office? What is the policy about sick days, holidays, and vacations? What are the opportunities for promotion? Is the company financially stable? What is the retirement plan or health insurance?

5. *Allow yourself ample time.* Perhaps most important, allow enough time to be able to *make* a choice. Waiting until the last moment to make decisions deprives you of the opportunity to find out what your options are, or to gather sufficient information to think about them. The whole point of "Playing Chess" is to take the time to work out and con-sider all the possibilities, which gives you more autonomous control and a better chance to make a great choice. In the example of a job, don't wait until you can't stand your old job a minute longer, or until unemployment is about to run out, and then take the first thing you can get. Begin *early* to look and compare, to give yourself time to choose, so you can find a job that is ideal. Playing chess works wonders in relationships, too.

MOLLY

Molly, a thirty-seven-year-old professional woman, explains how it affected hers: "Since learning to 'play chess' I find that when I meet someone new, I think: How would we be together? What kind of a friend or mate would this person be? Can I trust them? What would it be like to spend a lot of time with this person? Where are we likely to have problems? Where would we agree? Am I comfortable introducing him or her to my family and friends? It makes a huge difference in who I decide to spend more time with. For the first time in my life, I feel like I'm making a choice about my companions."

Autonomy is also called self-governing. Part of a governor's job is to analyze problems, develop options, decide among them, and put them into effect. A governor is responsible for taking care of a state the way you are responsible for taking care of yourself—you both try to use your resources to best advantage, and foresee problems, and prevent them if possible. To accomplish this, a governor spends time before an election focusing on the current problems and designing a campaign platform—a proposal of solutions. Similarly, the following exercise will help you make and define the choice to be responsible for your life—it contains a ceremony for committing to that responsibility.

EXERCISE
ELECTION FOR SELF-GOVERNOR

1. *Analyze the situation.* As candidate for self-governor, analyze where your life needs new management, more effective or efficient techniques, and damage control. View your life-style as though you were just about to take over, and decide where you would like to change it. For example, you might feel that your budget is seriously out of balance, or you might think your personal health and welfare (diet, exercise, dental care) are not as well managed as they might be.

2. *Propose some solutions.* Then, propose a "platform"—a plan, which may encompass a few months or a few years, for improving the governing of your life. Consider proposing

- an economic platform: if your budget is in trouble, propose some budget cuts, or a new source of income.
- a social welfare platform: for increasing your circle of healthy friends, or bringing your social life into balance.
- a health and well being platform: to improve your physical condition, adjust your eating habits, or take care of neglected doctor or dentist appointments.
- an environmental platform: to improve your surroundings, your house and/or yard, to get involved in more environmentally aware activities, or to surround yourself with healthier people.
- a mental and spiritual health platform: to take classes, try a new meditation, read some appropriate self-help books, or have stimulating and thoughtful discussions.

3. *Put your platform in writing.* When you have a plan for each item, write out your entire platforms ("As governor of my life, I will make the following changes:") and then post them where you will see them on a daily basis (Magical Tool 6: Repetition). After your election (see next step) do your best to keep your campaign promises.

4. *Make a commitment.* Design a simple ceremony to approve your platform, elect yourself governor, and induct yourself into control of your life. This ceremony will add power to your commitment by invoking your senses and using imagery to speak directly to your child mind. Make it a ceremony that is meaningful to you, and take your promise to govern seriously—giving up all dependence on anyone or anything else to do it for you. This is your official entry into autonomy. For example, you might engage sight by having a flag or campaign posters and touch by putting your hand on a symbolic object, such as a Bible or the AA *Big Book,* and promising to do your best to carry out your

platform or program. To engage your sense of hearing, you might play a tape of some dramatic music, such as "Pomp and Circumstance" or a Sousa march. The more your ceremony engages your feelings, and stirs you, the more powerful it is to your child self, or subconscious mind.

5. *Review your performance.* Periodically, every six months or once a year, check your progress against your campaign platform to see how you're doing. If your platform needs changing, or part of it is not working out as you hoped, as reigning governor you can propose new solutions by going back to steps 1 and 2.

This next exercise will help you learn to adapt and be flexible whenever you're trying to accept a change that you didn't choose or plans you had that fell through, or when you become aware of any rigid attitude you'd like to eliminate.

EXERCISE
ADAPTABILITY

1. *Choose a method for inner dialogue.* Pick your favorite of the "Trouble Spot," "Time Travel," "Negotiating Table," or "Adult-Child Dialogue" exercises and use it to discuss the upcoming change or the old, rigid belief with yourself and find out what your feelings are.

2. *Give yourself a chance to complain.* If you're facing a change, voluntary or not, you may have some resistance to it. If you're challenging an old, rigid belief, you will have some objections to changing it. Allow yourself some time to complain and be unhappy about the change. Express as many of the negative feelings and thoughts as possible, either verbally or on paper.

3. *Evaluate your complaints.* Allow yourself some time to consider the points you made in your complaining. Is there anything that you can do differently? Do you want to?

Have you made all the choices you can? Are you thinking clearly about the problem? Are you angry at anyone specifically? Are you resisting unnecessarily? If you have a choice, do you still want to change things? If you don't have a choice, can you see some alternatives? Do your options look different to you now?

4. *Befriend yourself to build trust.* Discuss the problem with yourself as helpfully as you would with another friend. Brainstorm for ideas, realistic or even silly, about what you could do to make things better. For example:

- I could move to Timbuktu and avoid the whole thing.
- I could talk to Harry and see if this is really necessary.
- I could ask Martha to help.
- I could find a genie and have him make my wish come true.
- I could win millions in the lottery and not have to worry about it.
- I could come up with three other plans, present them to my boss, and maybe get him to change his mind.

5. *Play chess.* Do whatever you can to check the facts about this change. Use "Playing Chess" and consider all the possibilities.

6. *Review and decide.* Once you've expressed your anger and disappointment, evaluated your feelings, brainstormed ideas, and checked the facts, you will be feeling much more in charge of yourself and this change. Review what you've discovered and make some decisions.

7. *Sell yourself on your new idea.* Once you've decided how much of the change is really necessary, pretend it's your own idea and sell it to yourself. Think of all the possible great outcomes of the change. Consider what you will learn from it. Figure out how you can maximize the benefits of making the change. When you've convinced yourself, make a commitment to your plan.

8. *Post and follow your plan.* Draw up a plan for making the best possible results come out of this change. Put the

plan where you can see it and read it every day (Magical Tool 6). Do your best to follow the plan when the change is made.

Thinking autonomously sheds new light on your life, including your relationships. Once you know how to think independently, you are freed from any need to be dependent. Even if you need someone's help, you can clearly consider all your options, decide on the most creative solution possible, and arrange to get the help you need on a clear, mutually satisfactory, independent basis. Remember, it's your choice.

CHAPTER 7

Autonomous Loving: Creating Healthy Relationships

The more whole you are, the more you can bring to a relationship. When you attempt to have the relationship fill in the gaps and incomplete places inside you, you are bound to become frustrated. . . . Taking time to nurture yourself is an essential ingredient in the nurturing of your couplehood.

DAVID GERSHON AND GAIL STRAUB

One reason it is so hard for us to free ourselves from dependent attitudes and behaviors in relationships is that almost every model and concept of relationships we have ever known is based on the ideal that the other person we love is supposed to take care of us, to "make it better" for us. Even after learning to take responsibility for our lives and to make more effective choices, and finding we can successfully handle most situations autonomously, when it comes to relationships (particularly intimate relationships) we can still find ourselves caught up frequently in our old dysfunctional destructive and dependent attitudes and behaviors.

We may find ourselves inexplicably obsessing on someone who isn't available or interested, or even feeling so needy or helpless that we are unable to object to being criticized, abused, or degraded. This behavior is a result of our being bombarded with images that imply love and dependency are the same thing: lovers should depend on each other to supply their needs, take care of them, and "make it better"; they should *need* each other ("You are my happiness," "I'd die without you"); and they are incomplete without each other and the two should "become one"—losing their individual personalities, friends, interests, and opinions in the process.

This dependent, dysfunctional image of love has been reinforced by generations of songs, poetry, plays, books, movies, and television soap operas—from *Romeo and Juliet* to *Dynasty* and *Twin Peaks*—that have celebrated a dependent model of romantic relationships emphasizing neediness, desperation, and the idea that only love (from a perfect substitute parent) can make life better. The ideal lover is supposed to love us no matter how unreasonable we are, always be there when we want or need them, always know exactly how to soothe our hurts, always know (and be prepared to give us) precisely what we want (even if we're not sure ourselves), and put our needs before his or her own needs. Dependent people in relationships are like the unsocialized, dependent infant who wants what he or she wants when she or he wants it, with no return offered, and they experience rage and hurt (like the red-faced, bawling infant) when their needs aren't met.

This "romantic" image of love is really a continuation of the search for a perfect parent to "make it all better." The problem with it is that it is based on powerlessness and helplessness. In this romantic image, you have to give up your power to take care of yourself in order to be taken care of, or to take care of someone else. This dependency-based romantic image, although it seems exciting and fulfilling at first, is not sustainable. The relationship cannot flourish. Since no one else can ever care for you as well as you can yourself (he can't know your needs and wants as well as you do, he can't tell what his caretaking feels like to you, and he also has his hands full with his own needs), one or both of you will wind up feeling cheated, used, neglected, unloved, and generally dissatisfied. Dependency creates dysfunctional relationships, in which the ground rules are:

you can't talk about it (it might upset the other person); it's hopeless (since you can't talk about it, you can't solve it together); and we're both helpless (we can't control our own behavior or outbursts of anger, or make effective choices).

Dysfunctional relationships happen because your first experience (and basic model) of intimate relationships was with parents who "made it better" and took care of you as a child (and perhaps did not encourage you to become self-sufficient and autonomous), or with parents who were *not* fully there to take care of you (as you felt they should be). Even the best parent/child relationship is unbalanced, with the parent having all the power of experience and ability and the child being dependent on the parent for survival. Because of this pattern, you either assume that there will always be someone there to take care of you and make life better, or you look to replace the care you never got and make the pain of neglect or abuse go away. Although your adult mind may outgrow this belief and know better, your subconscious child mind does not. When this happens, you unconsciously expect that whoever you fall in love with will be an ideal parent—just as your real parent was, or should have been.

On the surface, your adult, rational mind is looking for someone you can enjoy and have fun with, but secretly, the dependent, wounded, subconscious inner child mind is searching for a substitute, for the parent you never had, someone who will take care of you, make your old wounds better, care about your feelings, and accept you for who you are. If you come from a dysfunctional family where you suffered rejection or abandonment at an early age, when you begin to search for a romantic partner, all too often you find a substitute parent who is *too much* like the real parent who let you down, and you wind up repeating the old, subconscious patterns.

WARREN

Warren, thirty-four, a computer programmer, came into my office very upset about his relationship. He had grown up in a family where his father was alcoholic and abusive and his mother was given to uncontrollable rages, which had nothing to do with his good or bad behavior, but which he and his sister received the brunt of. Warren had a lover who, after a few months of happiness (right after they moved in together), became angry and abusive, punching holes in the walls, and threatening Warren. Although the lover was male, Warren realized that he had wound up in a relationship with someone just like his mother, with some overtones of his father. Warren was frightened enough by this to leave the relationship, get into therapy, and begin to examine and correct the old patterns he had based the relationship on.

Expecting a mate to be the perfect parent you always wanted places unrealistic expectations on the other person. Since no one can equal that, disappointment becomes inevitable. When neither can live up to these unrealistic expectations you feel on the one hand inadequate, pressured, and used, and on the other, unloved, uncared for, and abandoned.

You begin to learn about your relationship with your parents and then their relationship with each other during the critical early period of magical thinking, which makes it as difficult to change your old dependent relationship habits as it is to change your other dependency habits. What you learn about love, home, and family becomes deeply embedded in the subconscious child mind, and takes over and underlies your first reactions to solving relationship problems and challenges. When you later fall in love, and are faced with the stressful relationship complications of conflicting wants and needs, you fall back into the old patterns. They're such old habits that they feel natural and instinctive.

Our mistaken belief that someone else can make it better for us is at the root of most love problems we have with intimate relationships as adults—the mistaken expectation of parent/child love, where the child is dependent and powerless and the parent is in control and powerful.

We have already seen how this kind of dependency in adult intimate relationships can go wrong, resulting in abuse, misunderstandings, anger, or smothering. Even the most competent parents never take care of their children the way the *children* would want them to. As children, we are supposed to learn, with the help of encouraging parents, to take increasingly more autonomous risks and learn to be competent in life through those risk experiences. Ideally, the parent/child relationship matures to one of mutual respect and caring, where the child is obviously as capable, functional, and autonomous as the parent. If we let go of the dependent, childish view of love, and use the more mature model, we get a more autonomous picture of familial love. This kind of love is mutually caring, mutually giving, and mutually responsible, without the dependent, needy, or controlling imbalance of power present in the child/parent model. Remaining dependent robs us of our power to receive and give love at full capacity while retaining our self-esteem and sense of competence.

We can also be misled by our own initial romantic excitement and attraction. A romantic relationship—with the partner we hope and expect will provide us with the love, joy, and fulfillment of our dreams—that turns into a miserable and disappointing failure is a very painful experience. Not only is it a terrible disappointment of very high expectations, but it reminds us of whatever early childhood rejection and abandonment we experienced. The hurt of the failed relationship, coupled with the early childhood despair, can become an overwhelming pain of the type we have used addiction to escape. Most therapists and recovery counselors report that the pain of a troubled or failed relationship is cited by twelve-step members as the single greatest cause of many alcoholics' relapses.

And it's not romantic relationships alone that give us trouble; we can find ourselves repeating early patterns whenever closeness is present between us and others: with family, friends, and even co-workers. As soon as the feeling arises that we care about another, or want another to care about us, our old patterns and models of how people who are supposed to care about each other (our family) come into play. These early models, held in our deep inner mind, create dependent, problematic relationships, and must be changed if we are to be able to love autonomously.

THE SKILLS OF AUTONOMOUS INTIMACY

The good news is that while relationships are the most difficult aspect of our lives, learning the skills that make them work is one of the easiest. This is because all the skills you have learned so far, in confronting and building an autonomous relationship with yourself, are precisely the same skills you will need to zcreate and sustain autonomous intimacy with others on a longterm basis. Your inner relationship with yourself becomes your new model (and also standard or criterion) upon which you can build all other relationships. As you create this model within you, you can test it, correct it, and revamp it as needed. Building functional, dynamic, and rewarding relationships simply means learning to apply the skills you already know—risk taking, problem solving and effective choice making, coping with disappointment and failure, awareness, learning, and forgiveness—to relationships.

Risk Taking

Being in a relationship that is not based on playing old, dependent roles, but instead designed to actually *function* in your life, requires taking at least several risks. First is that of letting your partner know who you really are. If you don't, the risk you run (although you're usually unaware of it) is that you'll never feel loved for who you are but because you've learned to please your partner. When that is the case, you live in fear of being found out, that your beloved would reject you if he or she only knew the truth. As this fear eats at your self-esteem, the pressure and resentment build, leading eventually to an outburst of rebellion that can destroy the partnership.

The next is jeopardizing your wants and preferences. Instead of trying to guess what will please the other person (fill their wants and needs) while trying *not* to let your partner know what your wants and needs are, you must take the risk that your partner will not be willing or able to meet your needs (or you to meet your partner's). By taking this risk, you find out whether the two of you can negotiate mutually satisfactory solutions, and if so (by realizing you both can give and take no for an answer), you lay the foundation for the freedom to give from generosity rather than obligation.

Another is being honest when what works for you is different than the accepted role models. We all have different needs for closeness and space, for communication and silence, for accomplishment and relaxation. Squeezing yourself into a closer relationship than is comfortable for you, or feeling deprived in a distant one, leads to inevitable relationship failure. Feeling badgered by someone who is more verbal than you are or shut out by someone less verbal, or pressured by someone more driven to accomplish or frustrated by someone more inactive, inevitably becomes intolerable, unless you can discuss your differences and work together to find a mutually satisfactory solution.

These are personal risks of the most challenging kind, because you are exposing the most private aspects of your personality to the other person, and you risk being rejected. But, if you can do this before your investment in the relationship is too great, your disappointment is diminished, and you already know how to cope with failure and disappointment through feeling your feelings and then working on a new goal. However, the possible rewards are that you will build a *sustainable* relationship—one that you fit into naturally, that suits your needs and talents, and that makes demands on you that are within your range, so it will remain pleasant, satisfying, and functional in your life and the life of your partner. An autonomous, sustainable relationship—precisely because it is more easily managed and involves less struggle than a dependent, dysfunctional one—frees your energy for having fun together, building toward your future, and enjoying your present life.

The best you can achieve in dependency is approval for being "good"; but in autonomous intimacy, you can actually be valued and loved for your unique and different qualities.

Problem Solving and Effective Choice Making

In dysfunctional, dependent relationships, problems are solved through struggle—one person wins and gets her way, but then has to deal with covert anger continuously expressed by the other—or through passive sacrifice or denial—problems are endured or ignored, in the vain hope that they'll go away. In the "struggle" relationship, the partners fight a lot, usually about the same issues; one gets her way, and the other then "snipes" at her, making little sarcastic remarks when they're with friends. In the "sacrifice" relationship, a wife might insist that her husband give up golf and spend more time with her, which he does without complaint; but then he comes home later and later, perhaps having had a few more drinks, from the office each night.

In autonomous intimacy, problems are treated as opportunities to reach a new level of success: as challenges that, when solved, will yield a new and better way of life. The partners are willing to talk about what's wrong, what they want, and what they're willing or not willing to do, and they use effective choice making together to find a solution.

Coping with Disappointment and Failure

In intimate relationships, as in all aspects of life, you will make mistakes and encounter disappointment and failure. Even with the most well-intentioned, loving mate, you will not always get the response you want. Your sexual advances will be turned down occasionally, your need for sympathy will be met with irritation, your boundless enthusiasm for a cherished activity will be quashed by a mate who's disinterested, irritable, or exhausted. It happens in the best of relationships.

In a dependent relationship, these disappointments are often the cause of stored resentment, arguments, and major battles, because the basic promise of the relationship ("I'll make it better for you") has been broken and the partners feel angry and helpless. In autonomous relationships, where each person assumes the responsibility to take care of his or her own feelings, cope with disappointment, and develop another creative idea (so when your partner isn't enthusiastic about your achievement, you call a friend who will be), the problem remains a small, temporary setback, with no lingering aftermath.

Awareness

Because of their high level of fear and hopelessness, dependent people tend to block out problems and live in denial. In their relationships, this means that small problems can accumulate and eventually become years' worth of resentment, anger, and frustration. As an autonomous thinker, making the choice to be responsible for yourself, be aware of yourself, and evaluate your circumstances prevents this from happening.

Once problems accumulate and build up, they take much more energy and effort to correct. Acting autonomously in intimate relationships means being aware of problems when they're small and thus easily solved. Using your self-awareness to let you know when a problem is imminent, you can communicate what you feel, and open the problem up for discussion with an observation or a question: "You seem tense and anxious. Is anything wrong?" or "I'm aware that I got angry when you were too busy to listen to me last night. Can we talk about it?" Having awareness and acting on it means that your relationship problems can be solved early, when they are minor, and before the frustration of an unsolved problem causes resentment to build.

Learning

Because autonomous relationships do not follow predetermined patterns, they become a continuous learning process. In dependent relationships, we are busy trying to meet others' expectations and we are run by our old, rigid mental patterns, which leaves very little room for learning anything. Dependent people focus on defending themselves when a problem arises. Learning new things is thought to be dangerous and frightening. As an autonomous thinker, you welcome the opportunity to learn, which gives you the power to find out who your partner is on an intimate level and to communicate in special ways with each other.

In autonomous relationships, when a problem arises you need not fear it, because you know how to use effective choice making to solve it. When you use effective choice making, often the solution to the problem is a big improvement over the status of your relationship before the problem came up. With some experience of successfully solving your relationship issues and problems as they arise, you will begin to see each one as an opportunity to learn something new.

Forgiveness

The power to resolve and let go of old hurts, while learning to protect yourself from being hurt again, is one of the most useful skills when it comes to intimate relationships. No matter how much you care, and how hard you try, when you get close to your partner you are going to occasionally get hurt. Even people who are responsible and care about each other make mistakes, because you can't be 100 percent aware and because you don't always understand what's important to your partner. This emotional clumsiness can hurt, even when it's unintentional, so you need to know how to clear up the hurts when they happen.

By knowing how to express your feelings, and figuring out a way to prevent a similar hurt from happening again, you can make it possible to forgive each other. In true forgiveness, there is no lingering resentment, because the problem is solved. You have learned how to heal the hurt and prevent its recurrence, so you can forgive and wipe the slate clean. With forgiveness, autonomous intimacy can become like starting over with a clean slate.

JOE AND MARY

Joe and Mary, a married couple in their late twenties, were having a problem, because Joe forgot Mary's birthday and she was hurt. Joe apologized, and that helped, but Mary still felt unsure. After they talked a while, Joe realized that his family didn't celebrate birthdays, whereas Mary's family made a special occasion out of them. He "forgot" Mary's birthday, even though he knew it was important to her, because he didn't know what to do, and he helplessly "blanked it out" of his mind. After realizing how important it was to her, he agreed that next year he would ask Mary's friend Sue to help him buy a card and pick out a gift. Mary also decided to make sure her other friends knew when her birthday was, so someone would be sure to remember it. Once she decided this, and she heard Joe's plan, she was able to relax, forgive, and forget his mistake.

When you use risk taking, problem solving and effective choice making, coping with disappointment, awareness, learning, and forgiveness in your relationships, it becomes quite easy to maintain a loving, caring relationship of two equal, independently healthy partners, who mutually share their lives and enjoy each other. As you use these skills to make your relationship more mutual, more successful, and healthier, the relationship will display some dynamics that are characteristic of autonomous intimacy.

THE CHARACTERISTICS OF AUTONOMOUS INTIMACY

There are four basic characteristics of autonomous intimacy: intimacy with self, nondependent intimacy with others, warmth, and humor. When these characteristics are present, autonomous intimacy is also present. When these characteristics are not present, it is because dependency and dysfunction have blocked our ability to care for ourselves, be generous with each other, and be relaxed and open enough to enjoy each other.

Intimacy with Self
One reason for feeling dependent and powerless in romantic relationships is the fear of loneliness. When someone says, "I would rather be in a relationship than be alone," they're displaying

confused, dependent thinking, because that statement could mean "I would rather be in a relationship—with an addict, with someone violent and abusive, where I'm miserable, with someone who disgusts me—than be alone." This confusion is based on fear of loneliness and a mistaken idea that loneliness is dependent on other people. This fear can be so powerful that people *do* stay in toxic situations, believing it's worse to be alone.

How does this belief develop? We get confused because often being rejected or ignored by others can cause us to reject ourselves. For example, if Mary wants Bob to call her, and he doesn't, Mary criticizes herself: "I'm too fat, that's why he didn't call. No one will ever love me." When she does this, she feels frightened, alienated, and lonely, which she assumes is because she's alone. Confusing the hurt caused by her own self-criticism and self-rejection with loneliness, Mary feels miserable, and blames it on being alone. Her fear makes her vulnerable to a destructive, unsatisfying relationship. Believing that she doesn't deserve to be loved, and it's painful to be alone, she's vulnerable to the first person who flatters her. She's too panic-stricken to think clearly and make a thoughtful choice.

Mary's loneliness and pain are not the result of Bob's neglect, or of being alone, but a reflection of the quality of her inner relationship. Your interaction with yourself determines whether you feel good or bad, no matter if you are alone or with someone else. For a short time, the excitement of a new relationship can distract you from your inner pain, but the distraction is temporary. Sooner or later, even in a relationship, the pain will come back, unless you use the new technology, your magical tools, to correct your internal environment. It is not autonomy that creates loneliness, but inner alienation from yourself. Solitude can actually feel fine, and sharing your own company can be joyful. With the internal companionship of autonomy you never need to feel lonely, because when you're alone you know how to be a friend to yourself.

When you know you can count on yourself to be a friend, and you have mastered being intimate with yourself, fear of loneliness disappears. When you can enjoy your own company and meet your own needs, loneliness is no longer something to be afraid of, and without the fear of loneliness you have choice about when, where, and how you want to be with others. Instead of feeling panicky and desperate (which can cloud your thinking), dependent on others to keep you feeling OK, when you can depend on internal intimacy you feel more relaxed and are more able to make good, clear-thinking choices about whom you want to be with.

Healthy intimacy is closeness, a feeling of trust and safety that occurs between people (or your child self and your adult self) when they have had enough successful experience together to demonstrate that they care for each other and can rely on each other. True intimacy grows deeper as you realize that you can handle problems successfully together. Intimacy is your confidence in your partner, yourself, and the relationship.

Intimacy with yourself develops in a similar fashion. The more your experience with yourself shows you that you can count on yourself to be there and to care and support you, the more intimacy with yourself you will develop. The difference between intimacy and dependency is that intimacy happens between equals; dependency is based on one individual feeling powerless. When you choose true intimacy, you must give up the dependent dream that someone else (stronger and more capable than you are) can make it better, and accept your responsibility for taking care of yourself.

In recovery groups, *Thirteenth Stepping* means having inappropriate intimacy with a new member (sex with someone newly into recovery). But the *Real Thirteenth Step* as developed here means having appropriate intimacy (caring, responsible contact, and communication) with yourself. Here, as in moving from dependency to autonomy, the focus is taken off the other person and placed on yourself. When you make contact and communicate with your inner child in a loving, caring way, you soon become intimate with yourself, and as this internal intimacy develops, as you experiment with different kinds of interaction with your inner self, you learn what works best for you, and you learn from experience what true intimacy feels like.

This then becomes the pattern on which you base the intimacy you develop with another person.

Sensing neediness and dependency from you often scares other people off, because they have their hands full meeting their own needs, and they know they're too overloaded to carry any further burden beyond their own, except perhaps on a temporary basis in an emergency. Paradoxically, once you develop self-reliance and intimacy with your inner self, it becomes obvious to others (through their observation of the ways you act and relate) that you are well taken care of and will not place a burden of neediness or expectation to make it better on them. You'll find that (seemingly without any effort) you get more positive attention from more autonomous (and therefore happy and successful) people.

Would you rather join someone who's having a great time, or be responsible for taking care of someone who's in a mess? Would you want to be partners with a person who's *proved* they can have positive, successful experiences with intimacy (internally, and with friends and family), or with someone whose experiences have been negative and unsuccessful? "Self-image and self-love," writes clinical psychologist Catherine Solange, are "the key to romance. . . . The state of your love life very accurately reflects your willingness to love yourself and allow others to love you. . . . Self-love is ATTRACTIVE!"

Healthy, self-confident people recognize your self-esteem because it feels similar to their own. Because you have your inner relationship to compare to, you can recognize self-esteem in others.

Intimacy with Others

Once you've developed and enjoyed companionship with yourself, autonomous intimacy with others is much easier than you may believe. Because your own inner intimacy, caring, and responsibility form the model for your relationships with others, you now have a criterion against which to measure your other relationships. In other words, to determine how well you are doing, you compare the quality of your outside relationships with the quality of your inner relationship, and negotiate with your partner if you see a problem. The success of many of these minor negotiations is what ultimately tells you whether the two of you can work out a viable, sustainable relationship.

When two autonomous people meet and begin communicating to find out if they're a match and can create a sustainable, satisfying, and successful relationship, they are comparing their external interaction with the internal interaction they have already proven works for them. If all goes well, they collect more and more evidence that this new person can be trusted to keep him or herself emotionally healthy, and to relate honestly and reliably. The more success they have with each other, the more trust and intimacy they build together.

This mutual trust and intimacy form the foundation for a love that feels free, generous, and flowing. Here's how Riley Smith and I described autonomous love in our guide to noncodependent relationships, *How to Be a Couple and Still Be Free:*

Love doesn't limit the beloved.

Love is not possessive.

Love encourages growth and satisfaction in the beloved.

Love rejoices at the beloved's joy.

Let us support one another
Let us teach one another
Let us love one another—
without expectations.

It's okay to take whatever closeness or distance we need.

When you are open and honest with each other, you each feel truly loved for who you really are.

There are several characteristics of autonomous intimacy that stand out from the old dependent model of romantic love.

First, you are willing to make careful selections of the people you become close to, using effective choice-making techniques to determine if they are reliable and if your relationship is sustainable. You are not in the relationship out of fear of lone-liness, need, helplessness, or to have them "make it better," so you can take the time to get to know your partner *before* becom-ing emotionally invested, and be selective. It is a relationship of *choice*.

Second, you are aware that you are attractive because of your internal, real qualities, and not because of surface attri-butes or behavior. Your intimacy with and reliance on yourself creates your attractiveness.

Third, you value the content—that is, the connectedness, caring, committedness, and satisfaction—of your relationship over its form ("being in love," "being married," "being in a re-lationship"). It is not the fact of relationship that is important, but its results: you and your partner feeling mutual love, re-spect, teamwork, and reliability.

Fourth, you work problems and issues out, on the spot, according to what works best at the time, rather than trying to follow a preset pattern or model. You deal with issues and prob-lems as they arise, figuring the answers out as you go along, looking at long-term as well as short-term results, and adapting to new situations as they happen in a seat-of-the-pants operat-ing style. For example, if one of you gets a great job offer in an-other city, and the other doesn't want to move, you might decide to try living apart for a few months, or try the new city for a few months, to see what works best, and discuss how it feels as you go along.

Fifth, you value honesty and clear communication above pro-tecting yourself or your partner from hurt feelings, although you take care to express the truth as kindly and gently as you can, and still be understood.

Sixth, you consider your relationship to be an agreement or contract, in which each party has responsibilities and benefits, and which clearly states, in advance, what happens if the con-tract is broken. ("I will stay with you as long as it is healthy for me, and you agree to do the same. If either of us feels that some part of our relationship is becoming unhealthy, or uncomfort-able, we will bring it up for discussion. If we cannot solve the problem ourselves, we agree to bring in an objective third party to help. If nothing will fix it, we will renegotiate whether we want to stay together.") That is, you recognize that your relationship will not survive "no matter what," and that you must take responsibility for keeping it worthwhile for yourself and for each other. If either of you feels that your relationship is becoming detrimental, your responsibility is to say so as soon as possible, to give yourselves an opportunity to work the problems out.

Seventh, as with any viable contract, problems, confusion, and changes are resolved through discussion and negotiation. You bring up whatever seems to be a problem to either of you, and then you discuss it, use effective choice-making techniques, and work it out together.

Eighth, you understand that in order to be functional your relationship must be sustainable: that is, you (and your partner) must be able to do what is necessary to keep it going for a lifetime. You recognize that if you must ignore your needs or wants, or act in ways not natural to you to please your partner or society, that you will not be able to sustain such uncomfortable, atypical, self-depriving behavior for years. At the same time, you balance your need to be yourself with other considerations of what is good for you. (For example, you know you won't happily deny yourself classical music forever, but your partner prefers country/western. So, in the interests of sustainability, you find ways that you can listen to classical sometimes, and your partner can listen to country/western.)

Autonomous love is always inviting to others, because it puts no pressure on them to take care of you. Because each of you meets your own inner needs autonomously, and does not feel obligated to "make it better" for the other, and takes care of problems as they happen, and doesn't let them pile up into years of resentment, you can both relax and enjoy yourselves, and be free to have fun together.

Warmth

People often say that autonomous relationships—in which each person is responsible for taking care of him- or herself and not the other person—sound cold, because the fantasy of romantic love does not include the clear thinking of effective choice making or the responsibility of autonomy. But the actual experience of autonomy in interactions is anything but cold. Taking care of yourself without a struggle creates inner security, and the absence of struggle allows you to feel warmth toward another. Your personal inner security and comfort radiate out from you as the feeling others describe as "warmth." In this way, autonomously taking care of yourself generates intimacy that feels warm and inviting.

The freedom to love each other without obligation, coupled with mutual trust (based on real experience of each other) and lack of pressure, allow warmth to flow between you. Warmth is a spontaneous feeling of goodwill, respect, pleasure, and satisfaction that arises when relationships are based on autonomy. Because you are equals, together out of choice and both demonstrating and experiencing your love of yourself and your simultaneous love of your partner, and because you both take responsibility for yourselves and your actions, solving problems as they arise rather than allowing them to accumulate, you are freed from struggle and frustration. So, when you think of each other, your thoughts will be mostly of the good feelings you have when you're together. It is an accumulation of these good feelings, or emotional successes, over a period of time that we call *warmth*.

Warmth arises out of successful intimacy. In autonomous relationships, you will feel warmth both toward yourself (because of your history of successful intimacy with your inner child self), and toward your partner (because of successful intimacy you've experienced together). You can also have warmth in autonomous family relationships or autonomous friendships. As long as the successful history of autonomous loving is there, the warmth will be there, too.

You can tell you're experiencing warmth if you find yourself smiling with pleasure and appreciation when you think of your partner (or your inner child self). This warmth is, to me, the greatest reward of autonomous loving and living. To go through days being able to smile to myself about my experience of me, my experience of my spouse, and my experience of friends makes life feel very worthwhile and pleasurable—even when outside things go wrong. For example, one day when I was having a difficult time with this book, three of my friends called to tell me they loved me, they were "rooting for me," and they knew I could do it, and my husband came home with a bouquet of flowers. The warmth of those gestures, and the mutually supportive history they represented, made any problems I was having seem minor. Living and loving autonomously is not always easy, because it requires a high degree of self-awareness and self-care and you must think often about your actions before you do them, but it means being surrounded with loving, spontaneous warmth every day. Expressing this kind of undemanded, generous warmth feels equally good to the receiver and the giver.

Warmth is also the foundation of autonomous commitment, which is not something you do because you promised or you should; autonomous commitment is much easier than that. When such warmth and goodwill are present between you and another person, that relationship becomes very precious. You are willing to expend considerable effort to protect such a source of good feelings. That effort is the measure of your commitment. You don't get to feel the warmth because you're committed to each other; instead, you feel committed to each other because the warmth is there.

In a dependent relationship, with its attendant feelings of powerlessness, hopelessness, and helplessness, our memories are not as pleasant (because the relationship is based on struggle or sacrifice), our frustration level is higher (because we don't get what we want), and the experience of warmth is very fleeting. Some warmth is usually there in the very early days of the relationship (often based more on our fantasy of what we *want* the relationship to be than on our actual experience of what it is), when we have the first rush of passion and pleasant feelings, but it fades as our frustration grows. Without the foundation of warmth, commitment feels like hard work, and is not sustainable. Although people manage to stay together, they remain so out of obligation or fear of taking risks, and the relationship loses pleasure and meaning.

Humor

It may seem odd that one of the characteristics of autonomy is humor. But autonomous people are unafraid to be different and individual, which also makes them free to be humorous. People who have a solid feeling of self-love and self-worth feel free and secure enough to laugh at silliness in life and in themselves, without being sarcastic or negative. Autonomy is a function of the secure child mind, and children who know they are loved feel secure and become playful.

The most joyous and beloved comedians of all time—such as Sid Caesar, Jonathan Winters, and Lily Tomlin—make us laugh without criticizing or attacking others or themselves. This kind of humor is closely connected to warmth, and it is characteristic of autonomous intimacy. It takes a certain amount of self-acceptance to create healthy humor, rather than the hurtful kind; but then again, this loving, shared laughter also enhances your degree of self-acceptance. The paradox seems to be that having permission for childlike play also gives permission to be responsible and self-accepting. We laugh *together,* and it feels good.

Just as humor and merriment arise out of the freedom of autonomy, grimness arises out of dependency and obligation. In our parents' youth, relationships were believed to require sacrifice and compromise. We were taught, by word and example, to think of others' feelings and wants, seldom about our own. From a viewpoint of dependency, if we focus autonomously on being healthy ourselves it seems to eliminate caring about others and to deny these venerable teachings:

- others' feelings and wants must come first
- sacrifice and love are synonymous
- to care about yourself is selfish and stuck-up

- you are incomplete alone, and need another person to make you whole
- you can only care about yourself or others—not both at once

But viewed from a healthy, autonomous position based on self-esteem, these old ideas no longer make sense.

Instead, as autonomous, self-aware people, we know that we cannot be truly generous unless we ourselves are taken care of; when we are deprived, we will (consciously or unconsciously) resent giving. We know that sacrifice and martyrdom are counterproductive to healthy interaction—that it produces guilt to receive benefit at the expense of others' well-being and that sacrifice is not truly loving because it is unloving toward yourself.

The more we learn about being intimate with ourselves and autonomously intimate with each other, the less we struggle; the less we struggle, the more we laugh and play. There are times when an overwhelming feeling of warmth and caring flows over us, and many of those times are when we laugh. Both the warmth and the laughter arise spontaneously from the childlike inner self, when we treat ourselves and each other with kindness, respect, and caring—in short, when we are autonomously intimate.

A MODEL FOR THE AUTONOMOUS RELATIONSHIP

The basic attitude of an autonomous relationship is caring, since each partner cares about him- or herself, and each partner cares about the other. Caring about yourself is not selfish, but the foundation of true generosity of spirit and joy of giving.

Because your self-love creates the inner security that makes generous love possible, and because your internal intimacy combined with effective choice making enables you to choose people who are healthy and reliable to love, you have an abundance of love to give to others. You realize that you can not only love and care for yourself and love others at the same time, but that the only functional love is that in which you love yourself as much as you love others.

Operating from this abundance-based belief system, we are each fully able to care for ourselves, we are free to be individuals, and we are able to share with each other to our mutual benefit and enjoyment. The desperate, helpless, and dependent attitude that another person should focus his or her life on "making it better" for you or "making you whole," when examined in the light of this contentment-based, freely shared love, seems a selfish and greedy attitude.

Under your new autonomous model for relationships you may find a different outlook on life:

- Your ideal of love is much more unconditional and free.
- Love is based on cooperation, not martyrdom or sacrifice.
- Problems are solved through cooperative *negotiation,* where you and your partner have equal investments in *both* of you being satisfied.
- Relationships are unique and fulfilling for each individual within a couple and/or family.
- You understand that loving yourself is the necessary foundation for loving anyone else.
- Change and problems are welcomed as opportunities to learn.
- Love is seen as dependable—it is not necessary to try to trap or hold it.
- Trusting oneself becomes more important than trusting others.
- Every event of life is viewed as a challenge to respond in a positive, caring, and healing way.
- Self and others are accepted as fallible, imperfect, yet beautiful human beings.
- Jealousy, possessiveness, dishonesty, and coercion are seen as destructive—traits to work on and overcome.
- Hostile competition feels wasteful and ineffective.
- Cooperation is seen as the ideal way to interact.

- Families become open systems, in which love, honesty, and communication flow freely—both to members within the family and to others.
- Commitment becomes a voluntary and therefore reliable *expression* of an emotional attachment that has grown out of successful interaction, rather than a forced, guilt-based, and unrealistic *promise* based on fantasy and wishing.

As autonomous partners, you create your relationship to suit yourselves and each other. Each relationship is therefore unique and different from all others, because the partners are different from everyone else. Autonomy allows you to express your individuality. Partners with healthy self-esteem do not have to distort themselves or deny who they are for fear of not pleasing a partner, or to fit some idea of a relationship.

Since each person involved is unique, there are no rules that apply to all people and all situations. Therefore a universal model of the roles people play in the "traditional" autonomous relationship is not possible. This makes it difficult to formulate models for autonomous relationships. Each new relationship is different from the others.

Therefore, it is necessary to learn to build each relationship from scratch. Rather than follow old, dependent childhood patterns, you can relate "by the seat of your pants"—paying attention to signs that potential conflicts may be developing, exploring options and weighing their short- and long-term consequences, and choosing your actions consciously with an eye to taking care of yourself and providing mutual satisfaction.

Trouble Signs

In an autonomous relationship, each partner is responsible for stating his or her wants and needs, and for self-monitoring for signs of resentment, disappointment, or deprivation, which indicate that something about your own internal relationship or something in your relationship with each other is not meeting your needs.

When these signs occur—as they do when we become stressed, are too busy to pay attention, or find that some problem has activated an old, dependent behavior—it is the individual who *feels* them who is responsible for initiating the effort to make them better. For example, if you're feeling irritable, anxious, and frustrated, you do not blame your partner. Instead, you first use an inner-awareness exercise (such as "Finding Your Trouble Spot") to figure out what's wrong; then, if you want your partner's help in solving the problem, you can calmly discuss it. ("I realize that I haven't been getting enough sleep, because I've been staying up too late watching TV with you, can we talk about it?") If you are too upset to talk calmly, you handle your feelings first (on your own) with "Discharging" or "Time Out" (see below) until you are prepared to talk reasonably.

An autonomous couple regards fighting as a mistake, not an inevitable part of relationships, and uses effective choice making to find other ways to handle problems. If Joe and Mary have a fight, they break it off as soon as possible, and take a time out; when they've calmed down, they discuss two problems: what they were fighting about, and why it became a fight and not a discussion. As you get comfortable with caring for your inner self, and better at it, you will find you do not begrudge or resent this responsibility but embrace it, because you know it is the best way to care for yourself and to ensure a healthy, growing relationship.

Because you take responsibility for yourself, you know that in an autonomous relationship it's up to you to handle any problem that makes you uncomfortable:

- become aware of it
- discuss it with yourself and find possible solutions
- implement those solutions that require only your action
- if your partner's cooperation is desired, discuss the problem and ask for what you want
- negotiate for a *mutually satisfactory* solution

If you can't find a mutual solution in a reasonable time (an hour or so), you may need to make a temporary decision that you both can agree to, and come back later to try again until the problem is satisfactorily solved.

Commitment

"I'll love you forever" is a promise that may be unrealistic and impossible to fulfill—therefore, it is based on fantasy. It's difficult to predict how you'll feel in five years, never mind forever. Although it's romantic and pleasant to speak about unending love, the true commitment in self-governing love is about negotiating, respect, and fairness, because these activities increase and maintain the warmth in your relationship, which is the best guarantee of relationship commitment and sustainability. When an autonomous couple commits to having children, or making long-term investments and decisions, they "play chess" with the decisions before they are made, and provide for future possibilities as well as they are able. (If they want a baby, they consider their competence as parents—taking classes and baby-sitting for friends to learn more—and their financial responsibility, and they research the realities of child-rearing.) They realize that these serious decisions require serious thought, and that they are not taking care of themselves (or their future children) if they decide based on fantasy ("Wouldn't it be nice to have a baby? Babies are so sweet and lovable.") alone.

When you are committed to caring for yourself, you value honest communication, so you are unafraid to tell a partner when you are dissatisfied with something. Your mutual guarantee actually is: "No surprises—if I'm dissatisfied or unhappy, I'll let you know and give us both a chance to correct it. If we can't, then we get help, and if that doesn't fix it, then we renegotiate what we'll do about the relationship." This is a realistic, sustainable commitment that you can actually expect to meet, and it gives you the best possible chance of success.

Truthfulness

Autonomous people don't waste time ignoring developing problems and being "nice" until they can't stand it any more, and then blowing up with the frustration, saying, "You never listen to me!" or "You always do that!" Autonomous relationships are based on truth. Because partners tell the truth to each other as much and as often (although as gently) as possible, devastating surprises ("I've had it! I'm leaving you!") do not arise. If there are unsolved problems, you will be aware of them for a long time before they could damage the relationship, and the worst possible thing that can happen is that you'll mutually agree that the relationship is not sustainable, and part as friends.

One aspect of this truthfulness is that as an autonomous person you can also admit when you are wrong, forget, or make a mistake, because you have confidence that you are capable of handling failure and then finding a new solution.

As you become less dependent, your love of others becomes less possessive and less needy, more generous, more intimately connected, and more free and flowing. Your newfound autonomy is self-perpetuating, because the old, dependent ways become too difficult and painful in contrast. Once you know how to meet your own needs and to ask for what you want from others, going back to old, self-effacing, dependent methods of getting what you want, or back to denying yourself, is not at all appealing. As autonomous individuals, you each recognize that you are fallible humans who make mistakes, who can admit when you're wrong, and who are capable of learning better ways of handling problems and difficult interactions.

People who can take care of themselves easily and confidently are being taken care of not as an ideal of love but as a type of unpleasant bondage, suitable only for small children and the mentally handicapped or mentally ill.

By learning the basic skills of personal autonomy—your magical tools, risk taking, problem solving, coping with failure, awareness, learning, and forgiveness—you already have begun to learn the skills necessary for autonomous relationships. Applying those skills to your relationships, and then adding the techniques and exercises that follow in this chapter, will give you a complete model for how to develop the autonomous relationship that is perfect for you. As you practice the techniques and exercises that end this chapter, and add them to the tools you have already learned, you acquire expertise with the techniques and tools needed to reframe your definitions of love and relationships.

CREATING AND MAINTAINING AUTONOMOUS INTIMACY

In addition to the skills you already have mastered to help you maintain your autonomy in your relationships, and the characteristics of autonomous intimacy that indicate when your relationship is successfully autonomous, there are several techniques and exercises that you will find very helpful in maintaining the autonomous intimacy you have created. These techniques and exercises help you reclaim your own internal intimacy when you have lost it, communicate better with your partner to make negotiating and problem solving easier (as well as improve your general communication), and deal with people who are still living by dependent beliefs and patterns.

Setting Boundaries

Living autonomous love is not automatic or easy in a social atmosphere that doesn't support these values. Establishing the difference between what is good for you and what others want, need, or think about it is called *setting boundaries*. "The world is full of people," Joseph Campbell writes in *The Power of Myth,* "who have stopped listening to themselves or have listened only to their neighbors to learn what they ought to do, how they ought to behave, and what the values are that they should be living for." The ability to develop these values for yourself, and to communicate your limits to those who attempt to overstep them, will help you keep others from attempting to impose their beliefs and values on you. Setting boundaries is another aspect of what you have already learned: governing your own life, acting according to what you know is right for you, *even if your family, friends, or lover doesn't like it.* In short, although problems usually can be negotiated, taking care of you sometimes requires saying no.

"Boundaries," writes Jody Hayes, author of the codependency recovery book *Smart Love,* "represent the dividing lines between us and other people. Boundaries are important because they allow us to maintain a healthy sense of self as an individual, separate from everything else. Without this sense, you cannot achieve balance or maintain your own values and goals while encountering the influences and emotions of others." Boundaries and limits, of course, are only needed when you feel your rights are being denied, or the situation is physically, emotionally, or mentally unhealthy for you. Your personal boundaries can include these areas:

- insisting on privacy and time alone
- setting limits to physical contact ("Please don't tickle me. I won't be around people who are violent.")
- setting limits to emotional excess ("I won't talk to you if you yell.")
- setting limits on giving time, attention, money, sex, and so on ("I'm sorry you spent your whole paycheck and don't have your rent, but I can't loan you money.")
- saying no to requests or demands
- refusing to associate with certain behaviors, habits, attitudes, and actions ("I won't listen to racist jokes. Please don't smoke [or drink] in my house.")

Often, simply knowing what you want and communicating your wishes to your friend or partner is sufficient to set your boundary. Most other people want to know your preferences so they don't have to guess what your limits are, but in some cases, especially with people who are still in addictive and dependent behavior, setting boundaries is more difficult. When your limits and boundaries aren't respected, you need to let the other person know it. Boundaries are not demands—they do not require the other person to change—they are statements of your intent—the changes *you* will make if your boundaries are not respected.

Although your limits are not negotiable, some details are. When someone behaves toward you in a way that you find unacceptable, it is most effective to: 1) Tell them gently what you don't like. ("I would prefer it if you didn't smoke in my car.") With many people, a simple request will solve the problem. 2) Offer to negotiate. ("Your smoking is unpleasant to me, can we talk about it?") 3) If the other person will not negotiate, make a decision about how to fix your part of the problem, whether the other person likes it or not. In severe cases, it just takes making a unilateral decision. ("I'm sorry, but if you won't stop smoking in my car, I can't drive you anymore.")

Setting your boundaries is not a demand, because it requires *no action at all* on your partner's part. You can invite your lover or friend to negotiate the details with you, or to express an opinion, but your limits stand *no matter what your partner says*. Setting boundaries and honest communication go hand in hand, because healthy boundaries are an autonomous expression of your true needs (what is healthy for you), rather than a dependent adaptation to (or rebellion against) your partner's (real or imagined) wants.

Maintaining Autonomy with People Who Are Unaware

Once away from the insulated environment of family, friends, or twelve-step programs (and sometimes even in those venues), we encounter people who don't understand the ground rules we have adopted. Perhaps you are concerned that once you are aware and autonomous, you won't be able to relate to people who have not yet taken the Real Thirteenth Step. This is not true, because being more aware and in charge *increases* your effectiveness, even with those who are still addictive or dependent. The variety of people you can be successful with increases, too.

Being autonomous, and having self-esteem and the capacity to govern yourself, means you are not at the mercy of others' emotional confusion or uncontrolled behavior. You can let their problems be *only* their problems, and not take them on as your own. Here are some of the more common problem personalities and how to handle intimacy with each type.

Ambivalent personalities. Creating intimacy with potential friends or lovers who give mixed signals—first they seem to invite, then to reject us—can be frustrating. However, getting close to them is easier if we pay attention to *both* signals. The mistake we often make is to believe the invitations, and then get hurt by the rejections.

Handling ambivalence is a lot like taming a wild animal. It takes patience and inner calm. Go slowly, remain relaxed, move closer only when invited, and just stand your ground when rejected. Don't take the ambivalence personally: it's just that your new friend has a difficult time knowing what she wants. In this case, emotional autonomy means not becoming more emotionally invested (more in love or caring more) than the other person can match. You are being dependent if you become too invested and *then* demand that the other person match your investment.

Because your prime objective is to take care of yourself, you can only do this as long as it's not emotionally painful. If you find yourself getting hurt feelings, resenting your companion's ambivalence and lack of commitment or energy for the relationship, you're getting too invested and are in danger of being hurt. In that case, it is healthier to let this be a somewhat distant friendship and look for someone who's more easily available and more definite about her interest in you.

Dependent personalities. Surprisingly enough, creating intimacy can be difficult with clingy, overattentive people. It's a paradox that you have to have enough separation to create intimacy. A person whose whole world is centered on you, and who tends to give up his friends, activities, and life-style in favor of yours, loses his individual identity and is not really available for autonomous intimacy—that person wants a parent to make it better, not an equal partner.

Developing intimacy with dependent people requires boundary setting and resolve. It's easy to be fooled in the first rush of romance and passion, because for a short while all that closeness feels OK, and it's what we've all been told love is about. But before too long, you will begin to feel smothered by the other person's needs, unless you set careful limits.

If you realize someone you're in a relationship with is focusing entirely on you, and losing his identity in the process (he stops seeing friends, waits by the phone, changes schedules and activities to be constantly available), talk about it right away. Let your partner know that individuality is important, and encourage your partner to keep or develop a separate identity, too. The sooner you do this, the easier it is.

Passive personalities. People who resist by doing nothing (they agree to do it, but they're late, or they procrastinate) can be the most frustrating to be around, but they really are very easy to handle, if you know how. To fix this problem, all you have to do is interpret, out loud, what you think their inaction means. If your friend is silent, for example, you can say, "You're not saying anything, and I think that means 'no.' Is that what you mean?" Or, "If you don't have a suggestion, I'm going to _____ (present your solution). Let me know if you want a different solution, or you have some ideas." Or, "You're agreeing with me, but you've agreed before, and I'm afraid you won't keep your part of the bargain. Will you tell me if you don't want to do it?"

If your partner is passively not participating, maintain your autonomy: figure out what you want to do for yourself, *and communicate it out loud or in writing.* If a friend is habitually late, you can say: "You agreed to be here at 7. If you're late, I'm leaving at 7:15." This gives your friend the choice, clearly states your intent, and minimizes your inconvenience. When dealing with someone who is passive, ambivalent, or reluctant, simply take care of yourself, and don't try to please or control your partner. You'll find their passive behavior eventually disappears, because it becomes more of a problem for your friend than for you.

Calming the Abandoned Child

Most violent arguments and emotional blowups between people, particularly between partners in intimate relationships, occur because both parties involved have (often unconsciously) chosen to allow themselves to become so upset that their inner turmoil interferes with their thinking ability. They cease thinking or using effective choice making, and *react* to each other, to the past, and to current events. When we let upsetting events prevent us from thinking clearly, it is as though our unconscious child mind is *abandoned* by our rational, adult mind, and can only helplessly follow old, childhood patterns. Observing couples with relationship difficulties is often like watching two little children fighting: "You did so!" "I did not, and anyway you stink!" Or, "You did so!" "Well, you did it first!" Actually, fights are just loud, dramatic disagreements about something that we could solve if we could remain calm, and access our adult thinking. When we get upset, we stop thinking rationally and *interpret* events according to what happened in childhood, *respond* as we did when we were powerless little children in a world of adults, and *react* with childlike fear and helplessness. This helplessness often takes the form of rage, resentment, and frustration.

If you grew up in a dysfunctional family, where children were told what to do but not helped to figure it out for themselves, and you have not learned to parent your child self, you have no other choice but to abandon, shut out, or ignore your inner child self (your feelings, reactions, and magical thinking) because it's the only thing you know how to do. But even when you've done your inner work, used adult-child dialogue, and developed internal intimacy, you can still abandon your child self if you get upset and stop thinking, and your autonomous ideas may get bypassed.

There are several unmistakable signs that stress and conflict in a relationship have led to abandonment of your inner child self.

Blaming. Blaming or accusing your partner, your self, other people, or other circumstances for your relationship problems, rather than looking for solutions. As an autonomous adult, you know how to solve problems and that blaming doesn't help, but your dependent child self forgets if the adult is not there to remind it.

Helplessness. Helplessness is the passive form of blaming. "I can't do anything, because it's their fault." When being upset has caused you to stop thinking, you may feel your old powerlessness, frustration, and helplessness, because without thinking you cannot solve problems. For example, if you find yourself yelling just the way your alcoholic parent did, or having the same argument with your mate, without resolution, over and over again, you are probably reliving old helplessness.

Repeating old patterns. When you find yourself repeating old patterns and reacting in old, familiar dependent or destructive ways after a fight or problem, it's a clue that you're letting your panicky, overwhelmed, and abandoned childlike self be inappropriately in charge, and you're not using autonomous, adult thinking to solve your problems. Your child self is acting on the only patterns that are familiar. This will happen less often after you use your magical tools to develop and practice new patterns, and give your child self alternatives.

Addiction, obsession, compulsion. If you begin to feel in danger of reverting to your old, addictive behavior, you have probably not been open and available to your inner child self or aware of its needs. You have probably left it to cope with a problem that (although you could easily handle it with autonomous, adult thinking) is completely overwhelming to your child mind, which brings up the old, hopeless and helpless feelings. When you've completed recovery and developed the skills and attitudes of autonomy, relapse only happens when you forget (under stress, or because you haven't yet repeated your autonomy exercises enough to strongly develop your new habits) to use autonomous thinking and you stop taking care of your inner child self for too long a time.

Using mind-deadening (or accelerating) substances, obsessing on a person or action, and compulsively doing what you know is bad for you are all ways that your dependent child mind learned to escape overwhelming pain or responsibility. If you catch the signals early, relapse will never be a problem, because you'll know how to reconnect to your inner child (using "Finding Your Trouble Spot" or other self-awareness exercises) and resume autonomous thinking long before your old behaviors have been activated enough to cause you frustration, anger, or pain.

Autonomous relating requires learning how to keep your grown-up aspect present and in charge. When any of the signals above are present, know that your childlike mind is feeling abandoned and overwhelmed by facing your circumstances without access to your adult, rational thinking ability. When your partner exhibits these same signs, she or he is probably experiencing self-abandonment, too. It's as though you have surrendered your autonomy, you are out of control, and *no adult, competent person is in charge.* Everyone abandons their inner child from time to time; we get frustrated, tired, overloaded, careless, and upset, and forget to use our autonomous thinking. But if you know the steps to reactivating autonomous thinking, you can quite easily get back in charge.

When you notice signs of abandonment in yourself or your partner, it's time to take a break, calm down, and get control of your thinking. Being autonomous, learning to be *present* in your own life and to be in charge, means not abandoning your inner child when the going gets rough. In other words, you retain your ability to think and figure out how to take care of yourself. Whether getting in control takes five minutes or twelve hours, it's worth doing, because it stops the destructive behavior and gives you a chance to find solutions.

Techniques for Reconnecting After Abandonment

By using the following techniques to keep your grown-up rational and thinking mind present in the relationship, you can overcome the tendency to repeat old, dysfunctional patterns. Regaining the ability to think clearly will put you in a *creative* rather than a *reactive* mode, and keep your autonomy intact.

These effective ideas, some of which are time-tested and some new, will help you get back in charge.

No matter who is feeling abandoned, hopeless, destructive, or upset, you or your partner, these three techniques will give each of you (or you alone) a chance to restore your own internal balance before facing each other again. Although you cannot decide whether your partner chooses to use them, you can certainly choose to use them yourself, no matter which of you is upset. Taking a break gives either one or both of you time to regain your autonomy and thinking capacity, once feelings have gotten out of hand. "Discharging Your Feelings" is for you to use when you're emotionally upset, whether you're the only one upset or not. "When Your Partner Shows Signs of Abandonment" is for you to use when your partner seems upset. You can use these techniques alone or in combination with each other.

"Taking Time Out" works no matter who is getting upset, because if one of you takes a break, the other is automatically given one, too. This break gives each of you a chance to get beyond your reactions and upset, and to recapture your ability to think clearly. It's very helpful if the two of you discuss "Taking Time Out" before you need to use it, but even if you haven't discussed it in advance, it's a good thing to do. Taking a time-out is different from running away from an argument, because the technique includes coming back to discuss the issue.

TECHNIQUE
TAKING TIME OUT

1. *Separate from the situation or person.* To take a time-out, when either you or your partner is showing signs of abandonment, make the choice to separate yourself from the situation or person you feel hopeless or upset about. Announce that you're going to take time out, and that you will be back. Then, for five minutes to half an hour, walk around the block, take a shower, visit or phone an understanding friend, or just go into another room—long enough

to complete this exercise and then go back and deal rationally with the situation. If you're in public (at a party, at work, or at your in-laws' house, for instance) and you need a time-out, try taking it in the bathroom. (There is almost always a bathroom nearby, and people will not object if you excuse yourself to use it.)

2. *Talk to yourself.* Once you have separated yourself from the source of upset, use your inner dialogue techniques to 1) make contact with your inner self or your child mind, which is feeling abandoned, 2) listen to how your child feels until you feel calmer, 3) discuss the problem and develop as many solutions and options as you can. For example, if you're at a party with your partner and you are having a bad time, your options might be to: go home early (by yourself if necessary), seek out a friend at the party to talk to, volunteer to wash dishes or refill the refreshments, take a walk or a drive (if it's safe) and then come back, or perhaps even dance.

3. *Make a choice.* Once you have considered what your options are in this situation, make a choice about what to do and then do it. You might decide to help with the dishes, and after a short time you'll be talking and laughing with others. Or if it's an argument, knowing that there are several ways to solve it will make you feel much calmer. If you learn to take your time-out as early as possible, before you're too upset, this calmness will come to you rather quickly.

4. *Repeat to develop expertise.* With enough repetition and practice of this exercise, you can recapture your calmness, get back in charge, and exercise the options you have in just a few minutes.

If you or your partner is so upset that "Taking Time Out" doesn't work, a period of emotional discharge may be necessary. This is easiest to do with someone uninvolved in the problem, because anyone connected with the problem, such as the mate with whom you are upset, may not be able to listen to your *dumping* without taking it personally and reacting to it. Discharging *away from the person you're upset with* allows you to express your feelings in a way that doesn't aggravate the problem, and once your feelings are dealt with, you will be calm and able to think clearly enough to solve the problem. With normal amounts of anxiety, aggravation, or other upset, talking to a friend can be very helpful. But to avoid becoming dependent on others, also learn to discharge by yourself.

Be aware that in cases of rape, violence, child abuse, or other traumatic history, or where emotions have been pent-up for a long time, discharging is critically important, needs knowledgeable supervision, and can take some time to complete. In these cases, getting into group or individual therapy is essential.

TECHNIQUE
DISCHARGING YOUR FEELINGS

1. *Separate from the problem.* In order to discharge effectively, take a time-out, and *get away from the source of upset*, as in the previous technique. Find a secure place to be alone, or with an uninvolved neutral person. Remember, discharging your feelings at the person you are upset with will just tend to make the problem worse.

2. *Express your feelings.* Once you are in a secure place, discharge your feelings by *expressing them* in whatever way feels best to you—write, yell, talk, or cry. If you are alone, you can write or draw in your journal, talk or yell out loud, or discharge them physically: pound a pillow if you're angry, or cover your head with a blanket if you're scared. If you're with someone else—a friend, a sponsor, or a therapist—tell them how you feel.

3. *Wait for a release.* The most important thing is to keep expressing your feelings until you feel a letting go or release. This is the discharge, and you'll know when you get to it because you'll experience a feeling of relief. Along with

the relief, you may also discover the real or central reason for the feelings, which often comes in the form of a new idea. It is often accompanied by an *Aha!* feeling of discovery, or a *Whew!* feeling of relief. As soon as you reach release, you'll find that your thinking capacity returns, and you can go on with problem solving, either by yourself or with the other person.

If your partner is the one acting helpless or very upset or otherwise showing signs of an abandoned child, you cannot really fix it *for* him, because your partner's feelings are his own responsibility. This technique can help you make sure you don't make the problem worse.

TECHNIQUE
WHEN YOUR PARTNER SHOWS
SIGNS OF ABANDONMENT

1. *Listen to the problem.* Often people get loud or upset, or quiet and helpless, because they believe their opinion, point of view, or feelings are not being heard. If you believe this may be the case, try giving your partner a chance to talk. Say, "You seem upset; will you tell me about how you feel?" or, "You're so quiet. Please tell me what you think?" or just, "Please tell me about it," and then listen quietly. Listening is not the same as agreeing, and you might hear something useful in your partner's point of view. If you can listen without getting upset yourself, and remain calm, you may find that your partner will then become willing to hear your side of the story. However, if you cannot listen calmly right now, skip to step 3. If listening works, but you still think your partner is not thinking rationally, move to step 2.

2. *Try to contact the adult, rational mind.* If your partner seems very helpless, or very upset, try asking some

calm, rational questions. Questions about numbers, dates, details, and facts are most successful in engaging the rational, adult mind, because to think of the answers your partner must be distracted from his subconscious feelings. For example, if your partner is yelling and accusing you of something, try asking calmly, "When did I do that?" or "How often do I do that?" Often the answer to such a question will be much calmer, and the yelling will stop. If your partner can access the rational part of his mind at all, he will suddenly find himself thinking again and may be relieved to find that you're interested. If that doesn't work, or your partner is still out of control, try step 3.

3. *Take a time-out.* If your partner is becoming very angry or violent, and your presence seems to be prolonging the problem or making it worse, or if you find you can't listen calmly, take a time-out. Even if you didn't start the argument, or it's your house, or you're somehow *right,* you can be the one who takes care of yourself. Taking a break will give you both a chance to calm down and return to clearer, more rational thinking.

Active Speaking and Autonomous Communication

Many of us are aware of active listening skills: we know to respond and rephrase what the other person is saying to show that we're attentive and understanding. What is not often taught is that you must pay attention to the other person when *you're* communicating, too.

Intimacy and good communication require active *listening,* that is, being aware of what your partner is saying, and also active *speaking*—being aware of how your partner is *receiving* what you are saying. If you are not aware of your partner while you are speaking, you can be misunderstood, ignored, or confused by her reaction. When you know what to look for, your listener will give you many clues about whether he is understanding what you say and is interested in it, and how he is reacting to it. Active speaking will also help you correct bad speaking habits that make your communication less effective. By keeping the questions of the following exercise in mind, you can learn to practice active speaking, and pay more attention to significant clues from your listener.

EXERCISE
ACTIVE SPEAKING

1. *Do you have your listener's attention?* Is your listener looking at you, rather than somewhere over your shoulder, off into space? Does she seem to be alert and interested, rather than have glazed eyes or a vacant, bored expression? If the answer to these questions is yes, you're doing fine. If no, you've lost your listener's attention, and your speech is in vain. If this is the case, try asking a question—it brings wandering attention back instantly. You can try: "What do you think?" or, "Has that ever happened to you?" or, "How does that feel to you?" If you lose your listener's attention frequently, pay attention to your speaking habits. You may want to make a recording of yourself in conversation, so you can check to see if you are speaking in a monotone voice, interrupting others, being unclear, or over-explaining your points.

2. *Does your partner's expression seem appropriate?* When you are talking to someone, you probably have some expectations of how that person will feel about what you're saying. If you say, "I like you," you expect your caring to be returned, or at least appreciated. If your listener's expression seems to be the wrong reaction for what you are saying, try to find out what is happening. Is your partner thinking of something else? Did he misunderstand or misinterpret what you said? You can ask: "I thought I was giving you a compliment, but you don't look happy. Can you explain what you're feeling?" or, "You look like you don't understand. Do you have a question?" or, "I'm upset, and you're

smiling. What does that mean?" By doing this, you can make sure you are communicating effectively and that your listener understands what you are saying, and if there's confusion, you can clear up misunderstandings before they become problems.

Active communication shows that you care about your listener and are interested in his or her responses. If you're miscommunicating, boring, or even upsetting your listener, you won't waste a lot of time before you find out. By paying attention to your partner's reactions, responses, and clues, and by staying present and aware, you can figure out on the spot how to create better communication, and therefore, more intimacy.

An additional benefit of learning autonomy is that it gives you skills that help you communicate. When you get proficient at internal intimacy, your deepened awareness of yourself and sensitivity to your own feelings make you familiar with how much better you feel. Whether you're talking to a friend, solving a problem with a lover, meeting someone new, or making love, by paying attention to how you feel on the *inside* about what's happening on the *outside,* you can learn to interact skillfully:

- slow down when you're going too fast
- keep things mutual by letting your partner make some of the moves
- recognize and respond to subtle invitations for more closeness
- keep a good balance between seriousness and fun
- avoid inappropriate interaction (such as becoming too parental, too childish, or struggling for control)

The next exercise is specially designed to help you develop this interaction skill. Following the steps will help you learn to use your awareness to achieve autonomous communication.

EXERCISE
AUTONOMOUS COMMUNICATION

1. *Check-in with yourself.* During communication, learn to check-in with your inner self and find out how you feel. Use the self-awareness exercises with which you have become proficient (such as "Trouble Spot" or "Adult-Child Dialogue"), to check-in with your inner self as you talk to people. If you use these exercises often, you'll find you've become quiet good at doing them on the spot. While you are in the presence of the other person, your inner awareness will let you know how the conversation feels, whether you feel loved, appreciated, and comfortable, and whether the other person is indicating that it feels good or not. Keep this on-the-spot check-in simple, merely paying attention to how your inner self feels, whether you're comfortable, and if you feel you're putting out too much of the energy in the conversation or not enough.

2. *Debrief prior conversations.* Develop a habit of reviewing your conversations with your partner and friends after you have them. Take some time after having a significant discussion and review it with your inner self, using "Adult-Child Dialogue" or "Trouble Spot" to find out how your inner self feels about the conversation and the person you spoke with. Ask your inner self questions such as, "How did it feel when Ron said he wanted to slow the relationship down?" "Could I have responded more sympathetically when Amy said her feelings were hurt?" "What was going on when Billy was congratulating me that made me feel so uncomfortable about it?" Review your responses and decide what you would like to change about your communication.

3. *Act on what you learn.* Whatever you learn about your inner reactions, pay attention to them and value them. Your inner intuition and emotional awareness are valuable clues about how comfortable and balanced (and therefore healthy and autonomous) your interactions are, and they will

also help you be aware of which people feel best to talk with. If you feel that you're putting more energy into the conversation than your partner, learn to relax more—hold back, slow down, and give your companion a chance. If you're feeling overwhelmed by your partner, experiment with ways of balancing the energy. Speed up a little or try to be a little more aggressive in speaking. If you consistently feel you can't get in a word, try talking about it with your partner.

If a conversation problem persists, remember that it could be an indication of other potential problems. If someone is unresponsive in a conversation, odds are that person is going to be unresponsive emotionally and/or sexually, too. If in conversation your partner often feels hostile toward you, it may mean that he or she is angry most of the time. As you become more familiar with your internal, intuitive responses to people, and you learn to act on what you feel, you'll find you have more ability to create relationships that are more mutual, balanced, and successful.

The following exercise combines Magical Tool 3, Self-Love, with "Time Travel," to help you reassure your inner child self and enhance your friendship with yourself. Try it whenever you feel rejected, lonely, abandoned, or unloved. Loneliness is your emotional clue that you are feeling abandoned by yourself, and when that happens, you will also feel abandoned by others. No one else can meet your internal needs for intimacy and love better than you can, because only you know exactly what you want, and exactly how satisfying different kinds of interaction are to you. By doing this exercise, you can autonomously experience and experiment with both the giving and receiving of intimacy—how the love you give feels and how it feels to receive exactly the kind of love you want. By meeting your needs for conversation, companionship, and attention yourself, you free yourself from anxiety about being alone and simultaneously reduce your dependency on others. Then when you do have an opportunity to be with another person, you can be relaxed and open. Healing your abandonment through internal intimacy also means you will be more free to choose who you spend time with, because being alone feels good, and you will only spend time with those who treat you as well as you do.

EXERCISE
HEALING ABANDONMENT: INTERNAL COMPANIONSHIP

1. *Find the source of your loneliness.* Whenever you find yourself feeling abandoned or lonely, or you long for someone else to take care of you or "make it better," ask yourself what you would like someone to do or say to you. Take some time with this, because it will give you clues about the source of your loneliness. Make a list. Do you want someone

- to make you laugh?
- to tell you everything is OK?
- to share an experience with you?
- to protect you?
- to reassure you?
- to understand your feelings?
- to be sympathetic and supportive?
- to give you a hug?

Once your list is made, put it aside for a moment, and go on to the next step.

2. *Invoke the inner child.* Using "Time Travel," visualize yourself as a child, but instead of going back into your childhood, imagine bringing your child self into your present life. Picture your child with you wherever you are now—sitting with you in your apartment or house, or walking with you outdoors.

3. *Choose an activity.* Using your list from step 1 to help you, talk with your child self and figure out something you can do together. For example:

- bike riding
- walking or hiking
- snuggling in bed
- eating while soaking in a bubble bath (especially good with sloppy food)
- dancing to your favorite music
- doing a jigsaw puzzle
- going to the movies
- preparing a special dinner for one
- jumping rope
- going to a favorite restaurant
- taking a drive in the country
- going to a museum or gallery
- going to a play or concert

4. *Make a date and keep your commitment.* Once you find an activity that feels right, set a date and make plans with your child self just as you would with a friend. Plan to actually physically carry out this activity by being physically alone but mentally in touch with your child self, as though you were doing the activity with an imaginary playmate or companion. When the time arrives, keep your commitment to your child self and carry out your plans. Prepare whatever you need for your date—"Time Travel" your child self here to be with you and do what you promised. For example, if you are going for a walk in the woods, you would go walking alone, but imagine your child self is with you and mentally talk to him or her throughout the walk.

5. *Treat yourself like a friend.* Remember you and your child within are doing this together. Keep in touch, talk to each other (silently if you're in public), and *share* this experience. Be aware of the information from all five of your senses (Magic Tool 1): sight, hearing, touch, taste, and smell. *Be as attentive with yourself as you would be with a friend you love a lot.*

6. *Talk about your experience.* By imagining talking to your child self, find out what he or she thinks about your

time together. Laugh or cry together, share feelings. This may feel awkward at first, so give it a chance, take your time, build on the internal dialogues you have done in previous exercises. Like Julie Ann in the following example, you will find that spending time with your child self is fun.

JULIE ANN

Julie Ann, a twenty-six-year-old from an alcoholic, abusive family, who had been in CoDa and ACA for several years before coming for therapy, rushed into my office one day excited. "I had such a great time this weekend! I can't wait to tell you. I decided to go roller skating at the beach—by myself. At first, I had a tough time. I was hot and sweaty. It was noisy. I was irritated at everyone and everything. Then I remembered little Julie, my little girl within. I decided to bring her along. All of a sudden, everything changed. Little Julie saw pretty colors, the beautiful light on the sea, the clouds in the sky. She laughed and joked with me about the people we passed. She enjoyed the air rushing by my face. We had a wonderful time, and we stopped to celebrate wtih frozen yogurt on the way home. I can't wait to go with little Julie again. It was more fun than I sometimes have with my friends!"

7. *Give yourself all the time you need.* When you are learning to meet your own needs for love, give yourself plenty of time. Go slowly and give yourself a chance to overcome old shame, embarrassment, self-consciousness, and self-rejection left over from toxic childhood experiences, which taught you that you were unlovable and that you didn't deserve attention from anyone including yourself. If these feelings come up, they're just leftovers from your dysfunctional family experiences, and the legacy of a dependently oriented society. You can overcome them with love, caring, patience, and practice. Ask yourself the following questions: How does it feel when I pay attention to my-

self? What do I like best about spending time with my child self? What would I like to do next time?

8. *Repeat to develop an ongoing relationship.* Try this exercise several times with lots of different activities, until being *with yourself* becomes automatic (using Magical Tool 6, Repetition). Do this exercise often, until it becomes easy and natural to spend time with and love yourself, and you no longer feel dependent on others for companionship and love.

With practice, these exercises and techniques (added to the magical tools and autonomous thinking skills you already have learned) will make the intimate relationships in your life seem less mystifying and relationship problems will seem much easier to solve. The more you use these tools and techniques, the more confident and effective you will become at building warm, loving, mutual, autonomous relationships.

CHAPTER 8

Autonomous Living: The Promise and the Challenge

> *Original experience has not been interpreted for you, and so you've got to work out your life for yourself. . . . The courage to face the trials and to bring a whole new body of possibilities in to the field of interpreted experience for other people to experience—that's the hero's deed.*
>
> JOSEPH CAMPBELL

O nce you accept responsibility for taking care of yourself— and are no longer dependent on other people, substances, or habits that fill your days and nights—life presents a new and unexpected challenge, one that is unlike anything you have ever experienced or imagined before. Now that you have acquired the skills of autonomy and the sense of self-confidence and self-reliance they bring, life becomes much easier.

In the beginning, this is a great relief, and you just relax and enjoy life with a minimal amount of chaos and difficulty for the first time. After your new skills of autonomy become natural and automatic, life becomes a lot more fun. Because you have learned to make effective choices, and "play chess" to consider the short- and long-term consequences of your decisions, you no longer go from crisis to crisis. Since your life is much more predictable and calm, you have the energy to build healthier habits and thought patterns, experiment with new behaviors, and begin to enjoy life even more.

When you are no longer numbed out by addiction, exhausted by inner turmoil, or distracted by recurring problems, you experience a burst of enthusiasm and energy. Your child self, now feeling safer and more confident, becomes more playful, and you are willing to allow that playfulness to be expressed in your life. Because you feel more secure, you can venture further into life and new situations, experiment, succeed, have victories, fail, be disappointed, but through it all you'll have the confidence that you can rely on yourself, and adapt when things don't work out the way you planned.

As you begin to experience the childlike joy you didn't have in your early dysfunctional, dependent family, you begin to have more fun with friends, family, and co-workers. Your relationships, based on autonomous thinking and mutual respect, are also less chaotic and more positive and rewarding, because instead of struggling with people you know how to work out problems with effective choice making and negotiation. Your experience is similar to that of the people whose histories have illustrated each part of this book:

Susan, the floral designer who overcame her compulsive overeating, said: "You told me this would happen, but I never understood how good it would feel! Life is so much easier, and business problems no longer overwhelm me, now that I can handle my feelings directly. Now, when I get angry, I just fix the problem, and the anger goes away! No eating, no depression—I never knew life could feel this good."

Warren, the ACA who had been abused as a child and then in his adult relationships, found he could now tell quite easily when he was being mistreated, and break off relationships that felt abusive. He was now making new, healthier friends. He had a new feeling of calm inside, he was no longer having nightmares or flashbacks to his child-hood, and he was now spending his weekends playing and relaxing with his child self, and his new friends.

Suzanne, whose father had called her "selfish" when she took better care of herself, found that as she got more secure, her family treated her better, and so did others: "Even my boss treats me better now, and I can't believe I used to be so afraid of him! As soon as I stood up for myself, and refused to acknowledge him unless he spoke properly to me, he changed his attitude. All of my life is pleasant now, and I'm really enjoying having friends who treat me well."

Perry, who had been afraid of a new career change, said: "After I got over my old, childhood fear of being ridiculed, I found that my job search was actually enjoyable! I met a lot of new people in my field, and, since I wasn't unemployed, I took my time and found the perfect job. My life is so much more enjoyable now. I feel good about my work and I have more personal time to enjoy myself. I'm now having fun looking for a new, autonomous romance."

Carla, the formerly battered woman whose children were now grown, said: "I never would have believed an old broad like me could have a new love, but I feel like a schoolgirl! He treats me well, and when we have a problem, we work it out together. And I know that my relationship with me is the most important one, so that gives me the freedom to leave if this relationship ever gets abusive. Not that I think it will. Learning to take care of myself, and negotiate with others, has made all my re-lationships, even with my children, work better. I really like my life."

Like most of these people, you will probably have difficulty adjusting to this at first, after years of experiencing chaos and pain. It may take you a while to learn to trust your newfound calm and happiness, to believe it will last. In the early months, the calm and security of autonomous living seems fragile, as though you'll revert back to old behaviors at any moment. But as you learn that you can correct any errors you make, and sustain your new, healthy ways of living and relating, your feeling of competence and security in your new way of living will grow.

The relief of this new, uncomplicated, and straightforward style of living can last months or years, particularly if new dynamics such as a relationship, career, or life-style are being explored. For that period, it is enough just to have ended the chaos and be able to live functionally and effectively. But after a while, as your new happiness becomes commonplace and feels natural, you may begin to notice something—a feeling of emptiness where all the struggle and chaos, followed by excitement and joy, has been. A sense of restlessness, as if there were something you ought to be doing, something missing from your life. This calm life has begun to be a little *too* calm, and you begin to wonder: "What else is there?" It may even feel as though your whole *being* is asking, "Now what?"

This phase worries most people who hit it, because they mistake their restlessness and need to challenge themselves with their old drive to addictive behavior. They fear it means they're looking for a relapse, to get back into crisis. However, they (and you) need not worry. Once autonomous thinking, effective choice making, and functional relationships with your inner self and others become easy and natural for you, any fear that you will revert to addictive behavior is groundless. Even if you try, you'll find that it feels too bad to continue doing it.

In your addictive, dependent period, all your time was taken up by struggling, avoiding, being overwhelmed by responsibility, and trying to get someone or something else to make it better. There was never any question of what to do with yourself or your time. And since then your life has been taken up with enjoying your new achievements of autonomy, and your new ability to cope well with life. Now that the novelty has worn off, you are faced with a new situation, one you never had to face before: what to do with your time and energy.

Getting to this stage feels much like being healthy again after a long illness—for a while, it is enough just to feel well, to get up in the morning and sit in the sun. But soon, as your energy rises and your confidence in remaining healthy returns, you feel restless. You want to get back to your life, to your friends, to your accomplishments—just sitting and not feeling sick is no longer enough.

FINDING YOUR PURPOSE IN LIFE

When you begin to feel restless, as if there must be more to life (as many who learn to live autonomously eventually do), it is a signal that you need more challenge in your life—that just feeling good is no longer enough, that your individuality needs greater and more range to express itself more completely, and that you need a way to evaluate your ideas for creative expression before you act on your new energy and impulses. In short, you're looking for a new *purpose,* more meaning in your life.

Purpose is a very adult concept. Children have an automatic, built-in purpose: survival, and learning how to function in their world. Some adults never grow beyond this original purpose; the basic needs of survival (food, shelter, clothing, contact) occupy their entire lives. And indeed, in a chaotic, dependent, out-of-control life, just keeping the basics of survival together takes all your time and energy. But people who learn autonomous living, as you are now experiencing, have a *surplus* of energy. People for whom the basics of life are already established need more: they need a sense of meaning and a higher purpose than just survival. When you know how to think clearly, and be effective, a life based on just survival is boring—a person with self-confidence and self-esteem needs a challenge to feel satisfied, a way to express her or his uniqueness and individuality to him- or herself, to friends, and to the world.

Each of us has special talents and abilities that begin to beg for expression when the issue of survival ceases to occupy all our time. In *The Power of Myth,* philosopher/teacher Joseph

Campbell describes the "maturation of the individual, from dependency through adulthood, through maturity": "Some people are living on the level of the sex organs. . . . Then you come to . . . the will to power . . . centered on obstructions and overcoming the obstructions. Then there comes giving oneself to others one way or another." Finally, you begin "to work out your life for yourself . . . to face . . . a whole new body of possibilities."

When you learned autonomous thinking and effective choice making, your life began to work better, and you felt better about yourself, so your energy and enthusiasm rose. Because this success has enhanced your self-confidence, your capacity to meet and enjoy challenges is greater than it ever was. Your inner self is beginning to want to express itself to the world. But if your life's purpose is not evident to you already, how do you find out what it is? Where does a sense of purpose come from? Although finding a purpose that can encompass your whole life might seem impossible or overwhelmingly difficult and daunting at first—even for someone confident of your ability to rely on yourself to meet most challenges—you really don't have to look long or hard to find it. It is *your* purpose, remember. It comes from within you, and is not imposed or chosen from outside. Bernie Siegel describes this sense of purpose as being within all living things "directing" them "from within." It is what "makes it possible for the fertilized egg to know who to grow up to be, physically, intellectually, psychologically, and spiritually."

In human beings, Siegel writes, our sense of purpose takes the form of "an inner message, an inner awareness, that says, 'This is your path, this is how you can be the best human being possible.' If you follow it, you will achieve your full growth and full potential." To find your purpose, you need not look any further than your own inner self: "If you learn to listen, your inner voice will speak to you about your path, about . . . your . . . 'job on earth.'"

From this gradually grows a sense of purpose, what Dr. Siegel calls your "job on earth"—a sense of the significance of your life, and the responsibility that goes with it. Your purpose may be your livelihood, or it may have nothing to do with how you make a living. Your purpose may be a simple one, like making a good, healthy life for yourself and your children; or it may be more dramatic, based on what you learned by healing your own childhood experience. Many people have experienced the power that their inner purpose has to transform anxiety, anger, fear, and rage into powerful, life-affirming action:

Dr. Siegel knows about inner purpose because he experienced it himself: as a cancer specialist he was so discouraged and frustrated by the lack of success of medicine against cancer that he had the courage to look at patients who had experienced "miracle cures" and "spontaneous remissions," which no M.D. had ever done. Although he was ridiculed by the medical establishment, he persevered in his autonomous thinking, and out of it came his ECaP (exceptional cancer patients) recovery groups, and his book, *Love, Medicine and Miracles.*

For Carla, finding purpose meant going back to college at age fifty-five to get the law degree she had wanted before marriage and kids intervened.

Cleve Jones turned his rage, bitterness, and grief about AIDS into the Names Project Memorial Quilt, which has helped people throughout the world express, heal, and understand the grief resulting from this tragic epidemic.

For Marguerite, the young woman who was afraid to go out, it was volunteering to work with abused and abandoned children in a shelter.

Candy Lightner, after her thirteen-year-old daughter was killed by a drunken driver, used the power of her grief and rage to found Mothers Against Drunk Driving (MADD) to combat the problem and prevent the senseless deaths of other children.

For Warren, it was quitting his lucrative and successful career as a programmer to work part time and become a gardening landscaper.

Sojourner Truth, an African-American and former slave, was instrumental in developing the Underground Railway to guide slaves to freedom before and during the American Civil War.

Ron Kovic, a soldier who was paralyzed from the waist down in what he felt was a senseless war, turned first to alcoholism, but then recovered and channeled his resentment and rage into antiwar protest, and later wrote the best-selling book and Oscar-winning movie script, *Born on the Fourth of July*.

By having a life purpose, you are able to control your destiny, no matter what the force of the hardships you have incurred through dependency and addictive behavior. You already have everything you need to find your purpose, and you can begin at once, through the exercise that follows later in this chapter. You have already mastered the earlier exercises designed to help you communicate and listen to your inner self, your subconscious mind, and it is through these techniques, by focusing them on your inner purpose, that you can find your answers. By now, you may already be having many ideas but not be trusting them or taking them seriously. Many therapy clients knew what their "job on earth" or life's purpose was long before they got into recovery, but they were too distrustful of themselves or too hopeless and helpless to believe it or act on it.

Your purpose may make itself clear to you in one instant flash, or gradually, as if you were supposed to follow clues. Whether you get it all at once or a piece at a time, it will still take work and experience to bring it about. With the help of your magical tools, your inner, subconscious, childlike mind can become a source of inner wisdom. This wisdom is not rational or practical in nature, but more intuitive and spiritual. It can provide a way to see the *big picture,* or a more *detached* and *objective viewpoint* of the issues and problems of life. Combined with autonomous, adult thinking, "Playing Chess" and choice making, inner wisdom gives you one more viewpoint from which to evaluate your decisions and actions.

Access to inner wisdom, coupled with autonomous thinking, endows everything you experience with extra meaning. All the events, activities, and patterns of your life can be viewed from both perspectives. Using both viewpoints (intuitive wisdom and autonomous thinking) can even become the basis of your partnership with, instead of dependency on, the Higher Power spoken of in the discussion of the power of the Twelve Steps.

Many people have successfully changed their attitudes, livelihood, activities, and environment—but those who did thought ahead, "played chess," and did not proceed blindly. A partnership between your subconscious, inner wisdom and adult rational mind builds a successful life.

The Need for Stimulus

Another reason you will be compelled to find your purpose in life is that human beings need stimulus (a challenge from yourself, another, or your environment that causes you to think and react). Newborns die without enough stimulus. It keeps the mind alert and healthy. We all thrive on stimulus, and some of us crave more than others. In dysfunctional families, the need for stimulus that normally would lead us to take risks and seek to learn new things is often sidetracked into the drama of compulsion, addiction, and dependency, which supplies lots of action and excitement. It keeps us occupied, adrenalized, and stimulated, while (because the family creates drama according to an established pattern) it still feels familiar, predictable, and therefore safe. As we grow up, this need for the old, familiar excitement and stimulus remains one of the most tempting and compelling aspects of dependency, as Joy Davidson describes of her clients' experience in *The Agony of It All*:

> I began to see over and over again, a sometimes subtle, sometimes distinct straining toward the acting out of intense scenarios that were highly distressing and equally

stimulating . . . *not* out of a hidden wish to suffer or a belief that they deserved pain, but out of a *restrained or severely misdirected, but essentially healthy, drive for heightened stimulation.* . . . When we create our own exciting melodramas, . . . we set up or build upon potentially dramatic or explosive situations so that they are exaggerated, sensationalized, and pushed to the limits. As these scenarios become more volatile, they also become more thrilling . . . we are frequently unconscious of making it happen.

Replacing that excitement is essential, for without sufficient stimulus we cannot experience enough satisfaction. Health and sobriety, if we allow it to be dull and boring, cannot be sustained. Some people even fall off the wagon and revert to destructive behaviors, unhealthy relationships, and old addictions, because they don't know what else to do to relieve their boredom.

Having a purpose supplies plenty of stimulus. The challenge of real fulfillment becomes as exciting as the old addiction, compulsion, obsession, and drama, but with positive, healthy results. The popular image of excitement is often destructive, violent, and frightening. There are few positive images of excitement: of healing and growth, of helping others grow and change, of fighting for human rights, of saving the Earth, or of the challenge and satisfaction of building a healthy, productive life.

Having a higher purpose provides plenty of stimulus, because it constantly challenges us with new ideas and the necessity to work out new solutions to new problems. Because living according to a heartfelt purpose is motivating and energizing, and we feel enthusiastic about the next step toward our goal, our life feels stimulating and rewarding.

We are all used to thinking of excitement as nonproductive, but there is no need to manufacture melodrama as a source of stimulation, because life itself presents so many opportunities for excitement. As Carlos Castaneda's Don Juan said: "In a world where Death is the hunter, my friend, there is no room for regret or doubt. There is only room for decision." Life itself is a challenge: using our limited time on the planet for a purpose—to create something unique, special, and that feels good to us—is both exciting and satisfying. Joseph Campbell explains how stimulating and life-giving following your inner purpose can be:

> My general formula is "Follow your bliss." Find where it is, and don't be afraid to follow it . . . in doing that, you save the world. The influence of a vital person vitalizes, there's no doubt about it. . . . People have the notion of saving the world by shifting things around, changing the rules, and who's on top, and so forth. No, no! . . . The thing to do is to bring life to it, and the only way to do that is to find in your own case where the life is and become alive yourself.

Marsha Sinetar, who studied people with the courage to live fulfilling lives, says there is a "predictable sequence" to the "life-enhancing choices" those people made. In *Elegant Choices, Healing Choices,* she outlines the steps of the experience of living autonomously:

- We choose in a wholesome direction *despite* feeelings of fear or our need to cling to the familiar.
- Instead of avoiding those things we fear, we start proactively selecting those ways of being, thinking and acting that most efficiently take us toward what we consciously want.
- Our self-acceptance for our truest, "living self" increases . . . we move to present our real self to others, to live our real selves in our lives.
- Ultimately, our choices *flow* from this core-self, instead of being *forced*. . . . We are faithfully courageous and loving toward ourselves and—eventually—toward others. . . . Growing more closely attuned to our inner workings, we also grow more conscious and self-accepting.
- Soon we notice how our negative feelings can actually *help* us, provide information to us much as a mirror or photograph.

Danaan Parry, who worked with Vietnam War veterans of *both* sides to heal the aftereffects of the war, writes of the "new warrior" (his word for those who turn violent, destructive energy into life-affirming, purposeful, and stimulating action), and the challenge of disagreeing with those who think that dependency is safe:

> The new warrior . . . says, "I am going to show . . . that there is no real [problem] out there. That darkness exists within each one of us, and I will demand that we have the courage to look at it." So . . . warriors have to have the courage to put up with some pretty heavy flak from their own people. We are asking our own people to grow and not to project.

Life with a purpose can be new, different, and challenging, but it contains the vitality and stimulus that give life meaning. Life with purpose is constantly a new ballgame. Every situation you encounter is unique, requires clear thinking ability, and must be constantly checked against your purpose to see what steps you need to take. Many former therapy clients find that living life according to their inner purpose feels courageous and exploratory. Like Carla, they can now say, "I really like my life."

It *is* akin to living as a warrior, a new, exciting way to live that can satisfy the stimulus hunger that was once satiated by the drama of dependency. Your life no longer needs to be desperate to be exciting, because your purpose is stimulating enough. Look around you at the people who have the most fulfilling and rewarding lives. Then look at the ones who seem to have a definite purpose. You'll find both groups contain the same people.

Your Inner Purpose

Here's a guided fantasy (Magical Tool 2: Imagery) designed to help you communicate with your inner self and use clues contained in your personality characteristics, desires, and talents to find your "job on earth." It is not necessary to believe in a Higher Power to do this exercise, but imagining what a Higher Power intended often gives you a broader, more detached, wiser, not to mention kinder view of yourself and your life. The purpose of this exercise is to examine who you are from a different vantage point, as an all-knowing being might see it. For the purpose of the exercise, assume that an infinitely wise and creative being designed your own unique mix of traits to accomplish a specific goal. What could a benevolent Higher Power have possibly had in mind when you were created? Be careful, now, and don't insult or demean the special creation that you are. This is holy handiwork we're talking about.

EXERCISE
YOUR INNER PURPOSE

Imagine your Higher Power's plan. If you were an intelligent, loving God, or your Higher Power, who designed the Earth with a plan, and designed you just the way you are to fit into that plan, what purpose would you have?

Look for clues to your purpose in your inherent talents and qualities. What might a Higher Power intend them to accomplish? If you have trouble focusing on your talents and qualities, the following questionnaire is designed to help you find them. It will give you an opportunity to discover or review the kind of person you are, and what abilities come naturally to you (even if they sometimes get you into trouble). Read it over, choose one or several answers in each category that fit you best, and use each list to stimulate your own ideas. Some people have an instant "Aha!" when doing this exercise. Others take longer to ponder it before it makes sense. The point is to shake up your perception of yourself and your talents, qualities, and circumstances, and give you a chance to view them differently.

Using the following lists as guides, write your personal qualities, talents, desires, and circumstances down on a separate sheet of paper.

PERSONAL QUALITIES

Parents know that babies are born with different personality traits—one baby will be easygoing, the next more sensitive. Although these inherent qualities are further shaped (or sometimes distorted) by the growing-up experience, where they come from initially is a mystery. Approach this list as if you were made uniquely the way you are for a reason.

WHAT ARE YOUR PERSONAL QUALITIES?

- friendly, open, outgoing?
- solitary, quiet, reserved?
- communicative, verbal?
- a good listener, receptive?
- a dreamer, mental?
- a conscientious worker, productive?
- physically active, outdoorish?
- relaxed, meditative?
- practical, thrifty, cautious?
- courageous, bold, experimental?
- fun, enthusiastic?
- imaginative, creative?
- funny, witty?
- original, innovative (sometimes called "weird")?
- Do you work or play better alone or with others?
- Do you enjoy structure or openness more?
- Do you enjoy productivity or play more?

List the personality traits you have that were not on this list.

TALENT

All of us have special talents and abilities but may have been raised to discount them and may not even be consciously aware of them. After determining where your talents lie, add them to your list and try to imagine why a Higher Power might have given them to you in your particular combination.

WHAT ARE YOUR TALENTS?

- music (playing, singing, composing, appreciating, critiquing)?
- communication (conversation, public speaking, writing, explaining)?
- artistic (visual arts, dance, acting, directing)?
- mental skill or play (mathematics, spatial relations, puzzles, computer games or programming, crosswords)?
- good with your hands (mechanical, crafts, carpentry, pottery, needlework, sculpture)?
- sports (playing individual or team sports, coaching, refereeing, big fan, commentator)?
- negotiation (seeing both sides of a question, helping people understand one another, interpretation, brainstorming options)?
- nurturing (caring for children, the sick, the elderly, friends)?
- getting things done (efficiency, dedication, follow-through, determination, job satisfaction)?

List your talents that don't appear on this list.

DESIRE

Just as we were born with different qualities and talents, we are born with different wants. Why might a Higher Power have given you yours? There is a saying in mystical writings, "All wants lead to God." The belief behind it is, that if you seek to understand your deepest desires and follow them, you will find your path through life. This is what Joseph Campbell calls "following your bliss."

WHAT ARE YOUR DESIRES?

- clean up the environment?
- make a political difference?
- express yourself musically or artistically?
- travel?

- make a quilt?
- do Shakespeare in the park?
- make a film?
- be powerful?
- become a healer or health-care worker?
- grow a garden?
- follow a spiritual path?
- love and be loved?
- fly an airplane?
- save animals or human lives?
- get a college degree?
- write a book?
- teach and/or write philosophy?

List your desires that don't appear on this list.

CIRCUMSTANCES

Certain patterns seem to repeat in our lives, whether or not we want them to. Some are pleasant, some are not, but often the unpleasant, unwanted events turn out to be as valuable as the pleasant ones, because we may learn something new or break through some resistance that held us back. What if these patterns are happening repeatedly for a reason? What might a Higher Power be trying to teach or show you?

CIRCUMSTANCES THAT REPEAT IN YOUR LIFE

- people tell you their life stories (whether or not you ask)
- you often wind up teaching, talking to, organizing, or leading groups
- you are exposed to people vastly different from you, that some people might be contemptuous or afraid of
- you're drawn to churches, museums, forests, bookstores, farms, schools, hospitals, theaters, factories
- you find yourself repeatedly working with computers, plants, paintbrushes, horses, babies, heavy machinery, microscopes

- your career self-destructs, and you have to find something else
- you keep thinking about: helping AIDS babies or Mother Teresa, writing a play or novel, going to Brazil, having sex, organizing Eastern Europe, living in the woods
- you keep feeling that there's something you're supposed to be doing, but you don't know what it is

List the circumstances you repeatedly find yourself in that don't appear on this list.

PUTTING IT ALL TOGETHER

Fill in the blanks below with the appropriate words. You may have several words for each blank in the sentence. If you have lots of choices for each blank, you may want to write out the sentence several times, with several variations. When you've done this, your sentence may make perfect sense to you, or the result may be gibberish or sound silly. Keep adjusting the words so they make more sense. Experiment with it for a while. Allow your intuition to help out here. Make wild guesses, and play with the concept. Taking your list of traits, talents, desires, and events that seem characteristic of you, put them in a sentence form like this: I (your Higher Power) designed _____ (your name) to be a _____ (quality) person who can _____ (talent) and I put (him, her) in _____ (circumstance) often, because I want _____ (your name) to help me out by _____ (your desire).

Once your unconscious inner self gets the idea that you're considering your "job on earth," mysterious things will begin to happen. You'll notice qualities and talents in you that you never noticed before, or you'll view traits positively that used to feel negative. You'll view the circumstances of your life differently, as though they have more than just the obvious meaning, and you'll consider your desires more carefully, rather than just discounting them. Assume that both your character traits and the events of your life, if used appropriately, are positive and purposeful. After a while, a pattern will emerge, you'll begin to understand your "job on earth," and it might even surprise you.

This exercise, if you do it conscientiously, will begin to create change in your life. Marsha Sinetar says that by "growing more closely attuned to our inner workings, we also grow more conscious and self-accepting." Your acceptance of personal characteristics that may have been downgraded or ridiculed in your past, and a new openmindedness about the meaning of events in your life, will give you more options from which to choose.

As your awareness of your purpose grows, don't surrender your autonomy and just depend on your inner voice—apply autonomous thinking as in other matters, evaluate what your inner voice says, exercise choice making before you make drastic changes. If you follow this advice you will be able to work with the information you get from deep within, adjusting it to your outer reality and using your adult rational mind to make sure you're successful.

JASON

Jason, a thirty-three-year-old recovering lawyer who did this exercise, realized he wanted to be a playwright, but was afraid to quit his job and take the time he needed to write. Once he saw play writing as his "job on earth," he was able to quit the law firm he hated, work part time, and write. He has since won several awards and had plays produced in small theaters. He says, "I'm poorer in money, but I'm so much richer in happiness and satisfaction. This is the me I always wanted to be."

Endowing your life with a specific purpose makes a profound difference in everything you do because you can compare all your actions and decisions against a new criterion: Will this move you closer to or farther away from your purpose?

Finding your purpose in life is much like choosing your destination for a journey. As soon as you determine where you are going, many decisions are already made for you—what to spend your money on, what to learn for the journey, and which direction to go in. Each fork in the road you encounter is evaluated and chosen according to whether or not it takes you toward your destination.

Jason, the lawyer turned playwright, once said: "Ever since I was a small boy I knew my dad wanted me to be a lawyer. When someone asked me what I was going to be when I grew up, I *always* said "a lawyer," and I liked it that people were impressed. But I never thought about what a lawyer *was*. I don't like the work, it's too technical and not creative, I'm not interested, and I don't really care. I drag myself to work every day."

Like Jason, you may be living many parts of your life the way *others* think you should. Or you may be living in rebellion, according to what *upsets* certain people. Either way, you haven't made your own decision, you're living for others, not for yourself. For as long as you do it that way, you will feel dissatisfied. Jason says, "Some days it's really hard, and it's scary, sometimes, but I'm so much *happier* this way. *I know I'm doing what I was born to do.*"

The challenge of living your life toward a specific purpose is exciting enough that you will not be tempted to fall back into old, addictive/compulsive forms of stimulation. It's the autonomous, heroic way of challenging yourself—the rewards are a sense of satisfaction that comes from knowing you're doing what you were "born to do."

EVALUATING AUTONOMOUS LIVING

Sooner or later, you will probably reach a point where you're wondering: OK, I've taken the Real Thirteenth Step. I have now decided what I think is my purpose. So how do I know my purpose is correct? I can evaluate my individual choices and decisions, but how do I evaluate my life? If I don't live by others' ideas of who I am and what I should do, then what are the guidelines I do live by?

There are three criteria against which your choice of a higher purpose can safely be checked: results, experience, and ethics. Let's take a look at these checkpoints, and see how they are developed.

Results

Although the initial inspiration comes from within, there are also concrete, external clues by which you can evaluate whether you have chosen your purpose wisely. By paying attention to the results, the way a scientist doing a lab experiment would, you can know if you're on the right track in your life. Life is your laboratory, since all your actions have results.

By paying attention to whether the circumstances are working in your favor, you can tell how well you are doing. These circumstances include your stress level, your finances, your relationships, the time spent at leisure and work, and whether the steps you need to follow to achieve your life purpose are going smoothly or with difficulty.

For example, Jason is aware that his finances are not as abundant as they were when he was a lawyer, but he does make sufficient money to live comfortably, if simply, his stress level is less, he has more free time, more self-expression, and he is more relaxed and pleasant in his relationships. These results, for Jason, mean that his life works better *in the ways that are important to him* than it did as a lawyer, when his stress level (resulting from frustration with his job, commuting, and pressure to perform) was extremely high, he had little free time, and consequently he had less patience and energy for his relationships.

Sometimes things in your experiment with purposeful living will go wrong, even when your purpose is good and your attempts are honest. Or your results may be mixed and inconclusive. When you get a negative result, to analyze whether you need to reevaluate your purpose you can ask yourself two questions:

Is this an important result? One negative, amid a lot of positives, may not be important. Also, in some circumstances, a certain number of negative results are to be expected. All successful people have many stories of failure and rejection—but not one of them gave up and scrapped their work because of failure. They just reevaluated, corrected errors, and tried again. In your case, some negative results you can learn from, and thus improve your work; others you'll consider, find that you don't agree, and ignore them and persevere.

How does this affect my original idea? Is the result so different from what you expected that you want to reevaluate what you are doing in life, or could it just give you some new ideas about how to do it more effectively, if you approach the situation more creatively?

Marsha Sinetar discovered that people with purpose often learn how to use negative results in a positive way: "Soon we notice how our negative feelings can actually *help* us, provide information to us much as a mirror or photograph."

In addition to the concrete, observable results, there are other, internal results that help you decide whether your purpose and your autonomous living are going well. Your disappointment, dissatisfaction, anger, grief, frustration, and fear, if you pay attention to them and learn from them, are all *clues* to whether or not your life is satisfying and healthy for you. So are your positive emotions, such as happiness, fulfillment, satisfaction, contentment, and excitement.

Carla, for example, who enrolled in law school at age fifty-five, is experiencing a lot of stress, and has less free time than ever, but she feels a very high degree of inner satisfaction, which tells her that what she's doing is good for her, and worth the stress and hard work she has to go through to achieve her purpose.

Carla is sure that she has found the right purpose because of her feeling of deep inner satisfaction, which, according to the dictionary, is "a state of well-being consequent upon having achieved a goal, or gratified an appetite or motive." Knowing you can cope with the world on your own terms, focusing on your life purpose and achieving goals on the way to making your purpose a reality, produces a high degree of satisfaction. It gives you a specific goal or goals you can strive for, and a way to know when you've achieved each goal.

Many frightened, dependent people *never* feel satisfied or content. Their feeling of dissatisfaction, of emptiness, comes from not having a purpose, because without a clear idea of purpose they cannot know when they reach goals. It's similar to never knowing when your journey is finished because you never decided on a destination, or never getting the satisfaction of graduation because you never chose a major subject in which the university could say you had completed the requirements. Addiction, obsession, and compulsion are often ineffective attempts to quench your longing for satisfaction, for completion of some goals.

In contrast, life lived in quest of your higher purpose, guided by internal wisdom and evaluated by autonomous thinking, gives you a way to feel satisfied by giving you goals you can reach.

Another result or positive sign that you have chosen your purpose well is fulfillment. Fulfillment is the difference between feeling that life is empty, meaningless, and out of your control, and feeling that it is significant, rewarding, deeply nourishing, and sustaining, and that you are getting what you want out of it. Fulfillment and satisfaction produce a feeling of internal warmth, much like the feeling that arises from autonomous loving. When you have a sense of purpose, and you are working to bring that purpose into reality, each step or small achievement along the way makes you feel better about yourself. You can judge the appropriateness of your purpose and the way you are carrying it out by your inner sense of pride in yourself, feeling worthwhile and valuable as a person, and your level of enjoyment or happiness.

Because your sense of purpose has meaning for you in terms of your own personal value system, to work toward achieving that purpose helps you feel worthwhile as a person and gives you a life of which you can feel proud, not because it pleases others but because you feel it has intrinsic value. That is, whether anyone knows you're doing it or not, it feels worth doing. Joseph Campbell writes that when you follow your bliss you have a feeling that "the life that you ought to be living is the one you are living" and a sense that "no matter what happens, this is the validation of [your] life."

Experience

The second criterion for evaluating your higher purpose is experience. As you experience bringing your idea or fantasy of your purpose toward the reality of fulfillment, both the original idea and the final expression of it will change. In the beginning, your purpose is a dream, a fantasy. It is real only in your mind, and until you *experience* it, you can only *imagine* it. Anything that exists only in your imagination is bound to need some adjustment as you begin to make it a reality.

For example, Carla's dream of being a lawyer is *only* a dream as long as she's in law school. But, the more she learns in school, the clearer her idea of what a lawyer does and all the ways you can be a lawyer will change. By the time she graduates, works in some law offices as a legal clerk, and passes the bar, she'll have a much better idea of what she wants. Instead of thinking she wants to be "a lawyer," she'll know whether she wants to be in corporate, insurance, civil, or criminal law, and she may have an idea that she'd like to be in private practice rather than in a big firm. Even if she starts out dreaming about lots of money and a lovely office with antique furnishings and a great secretary, she may find herself, years later, in a plain little office, making modest money, because she gets the most satisfaction out of helping battered women and children, which is not the most prestigious or lucrative work. This may be far from Carla's original dream, but because she made the choices according to her inner sense of what was most important she'll still be certain that it's the right thing for her to do. Her inner satisfaction is more important to her than external evidence of success. Watching her vision change as she brought it into reality, and her reality change as her vision affected her decisions, affirmed for her that she was on the right path.

No matter what your life purpose turns out to be, the reality of it will change as, in the experience of making your dream come true, you learn more about how it works. This evolution of experience happens not only with your main purpose but also with every little goal you strive for. Knowing that you can *adapt* your goals as you learn more means that your autonomous thinking will remain based on reality, even as your reality changes. Only if your idea of your original goal is so rigid that you cannot accept the need to adapt it to make it more realistic or more possible for you to accomplish, do you need to reevaluate it as your life purpose.

Ethics

Taking care of yourself and being responsible for yourself means creating your own standards for ways of treating yourself and others that are healthy and make both your inner, subconscious self and your outer, rational self feel good. When you are aware of and intimate with your inner self, treating others or yourself badly is too uncomfortable. People with healthy internal intimacy do not need outside rules to tell them how to behave. Once your internal intimacy is in place, your inner standards of behavior will cause you to stay well inside of the law, as long as the law is sensible and just, and cause you to behave in a highly conscious manner. Lying, stealing, and coercing or using others just feels too bad to do. Inner intimacy and self-reliance develops a set of inner values that will guide you well.

Anyone who regularly considers effective choices, "plays chess," values the warmth in relationships, and compares their internal and external relationships continuously will live by a far higher standard of ethical behavior than anyone could impose via "rules to live by" from outside. Such standards imposed or accepted from without can never be completely right for you or fully match your personal criteria. Inherent in your life purpose is a set of values and standards—comparing your life frequently to these standards, and living by your internal values, is living ethically. Most dependent people operate (by either complying or rebelling) on a moral basis. For this discussion, morality can be defined as rules for conduct that originate outside oneself—for example, the law codes, the Ten Commandments, and "what Mom and Dad say is right." Morality is dependent and reactive.

Because the premade, rigid rules of morality cannot apply to every situation, people who blindly, dependently, follow an outside morality reach a crisis of conscience eventually, when they encounter a situation for which their "rules to live by" are inadequate. Sooner or later, there is a situation that can't be covered by the rules in advance. For example, the Ten Commandments' order to "Honor thy father and thy mother" can precipitate a moral crisis in someone who suddenly remembers being abused by his or her own parents. "Keep coming back," although appropriate for newly recovered people, doesn't work for every member forever.

There is no substitute for the ability to think for yourself, and there is no one who can make your decisions better than you can. In using your ability to make effective choices to create your own personal inner values, awareness, and purpose, you develop an ethical evaluation ability that will not fail you in time of crisis. You can evaluate each situation as it arises, and use your ability to make effective choices combined with your inner values to come up with a response that suits the situation. Dr. Nathaniel Branden, a pioneer in self-esteem studies, describes autonomous ethical self-evaluation in *Honoring the Self:* "Living by one's own mind . . . we do not attempt to live by unthinking conformity and the suspension of independent critical judgment. We take responsibility for the ideas we accept and the values by which we guide our actions."

Though you may not realize it, you have begun the work of formulating your own ethics. As you read and learn about people you admire, *if you evaluate what you learn and choose what to adopt as your own,* you can develop your personal ethics further. When you study the lives of people who live ethically, you are using Magical Tool 5: Environment to influence and develop your own ethics.

Once your ethics are developed, they form the criteria against which you can evaluate your life purpose, as well as all your other behavior. Ethics are what you as an individual feel you must do to make your life worth living, and to maintain your self-esteem. Ethics are autonomous and creative. Whereas morality is obeying someone else's rules, being ethical requires evaluating your own life and actions and requires thinking rather than blind obedience. It is a sense of personal ethics that prompts people to confront behavior they find unacceptable, even though everyone else does it, as when someone speaks out against war when the whole country is excited about it. Once you become aware of and develop your personal ethics, you become your own guide and teacher. You are free to ask others' opinions of your actions, thoughts, and behavior, but the final judgment of rightness of your actions and your life purpose belongs to you, as an autonomous person.

Living by ethics requires a solid sense of self-esteem and self-worth, plus judgmental ability and the capacity for making decisions on the spot. To live ethically, you must *think* about the implications of your actions. A sketchy, incomplete attempt at personal ethics is made in twelve-step programs in the experience of taking "personal inventory." Twelve-step programs, because they are reluctant to tell people what to do but still offer the Steps as guidelines for living, straddle the fence between morality and ethics—they teach you a little about setting criteria for yourself, but they don't complete the experience. Only autonomous thinking does that. Morality developed as humankind became social, and needed to learn to live together without constant struggle between individuals. The earliest, most primitive societies developed rules each person must live by or suffer punishment. People were expected, and if necessary coerced by force, to accept and adapt to these rules in order to reduce crime, conflict, and exploitation. We still operate by that system today, on a social level.

But living solely by such rules and following them blindly is dependent, because it leaves the vital question of what behavior is acceptable up to others. It means you don't trust yourself to make your own decisions. For people who are out of control of their behavior, laws and rules are essential, both to keep them from damaging themselves and to protect society from them. However, as we have seen, in our society these rules can be ignored, abused, and misused.

For autonomous people, who are sensitive both to their own needs and feelings and to the well-being (as opposed to the demands or wishes) of others, the laws of society are far below the level of life on which they live. As an autonomous person, you are already monitoring your own behavior to the point where you would not intentionally injure yourself or another, and you've reduced your level of mistakes and unconscious behavior considerably by practicing effective choice making and maintaining your internal intimacy. You are ready for more than just obeying the rules of others. Instead of just following the minimum acceptable standard, you can now begin to live according to your own internal values, and contribute to a better world (another way to take care of yourself) through your behavior and actions.

These three criteria—results, experience, and ethics—if you use them, will help you evaluate the effectiveness and suitability of your inner purpose. In addition, because you now know how to build successful, autonomous, supportive relationships with people who will tell you the truth, the responses of those friends you know to be supportive of you can give you another viewpoint from which to evaluate your goals and your purpose. This is not to say that you allow friends to tell you what to do; rather, you include the opinions of selected friends in with the other criteria you use for evaluating the success, appropriateness, and effectiveness of your goals and overall purpose.

THE REWARDS OF AUTONOMOUS LIVING

A distinguishing feature stands out in the lives of autonomous people—although there are struggles and disappointments, there is also an experience of joy. As an autonomous person, you experience what noted humanistic psychologist Abraham Maslow called "self-actualization." That is, because you are in charge of your own life, you have the ability to exercise your potential, and be the best person you can be, by your own definition.

According to Maslow, when our needs for survival are met, and we experience safety and security and successful intimacy with others (in short, when we are successfully autonomous), we can become self-actualized, which allows us to have "peak experiences"—what most of us would call joy. Joy occurs when we are comfortable with who we are, and feeling in the right place and time within life.

Many people who say they want autonomy find that they are frightened by joy. Because the kind of joy that wells up from deep inside feels unfamiliar to people who grew up in dysfunctional families where they were discouraged from intimacy with themselves, many of them long for, yet fear, true happiness. Years of pain, failure, and feeling unable to cope with life convinced them that being happy always led to disappointment or suffering.

To be able to experience joy, you must understand that happiness, like sadness, anger, or fear, doesn't last. Healthy emotions are changeable, like mental weather conditions. When emotions are felt, rather than repressed, they evolve and flow. Happiness will give way to thoughtfulness, sadness to nostalgia, anger to determination. Emotions are momentary reactions to events, interactions, and circumstances.

However, there's no need to fear losing your happiness. Once you learn what makes you happy, you can create happiness often. Sadness, anger, and fear are not the only feelings you can feel in response to life. You can be surprised by spontaneous good feelings, too. When you live autonomously (so you're no longer living in chaos) and you make effective choices (which minimizes your disappointment), when you have autonomous relationships that surround you, inside and out, with warmth and you are living life with a purpose (which gives you satisfaction), then happiness comes back to you, over and over again.

This recurring happiness and inner joy can only be achieved

by meeting your own needs completely enough to create sufficient self-confidence and satisfaction to allow you to develop fully your potential as a person. It is the lifelong experience of recurring joy and satisfaction that allows you at the end of life to say, like Edith Piaf, *"Je ne regrette rien"* (I regret nothing).

You now have a choice: you can be the autonomous hero of your life, or you can be the dependent, helpless victim of your past and your circumstances. Your reward and motivation to choose this heroic journey is joy. My wish for you is that you will be the most you can be and claim your full share of joy.

Recommended Reading

W ith most of my clients, I find that once they've become accustomed to the Real Thirteenth Step they are committed to lifelong learning and growth. This doesn't surprise me, because following my own "job on earth" (or inner wisdom) led me to learn and teach psychology, which in turn led to an unending study of spirituality and philosophy. I found the teachings of all three to be compatible, all essentially recommending that one follow various versions of the Real Thirteenth Step. The following recommended reading list offers some of the paths my clients and/or I took, and these books in turn lead to others. Friends and clients and I are constantly sharing new discoveries of books and ideas. As warriors of the mind, we enthusiastically welcome all new thought, because it both exercises our judgment and stimulates our own creativity. Please share the following book list in that spirit. May you have as much growth, satisfaction, and joy in your continuing life adventure as I have in mine.

In addition to the books that follow, try reading some current events and alternative publications. *The Utne Reader,* a magazine digest of the alternative press, gives a broad sampling of nonmajority views in print. Popular educational magazines, such as *In Health, Psychology Today,* or *Omni,* are entertaining, easy to read, and give a light overview of new research and ideas. *Parabola* is an excellent journal focused on the search for meaning.

Alcoholics Anonymous World Services. *Alcoholics Anonymous.* New York: A.A. World Services, 1976.

Alcoholics Anonymous. *Twelve Steps and Thirteen Traditions.* New York: A.A. World Services, 1982.

Bass, Ellen, and Davis, Laura. *The Courage to Heal: A Guide for Women Survivors of Sexual Abuse.* New York: Perennial Library, 1988.

Beattie, Melody. *Beyond Codependency: And Getting Better All the Time.* San Francisco: Harper & Row, 1989.

Black, Claudia, Ph.D. *It Will Never Happen to Me.* Denver: M.A.C., 1982.

Bradshaw, John. *Bradshaw on the Family.* Deerfield Beach, FL: Health Communications, 1988.

———. *Healing the Shame That Binds You.* Deerfield Beach, FL: Health Communications, 1988.

———. *Homecoming: Reclaiming and Championing Your Inner Child.* New York: Bantam, 1990.

Branden, Nathaniel. *Honoring the Self: Personal Integrity and the Heroic Potentials of Human Nature.* Los Angeles: Jeremy P. Tarcher, 1983.

Campbell, Joseph, with Moyers, Bill. *The Power of Myth.* New York: Doubleday, 1988.

Cappacchione, Lucia. *The Power of Your Other Hand.* North Hollywood, CA: Newcastle, 1988.

———. *The Picture of Health.* Santa Monica, CA: Hay House, 1990.

Carlson, R., and Shield, B., eds. *Healers on Healing.* Los Angeles: Jeremy P. Tarcher, 1989.

Cermak, Timmon. *A Time to Heal: The Road to Recovery for Adult Children of Alcoholics.* Los Angeles: Jeremy P. Tarcher, 1988.

Chandler, Mitzi. *Gentle Reminders: Daily Affirmations for Co-Dependents.* Deerfield Beach, FL: Health Communications, 1989.

Covington, Stephanie, and Beckett, Liana. *Leaving the Enchanted Forest: The Path from Relationship Addiction to Intimacy.* New York: Harper & Row, 1988.

Crawford, Christina. *Survivor.* New York: Donald I. Fine, 1988.

Davidson, Joy. *The Agony of It All.* Los Angeles: Jeremy P. Tarcher, 1988.

Davis, Bruce, and Davis, Genny. *The Magical Child Within You.* Berkeley: Celestial Arts, 1982.

Ellis, Albert. *Humanistic Psychotherapy.* New York: Julian Press, 1973.

Engel, Lewis, and Ferguson, Tom. *Imaginary Crimes: Why We Punish Ourselves and How to Stop.* Boston: Houghton Mifflin, 1990.

Feinstein, David, and Krippner, Stanley. *Personal Mythology: The Psychology of Your Evolving Self.* Los Angeles: Jeremy P. Tarcher, 1988.

Forward, Susan. *Toxic Parents: Overcoming Their Hurtful Legacy and Reclaiming Your Life.* New York: Bantam, 1989.

Friedman, Sonya. *Men Are Just Desserts.* New York: Warner Books, 1983.

Fromm, Erich. *The Art of Loving.* New York: Harper & Row, 1956.

Gawain, Shakti. *Creative Visualization.* Mill Valley, CA: Whatever Publishing, 1982.

———. *Living in the Light.* Mill Valley, CA: Whatever Publishing, 1986.

Gershon, David, and Straub, Gail. *Empowerment: The Art of Creating Your Life as You Want It.* New York: Dell, 1989.

Goodman, Gerald. "The 12-Step Program," *The Self-Helper.* UCLA, Summer 1989.

Hay, Louise. *You Can Heal Your Life.* Santa Monica, CA: Hay House, 1984.

Hayes, Jody. *Smart Love: A Codependence Recovery Program Based on a Relationship Addiction Support Group.* Los Angeles: Jeremy P. Tarcher, 1989.

Helfer, Ray E. *Childhood Comes First: A Crash Course in Childhood for Adults.* East Lansing, MI: Ray Helfer, 1984.

Irwin, Ben. "Jack Lemmon: Friendly, Popular, Unique," in *Sober Times*. San Diego, CA. April 1990.

Keyes, Ken. *A Conscious Person's Guide to Relationships.* Coos Bay, OR: Living Love Publications, 1979.

Kirsten, Grace, and Robertiello, Richard. *Big You, Little You.* New York: Dial Press, 1975.

Langer, Ellen. *Mindfulness.* New York: Addison-Wesley, 1989.

Lerner, Harriet. *The Dance of Intimacy: A Woman's Guide to Courageous Acts of Courage in Key Relationships.* San Francisco: Harper & Row, 1989.

Maslow, A. H. *Toward A Psychology of Being.* 2d ed. New York: Delacorte Press, 1978.

Miller, Alice. *For Your Own Good: Hidden Cruelty in Child-Rearing and the Roots of Violence.* New York: Farrar-Strauss, Giroux, 1980.

Munsen, Jim. "From Denial to Surrender," in *Science of Mind Magazine.* Los Angeles. Feb. 1990.

Parry, Danaan. "Peace and the Warrior," *In Content* no. 20 Winter 1989. Content Institute Bainbridge Island, WA.

Peck, M. Scott. *The Road Less Traveled.* New York: Simon and Schuster, 1978.

Peele, Stanton. *The Diseasing of America.* Lexington, MA: Lexington Books, 1989.

Pollard, John K. *Self-Parenting.* Malibu, CA: Generic Human Studies Publishing, 1989.

Ray, Sondra. *I Deserve Love.* Berkeley, CA: Celestial Arts, 1976.

Roberts, Denton. *Able and Equal.* Spokane, WA: Human Esteem Publishing, 1984.

Rossman, Martin L. *Healing Yourself: A Step-by-Step Program for Better Health Through Imagery.* New York: Walker and Company, 1987.

Sandor, R. S. "A Physician's Journey," in *Parabola.* New York. Vol. XII, #2, May 1987.

Satir, Virginia. *Peoplemaking.* Palo Alto, CA: Science & Behavior Books, 1972.

Schaef, Anne Wilson. *When Society Becomes an Addict.* San Francisco: Harper & Row, 1987.

Segal, Jeanne. *Living Beyond Fear.* New York: Ballantine, 1989.

Siegel, Bernie S. *Peace, Love and Healing.* New York: Harper & Row, 1989.

Siegel, Ronald K. *Intoxication: Life in Pursuit of Artificial Paradise.* New York: E. P. Dutton, 1989.

Sinetar, Marsha. *Ordinary People as Monks and Mystics.* Mahwah, NJ: Paulist Press, 1986.

_____. *Elegant Choices, Healing Choices: Finding Grace and Wholeness in Everything We Choose.* Mahwah, NJ: Paulist Press, 1988.

_____. *Living Happily Ever After: Thrive on change, Triumph Over Adversity.* New York: Dell, 1990.

Smith, Riley K., and Tessina, Tina B. *How to Be a Couple and Still Be Free.* North Hollywood, CA: Newcastle Publishing, 1987.

Solberg, R. J. *The Dry Drunk Syndrome* (pamphlet). Hazelden, 1983.

Szasz, Thomas, M.D. *Heresies.* New York: Anchor Books, 1976.

Wegner, Daniel M. *White Bears and Other Unwanted Thoughts: Suppression, Obsession and the Psychology of Mental Control.* New York: Viking Penguin, 1989.

Weil, Andrew. *Chocolate to Morphine.* Boston, MA: Houghton Mifflin, 1983.

Whitfield, Charles L. *Healing the Child Within.* Pompano Beach, FL: Health Communications, 1987.

Zweig, Connie, ed. *To Be a Woman: The Birth of the Conscious Feminine.* Los Angeles: Jeremy P. Tarcher, 1990.